ANCIENT INDIA

ANCIENT INDIA
A History of Its Culture and Civilization

by
D. D. KOSAMBI

PANTHEON BOOKS

A Division of Random House

NEW YORK

FIRST AMERICAN EDITION

Library of Congress Catalog Card Number: 66-13018

MANUFACTURED IN THE UNITED STATES OF AMERICA

Contents

CONTENTS

Illustrations

vii

Preface

IT is doubtless more important to change history than to write it, just as it would be better to do something about the weather rather than merely talk about it. In a free parliamentary democracy every citizen is supposed to feel that he, personally is making history when he elects representatives to do the talking and to tax him for the privilege. Some have now begun to suspect that this may not suffice, that all history may terminate abruptly with the atomic age unless a bit more is done soon.

Much that has been talked about India's glorious past, unhampered by fact or common sense, is even more free than Indian elections. Discussion eddies around obscure dates and deservedly obscure biographies of kings and prophets. It seems to me that some something more might be achieved in the way of charting the main currents of Indian history, notwithstanding the lack of the kind of source material which, in other countries, would be considered essential by the historian. That, at any rate, is what this book attempts to do, with the minimum of scholarly display.

I am especially grateful to Mr. John Irwin for special advice in making the book fit its avowed purpose, in choice of illustrations, and in seeing the work through the press. To him and to Professor A. L. Basham, my gratitude is also due for initiative in finding an English publisher. Mr. Sunil Janah was kind enough to permit the inclusion of a few of his brilliant photographs of Indian tribal and rural life. My thanks are due also to Miss Margaret Hall for her painstaking revision of maps and drawings; and to Mr. Semyon Tyulaev for tracing and photographing illustrative material in the USSR.

Any claim this book may have to originality rests on field work done as a free agent. To those friends and pupils who have shown faith in my methods and supported them with heartwarming enthusiasm, I owe more than can be expressed in a few lines.

House 803,   D. D. KOSAMBI
Poona 4, India,
July 31, 1964.

CHAPTER ONE

The Historical Perspective

1.1. The Indian Scene

A DISPASSIONATE observer who looks at India with detachment and penetration would be struck by two mutually contradictory features: diversity and unity at the same time.

The endless variety is striking, often incongruous. Costume, speech, the physical appearance of the people, customs, standards of living, food, climate, geographical features all offer the greatest possible differences. Richer Indians may be dressed in full European style, or in costumes that show Muslim influence, or in flowing and costly robes of many different colourful Indian types. At the lower end of the social scale are other Indians in rags, almost naked but for a small loincloth. There is no national language or alphabet; a dozen languages and scripts appear on the ten-rupee currency note. There is no Indian race. People with white skins and blue eyes are as unmistakably Indian as others with black skins and dark eyes. In between we find every other intermediate type, though the hair is generally black. There is no typical Indian diet, but more rice, vegetables, and spices are eaten than in Europe. The north Indian finds southern food unpalatable, and conversely. Some people will not touch meat, fish, or eggs; many would and do starve to death rather than eat beef, while others observe no such restrictions. These dietary conventions are not matters of taste but of religion. In climate also the country offers the full range. Perpetual snows in the Himālayas, north European weather in Kaśmir, hot deserts in Rājasthān, basalt ridges and granite mountains on the peninsula, tropical heat at the southern tip, dense forests in laterite soil along the western scarp. A 2,000-mile-long coastline, the great Gangetic

1

river system in a wide and fertile alluvial basin, other great rivers of lesser complexity, a few considerable lakes, the swamps of Cutch and Orissā, complete the sub-continental picture.

Cultural differences between Indians even in the same province, district, or city are as wide as the physical differences between the various parts of the country. Modern India produced an outstanding figure of world literature in Tagore. Within easy reach of Tagore's final residence may be found Santāls and other illiterate primitive peoples still unaware of Tagore's existence. Some of them are hardly out of the food-gathering stage. An imposing modern city building such as a bank, government office, factory, or scientific institute may have been designed by some European architect or by his Indian pupil. The wretched workmen who actually built it generally used the crudest tools. Their payment might be made in a lump sum to a foreman who happens to be the chief of their small guild and the head of their clan at the same time. Certainly these workmen can rarely grasp the nature of the work done by the people for whom the structures were erected. Finance, bureaucratic administration, complicated machine production in a factory, and the very idea of science are beyond the mental reach of human beings who have lived in misery on the margin of overcultivated lands or in the forest. Most of them have been driven by famine conditions in the jungle to become the cheapest form of drudge labour in the city.

Yet in spite of this apparent diversity, there is a double unity. At the top there are certain common features due to the ruling class. The class is the Indian bourgeoisie, divided by language, regional history, and so on, but nevertheless grouped by similarity of interests into two sections. Finance and mechanised factory production are in the hands of the real capitalist bourgeoisie. Distribution of the product is dominated primarily by the petty-bourgeois class of shopkeepers, formidable by reason of their large number. Food production is overwhelmingly on small plots. The necessity of paying cash for taxes and factory goods forces the peasant into a reluctant and rather backward wing of the petty-bourgeoisie. The normal agrarian surplus is also in the hands of middlemen and money-lenders who do not generally rise into the big bourgeoisie. The division between the richest peasants and moneylenders is not sharp. There are cash crops like tea, coffee, cotton, tobacco, jute, cashew, peanuts, sugar-cane, coconuts and others tied to the international market or to factory production. These are sometimes cultivated by modern capitalist owners by mechanised techniques on large plots of land. High finance, often foreign, determines their prices and skims off the main profit. On the other hand, a considerable volume of consumer goods, especially utensils and textiles, is still produced by handicraft methods and has survived competition with factory production. The political scene is dominated entirely by these two sections of the bourgeoisie, with a class of professional (lawyers, etc.) and clerical workers as the connecting link with the legislatures and the machinery of administration.

We must note that, for historical reasons, the government is also the greatest single entrepreneur in India. Its assets as a large capitalist equal those of all private Indian capitalists together, though concentrated in particular types of investments. Railways, air services, posts and telegraphs, radio and telephone, some banks, life insurance, and defence industries are entirely in the hands of the state, as to some extent are the production of electricity and coal. Oil wells are state owned. The major oil refineries are still in the hands of foreign companies, though state refineries will soon be in full production. Steel was mostly in private ownership, but the state has begun its own large-scale iron and steel production. On the other hand, the state does not produce food. When scarcities (often artificially created by shopkeepers or middlemen) threaten to drive cheap labour out of the cities the state distributes imported grain by rationing in the major industrial centres. This satisfies both the large and the petty bourgeoisie without interfering with the profits of either. The obvious cure and stabiliser for the uncertain food situation would be to collect agricultural taxes in kind, with storage and distribution of food effectively in the hands of the government. Though suggested often enough—and indeed the practice in ancient India—nothing has been done in this direction. The imported grain is neither unloaded by efficient suction pumps nor stored in modern grain elevators, nor even mechanically cleaned. The production of consumer goods is in private hands. State interference is necessary even here for two reasons. First, without it the economy would be shattered by unrestricted greed and uncontrolled production, particularly as many raw materials and almost all machinery have to be imported against very scarce foreign exchange. Secondly, the bourgeoisie came to power with full knowledge of the economics of scarcity, of restrained production and the black market, learned during the shortages caused by the two great world wars; in fact, these wars and shortages were the cause of capital accumulation and ultimately of the transfer of power from British to Indian hands. The state, for example, is now being forced to become a large-scale monopolist producer of antibiotics and drugs, a field where private enterprise showed its greed and contempt for human welfare in the deadliest fashion. The government, by exercising its regulating functions and by planning future development, seems to stand above all classes. The administration and top bureaucracy inherited from British

3

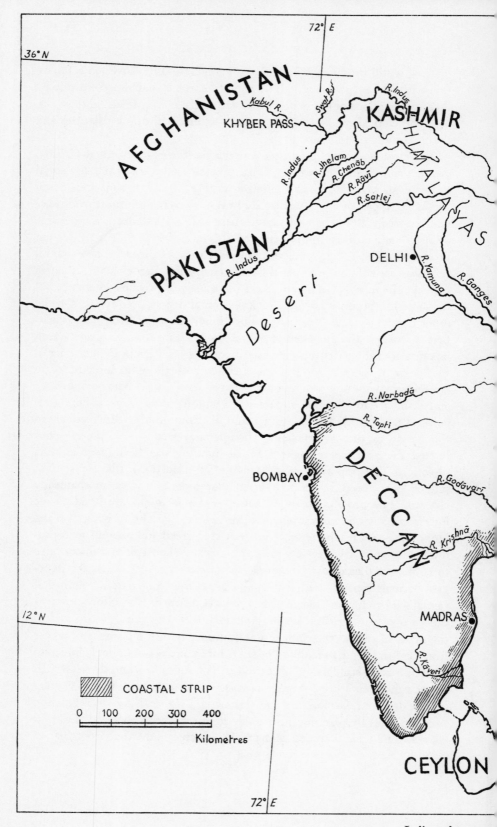

India and surroun.

96° E

36°N

TIBET

NEPAL

BHUTAN

R. Brahmaputra

YUN-NAN

R. Ghagra

BANĀRAS

R. Ganges

ASSAM

PATNA

R. Son

BIHAR

E. PAKISTAN

BENGAL

CALCUTTA

BURMA

R. Irrawaddy

R. Salween

R. Mahānadi

ANDAMAN
ISLANDS

12°N

96° E

ng regions.

rule always behaved and regarded itself as above anything Indian. Of course, the government in the final analysis is manned exclusively by members of one class. Thus what and how the government controls depends also upon who controls the government. Recent border incidents with China enabled the central state authority to assume extraordinary dictatorial powers which could bring socialism or any other goal rapidly within sight. If, then, the country finds itself as far away as ever from socialism, there may be some ground for the sarcasm that the road is not being travelled in the right direction. Nevertheless, the most carping of critics must admit that there has been progress since independence, no matter how much more could and should have been achieved. The needless man-made famines which killed millions in Bengal and Orissā during the last years of British rule seem as unreal now as any other evil nightmare of colonial misrule.

1.2. The Modern Ruling Class

The most noticeable feature of the Indian city bourgeoisie is the stamp of the foreigner. Fourteen years after independence English still remains the official language of administration, big business, and higher education in India. No significant attempts have been made to change over, beyond pious resolutions in shiftless committees. The intellectual apes the latest British fashions not only in clothing but even more in literature and the arts. The Indian novel and short story, even in the Indian languages, are modern creations based upon foreign models or foreign inspiration. The Indian drama is more than two thousand years old, but the literate Indian stage today, and overwhelmingly the Indian cinema, is patterned after the theatre and movies in other countries. Indian poetry has, however, resisted the change somewhat better, though foreign influence is demonstrable in choice of themes and freer metres.

The magnificent treasure of European (continental) literary and cultural tradition is generally ignored by this intelligentsia, except at third hand through badly chosen English books. The fact is that the entire bourgeois mode in India is a forced extraneous growth. The country had an immense feudal and pre-feudal accumulation of wealth which did not turn directly into modern capital. A great deal was expropriated by the British in the eighteenth and nineteenth centuries. Only when it reached England did it bring about the great industrial revolution in that country and become converted into modern capital in the strict sense of the term by being tied to mechanised production. The change increased the drain upon India's resources because the administration and military establishment steadily became heavier. The money disbursed as pensions, dividends, and interest

6

went mostly to England. Moreover, India's raw materials were paid for at the conqueror's price. Indigo, jute, tea, tobacco, cotton were planted so extensively as to transform the economies of whole districts. Control remained in the hands of the foreigner, especially as the processing was done in England. A part of the finished product was sold at very favourable prices in the vast Indian market. The profits were pocketed by the financiers of London and the manufacturers of Birmingham and Manchester. There was inevitably a secondary growth of finance in the new cities of Bombay, Madras, and Calcutta. The discovery was made in the second half of the nineteenth century that Indian labour could be trained to work cheaply on machines. The textile mills of Bombay and the jute mills of Calcutta were the result of this discovery and of the taxes that had to be imposed upon British cloth to pay for suppression of the 1857 revolt. A class of mechanical workers was also needed for the railways. The first Indian colleges and universities were due to the still earlier discovery that it was decidedly cheaper to train Indian clerical workers for administration and the counting houses than to import clerks from abroad. The Indians not only learned quickly but worked honestly and efficiently for a third to a tenth of the salary of a foreigner. Of course, all higher posts were reserved for the ruling class of conquerors. Eventually, the Indian intermediaries saw that they could start their own mills. The first in the field were the Pārsis of Bombay, many of whom had made considerable fortunes as trade associates of the East India Company—especially in the opium trade thrust upon China. From 1880, Indian nationalism of a new type and Indian political figures formally inspired by Edmund Burke and John Stuart Mill became increasingly prominent along with the great Indian financiers and mill-owners.

Though this bourgeoisie began as compradors for the foreign traders, it was formed out of more than one class, from a much older Indian society which already had its class divisions. A good deal of modern Indian capital is, in fact, transformed primitive feudal and moneylender's accumulation. In recent times even India's feudal princes have had to turn their crude hoarded wealth into shares and stocks or sink into poverty. The feudal, moneylending, and trading families, especially their womenfolk, never lost the outward forms of their religious superstition. The intellectuals and professionals derive from other groups which belonged to neither of the two. They felt the strong need to foster patriotism and national pride during the struggle for shaking off British colonial rule. This led the new intelligentsia to discover its country's past, sometimes to invent a glorious past where none was known. (The same problem never arose in Japan, also an oriental country recently modernised. The Japanese national tradition was always strong and well documented. Japan's change to industrialisation took place under a national, indigenous bourgeoisie without foreign occupation. Nevertheless, the Japanese intelligentsia also took vigorously to the study and copying of Western culture in their Meiji era. This shows that such cultural changes have deep underlying causes. Military occupation or the attractiveness of copying new fashions will not explain the phenomenon.) The very same Indian bourgeoisie, however, drove out the powerful British rulers of India after a bitter and protracted struggle. The expulsion would not have been possible unless a great segment of the Indian people had accepted the leadership of the advanced wing of this bourgeoisie. The struggle was not armed on the Indian side. The methods and ideology of Mahatma Gandhi, who conducted the liberation movement, as also of many predecessors like Tilak, seem peculiarly Indian, despite the clear line that connects Gandhi to Tolstoy and so to Silvio Pellico. Without such methods, it is doubtful whether the leadership would have been as effective under the specific conditions prevailing in India from the beginning of this century. So the very fact that Western culture has increased its appeal for the Indian middle class in spite of and immediately after this conflict has special significance and some deep-rooted cause. The basis of cultural change has to be looked for outside the formal manifestations which are generally taken as the essence of culture.

The new Indian bourgeoisie was technically backward compared with that of Japan, let alone of Germany or England. No new mechanical device or significant inventions lie to its credit. The machinery for modern industrial production, the financial system, and even the political theories were imported bodily from England. Because there was already a large class of poor, landless, Indian workers, the new bourgeoisie developed much more rapidly than the Indian mechanised proletariat. The real problems of industrialisation were faced only after liberation. India has shown more advance in this direction during the last fifteen years than under the whole period of British rule. The rest of the story lies in the future. Let us turn back to the more remote past, with which the Indian bourgeoisie had nothing to do, though it sometimes influences their mental imagery profoundly, while never interfering with the desire for quick profit without hard work or mastery of technique.

1.3. The Difficulties Facing the Historian

What has been said so far might lend colour to the theory sometimes expressed that India was never a nation, that Indian culture and civilisation is a by-product of foreign conquest, whether Muslim or British. If this were so, the only Indian history worth writing would be the history of and by the conquerors. The textbooks that the foreigner has left behind him naturally heighten this impression. But when Alexander of Macedon was drawn to the East by the fabulous wealth and magic name of India, England and France were barely coming into the Iron Age. The discovery of America was due to the search for new trade routes to India; a reminder of this is seen in the name 'Indians' given to the American aborigines. The Arabs, when they were intellectually the most progressive and active people in the world, took their treatises on medicine and a good deal of their mathematics from Indian sources. Asian culture and civilisation have China and India as their two primary sources. Cotton textiles (even words like 'calico', 'chintz', 'dungaree', 'pyjamas', 'sash' and 'gingham' are of Indian origin) and sugar are India's specific contribution to everyday life, just as paper, tea, porcelain, silk are China's.

The mere variety that India offers is not enough to characterise the ancient civilisation of the country. Africa or the single province of Yunnan in China offer as much diversity. But the great African culture of Egypt has not the continuity that we find in India over the last three thousand years or more. Egyptian and Mesopotamian culture as we trace them back from today does not go beyond the Arabic. Also there is no Yunnanese civilisation as such. China's development amounts to the predominance of the Han people over the rest with an early, stable imperial system. The many other nationalities of China did not make comparable contributions of their own. The Incas and Aztecs vanished soon after the Spanish Conquest. The culture of Mexico, Peru, and Latin America in general is European, not indigenous. The Romans left their mark on world culture through direct conquest of the Mediterranean basin. The continuity was preserved mainly in those areas where the Latin language and culture was carried forward by the Catholic Church. In contrast, Indian religious philosophy was welcomed in Japan and China without the force of Indian arms, even though almost no Indians visited or traded with those lands. Indonesia, Viet Nam, Thailand, Burma, Ceylon certainly owe a great deal of their cultural history to Indian influence without Indian occupation.

The continuity of Indian culture in its own country is perhaps its most important feature. How Indian culture influenced other countries is a matter for other books. Our task here is to trace its origins and the main character of its development in India.

At the very outset we are faced with what appears to be an insuperable difficulty. India has virtually no historical records worth the name. Chinese imperial annals, county records, the work of early historians like Ssu-ma Chien, inscriptions on graves and oracle-bones enable the history of China to be traced with some certainty from about 1400 B.C. Rome and Greece offer less antiquity, but far better historical literature. Even the Egyptian, Babylonian, Assyrian, and Sumerian records have been read. In India there is only vague popular tradition, with very little documentation above the level of myth and legend. We cannot reconstruct anything like a complete list of kings. Sometimes whole dynasties have been forgotten. What little is left is so nebulous that virtually no dates can be determined for any Indian personality till the Muslim period. It is very difficult to say over how much territory a great king actually ruled. There are no court annals in existence, with a partial exception for Kaśmir and Cambā. Similarly for great names in Indian literature. The works survive, but the author's date is rarely known. With luck, it may be possible to determine roughly the century to which the writing belonged; often it can only be said that the writer existed. Sometimes even that is doubtful; many a work known by a particular author's name could not possibly have been written by any one person.

This has led otherwise intelligent scholars to state that India has no history. Certainly, no ancient Indian history is possible with the detailed accuracy of a history of Rome or Greece. But what is history? If history means only the succession of outstanding megalomaniac names and imposing battles, Indian history would be difficult to write. If, however, it is more important to know whether a given people had the plough or not than to know the name of their king, then India has a history. For this work, I shall adopt the following definition: *History is the presentation in chronological order of successive changes in the means and relations of production.* This definition has the advantage that history can be written as distinct from a series of historical episodes. *Culture* must then be understood also in the sense of the ethnographer, to describe the essential ways of life of the whole people. Let us examine these definitions more closely.

Some people regard culture as purely a matter of intellectual and spiritual values, in the sense of religion, philosophy, legal systems, literature, art, music, and the like. Sometimes this is extended to include refinements in the manners of the ruling class. History, according to these intellectuals, is based upon and should deal only with such 'culture'; nothing else matters. There are difficulties in taking this type of culture as the mainspring of history. Three of the greatest such formal cultures combined in Central Asia: Indian, Chinese, and Greek; supplemented with two great religions, Buddhism and Christianity. The region had a central position in trade with high political importance under the Kushāna empire. The archaeologist still digs up beautiful relics in Central Asia.

But the original contribution of this well-developed Central Asia to human culture and to the history of mankind remains small. The Arabs coming from a decidedly less 'cultured' environments did much more to preserve, develop, and transmit to posterity the great discoveries of Greek and Indian science. Even the occasional Central Asian such as Al-Birūni who participated in the process wrote in Arabic as a member of an Islamic culture, not of the Central Asian. The 'uncultured' Mongol conquest which destroyed the efflorescence of Central Asia beyond recovery had no such effect upon Chinese culture, which was only stimulated to further advance.

Man does not live by bread alone, but we have not yet developed a human breed that can live without bread, or at least some form of food. Strictly speaking, unleavened bread is a late neolithic discovery, a considerable advance in the preparation and preservation of food. 'Give us this day our daily bread' still forms part of the Christian's daily prayer, though Christian theology places the world of the spirit above all material considerations. The basis of any formal culture must lie in the availability of a food supply beyond that needed to support the actual food-producer. To build the imposing *ziggurat* temples of Mesopotamia, the Great Wall of China, the pyramids of Egypt, or modern skyscrapers, there must have been a correspondingly imposing surplus of food at the time. Surplus production depends upon the technique and instruments used—'the means of production', to adopt a convenient though badly abused term. The method by which surplus—not only surplus food but all other produce—passes into the hands of the ultimate user is determined by—and in turn determines—the form of society, the 'relations of production'. The negligible surplus of primitive food-gatherers is often divided and shared out by the women of the gathering group. With further development, the apportioning is the function of the patriarch, tribal chief, head of the clan; often through family units. When the surplus is large and concentrated, a great temple or the Pharaoh may decide upon its gathering and distribution, through priestly guilds or the nobility. Production and exchange in a slave society remain in the hands of those who own the slaves, but this class may again have developed out of former priests, nobles, or clan chiefs now performing new functions. The feudal baron controlling serfs is the main agent under feudalism. His counterpart, the trader and financier, must deal also with the craftsmen's guilds. The trader class may transform itself through manufacture to usher in the capitalist age in which man's labour becomes a commodity, too, while his person remains free. In all this, form and content may differ. Britain has the complete range of feudal nobility, lords and knights—though no serfs now remain as primary producers. For all that, English society is fully bourgeois, the first and most important development of the full modern bourgeoisie. Edward VII may have been crowned on the wooden chair of Edward the Confessor in the latter's Abbey; but the England over which these two kings reigned had meanwhile changed beyond all recognition. The last great modern bourgeoisies, namely those of Germany and Japan, even strengthened certain feudal forms while demolishing feudalism under cover of absolute loyalty to the emperor.

Our position has also to be very far from a mechanical determinism, particularly in dealing with India, where form is given the utmost importance while content is ignored. Economic determinism will not do. It is not inevitable, nor even true, that a given amount of wealth will lead to a given type of development. The complete historical process through which the social form has been reached is also of prime importance. The gold and silver of the Americas which had kept the Amerinds in savagery only strengthened feudal and religious reaction in Spanish hands. A fraction of the same wealth pirated by Drake and other English sea-captains was of immense help in lifting England out of the feudal into the mercantile and bourgeois era. At every stage the survival of previous forms and the ideology of the top classes exert tremendous force—whether by tradition or revolt against tradition—upon any social movement. Language itself was formed out of the process of exchange, new goods, fresh ideas, and corresponding new words all going together. Any important advance in the means of production immediately leads to a great increase in population, which necessarily means different relations of production. The chief who can regulate single-handed the affairs of a hundred people could not do this for a hundred thousand people without assistance. This would imply the creation of a nobility or a council of elders. The district with only two primitive hamlets needs no government; the same district with 20,000 large villages must have one and can support it. So, we have a peculiar zigzag process, particularly in India. A new stage of production manifests itself in formal change of some sort; when the production is primitive, the change is often religious. The new form, if it does increase production, is acclaimed and becomes set. However, this must also lead to a decided increase of population. If the superstructure cannot be adjusted during growth, then there is eventual conflict. Sometimes the old form is broken by a revolution in the guise of a reformation. Sometimes the class that gains by preserving the older form wins, in which case there is stagnation, degeneracy, or atrophy. The early maturity and peculiar helplessness of Indian society against later foreign invasions bears testimony to this general scheme.

1.4. *The Need to Study Rural and Tribal Society*

How is a history of India to be written when so little documentation is available? For that matter, how was the history of a vanished civilisation like that of Rome written in modern times? The documents existed, but many words had no meaning to modern people. This meaning was acquired by the comparative study of surviving antiquities. That certain individuals really existed was taken as proved by their coins, statues, tombstones, monuments, and inscriptions. The confirmation in turn gave weight to the documentary record. Archaeologists dug up many buried remnants of the past. Literary sources are now regarded as trustworthy only to the extent that they can be substantiated by archaeological methods. Finally, archaeology helps documents to tell us how the people of a vanished age actually lived, though the meaning of certain key words has changed. Digging up the past and the scientific study of primitive people in other parts of the world also makes possible the reconstruction of a culture that existed before any written records. This is labelled prehistory.

All these methods can still be employed in India, though they will not suffice. Indian archaeology is not advanced enough to solve the really important questions, nor even to ask some of them. Nevertheless the country has one tremendous advantage that was not utilised till recently by the historian: the survival within different social layers of many forms that allow the reconstruction of totally diverse earlier stages. To find these strata one has to move from the cities into the countryside. The influence of education, recent political developments, the cinema, radio, and trade dominated by production in the cities have at times to be discounted. Many changes have been brought about by new forms of rapid transport over great distances; namely, the railways in the second half of the nineteenth century and motor transport on roads since 1925. It is not difficult to allow for all these, particularly in the more distant rural parts of the vast land. There are local differences of detail. Some parts of the country skipped a stage or two; sometimes the changes came in the wrong order. However, the main outline remains the same, so far as the really important basic developments go.

India is still a country of peasants. Agrarian development is extensive, though still with primitive technique. Most of the land is overgrazed and overfarmed after two thousand years of cultivation. The yield per acre is abysmally low because the methods are primitive and holdings too small to be economic. From the air, a main feature of the land is the lack of transport. The tight network of roads and railways that one sees in western Europe or the U.S.A. is lacking. This means that a significant part of the

13

production is local and locally consumed. It is precisely this backward, inefficient and local nature of production that has allowed so many older tribal groups to survive, albeit upon the verge of extinction. The whole rural economy is dominated by the seasonal rain, the monsoon. This causes from 20 to 200 inches of yearly precipitation in various parts of India. Anything less means a famine area, or irrigation. The rainfall is mostly compressed into four months, June–September. But the onset of the monsoon is later in the north than in the south. On the east coast the final monsoon comes in two separate waves. These differences generate a some-what different annual cycle for each locality. In spite of the heavy rains, most of the country bears (from the air) the semblance of a desert as compared to the green fields of Holland or England. The grass has vanished; the water flows off rapidly, leaving the top soil eroded. This is a modern feature; deforestation became serious at the end of the last century. For the older period with which we are concerned it must be realised that the problems caused by the seasonal rains were different in different parts of the country. Desert or near-desert conditions prevailed in the lower Panjāb, Sind, and most of Rājasthān; but the soil is alluvial and so fertile that irrigation or a little rain gives rich harvests. In the Gangetic basin the soil is also alluvial and most fertile, but there (as to a lesser extent in the upper Panjāb) the rainfall is heavier. This meant heavy forest and swamp in older days, particularly in the eastern United Province (now Uttar Pradesh), Bihār, and Bengal. Along the western coastal mountains and the hills of Assam the forest still exists in spite of heavy cutting. In the flat coastal area, now denuded of forest, three crops a year are possible; but the dense population is unable to subsist merely by con-suming the local production; the economy hinges on cash crops like the coconut. Mineral resources are only now being developed in the forests of central India and some wild areas of the peninsula to something like their proper extent. Here the tribal people still form the object of study for ethnographers (e.g. Bhil, Todās in the Nilgiris, Santāl, Orāon, etc.). The peninsular (Deccan) plateau has not and never had the cover of dense forest, being broken up by bare hills: basalt in the western portion, granite farther to south-east. The average soil here is not so fertile; though the black soil in its localised areas is excellent for many crops, particularly cotton, it needs the heavy plough to bring it under regular cultivation. Gujarāt has its own peculiar loess soil. Such differences are reflected in the historical development of these regions, which followed a different course in each case.

This varied topography and the generally warm climate has allowed an extraordinary inner differentiation—due to different local history—among the peasantry. The main feature of Indian society, seen at its strongest in the rural part, is *caste*. This means the division of society into many groups which live side by side, but often do not seem to live together. Members of different castes cannot intermarry by religion, though the law now permits complete freedom in this respect. This great advance is due to the bourgeois mode, because of which caste has begun to disappear in the cities, except for political or economic cliques. Most peasants will not take cooked food or water from the hands of persons of a lower caste. That is, caste has a rough hierarchy. In practice, the number of such caste groups goes into the thousands. In theory, there are only four castes: The brahmin (*brāhmana*) or priest caste; the *kshatriya*—warrior; *vaiśya*—trader and husbandman; and *śūdra*, the lowest caste, which corresponds in general to the working class. This theoretical system is roughly that of classes, whereas the observed castes and sub-castes derive clearly from tribal groups of different ethnic origin. Their very names show this. The relative status of the small local castes depends always upon the extent of, and the caste's economic position in, the common market. A Joulāhā of Bihār suddenly transported to some village of Agris in Mahārāshtra would have no definite status automatically assigned to him. But in Bihār his preliminary status is decided by that of his caste within the range of villages with whom he is in normal contact. This goes roughly by the relative economic power of the various castes. The same caste may have different positions in the hierarchy for two different regions. If this differentiation persists for some time, the separate branches may often regard themselves as different castes, no longer intermarrying. The lower one goes in the economic scale, the lower the caste in the social scale on the whole. At the lowest end we still have purely tribal groups, many of whom are in a food-gathering stage. The surrounding general society is now food-producing. So food-gathering for these very low castes generally turns into begging and stealing. Such nethermost groups were accurately labelled the 'criminal tribes' by the British in India, because they refused as a rule to acknowledge law and order outside the tribe.

This stratification of Indian society reflects and explains a great deal of Indian history, if studied in the field without prejudice. It can easily be shown that many castes owe their lower social and economic status to their present or former refusal to take to food production and plough agriculture. The lowest castes often preserve tribal rites, usages, and myths. A little higher up we see these religious observances and legends in transition, often by assimilation to other parallel traditions. Another step above, they have been rewritten by brahmins to suit themselves, and to give the brahmin caste predominance in the priesthood, which in the lower castes

15

is generally not in the hands of brahmins. Still higher we come to what is called 'Hindu' culture, the literate traditions that often go back to much older times. But even these stories of gods and demons are basically much the same in the lower groups. The main work of brahminism has been to gather the myths together, to display them as unified cycles of stories, and to set them in a better-developed social framework. Either many originally different gods and cults are identified (syncretism) or several deities made into a family, or into a royal court of the gods. At the very top come the philosophical developments formulated by the great religious leaders of Indian history. These last were, in general, a considerable advance for Indian society when the particular doctrine was first propounded. The same doctrine would later contribute heavily to India's being kept backward when society had gone farther ahead, because leaders of the crystallised religious sects refused to budge from what they proclaimed to be the founder's position. The religions themselves do not constitute history, but their rise and change of function is excellent historical material. Indian society seemed to develop more by successive religious transformation than by violence; it failed to develop further for much the same reasons, even when considerable violence was superimposed later on. Most of the surviving ancient Indian documents are overwhelmingly religious and ritualistic. The writers were not concerned with history or with reality. Trying to extract history from them without some previous knowledge of the actual structure of Indian society at the time of writing gives either no results or the ludicrous conclusions that may be read in most 'histories' of India.

1.5. The Villages

Not only caste but the emphasis upon religion and the total lack of historical sense have to be explained. The last is rather simple and is bound up with rural production and 'the idiocy of village life'. The succession of seasons is all-important, while there is little cumulative change to be noted in the village from year to year. This gives the general feeling of 'the Timeless East' to foreign observers. The bullock-cart and village huts seen in Bhārhut sculptures of about 150 B.C. or the plough and ploughman in Kushāna reliefs of A.D. 200 would cause no comment if they appeared suddenly in some modern Indian village. This makes it easy to forget that the very formation of a village economy with the plough used on fixed plots of land implies a tremendous advance in the means of production. The relations of production had to become correspondingly more involved than at the food-gathering stage. The modern Indian village gives an

16

unspeakable impression of the grimmest poverty and helplessness. There is rarely a shop except in villages that serve many others as a market centre; no public building apart perhaps from a small temple which may be an outdoor shrine open to the elements. Consumer goods are purchased from the rare itinerant vendors or at the weekly market day at a few key villages. Sale of village produce is mostly in the hands of middlemen who are at the same time moneylenders. Their grip on the rural economy and the resulting indebtedness of the peasantry is a problem still untouched by any agency, government or private, except for the usual empty schemes on paper. Once the monsoon season is over, most villages experience a progressive scarcity of water; good drinking water is scarce at all seasons. Hunger and disease are the massive concomitants of this India. The lack of medical attention and hygiene brings out most sharply the traditional apathy of the village—always a basic factor in the political economy of the country and a secure foundation for despotism. The surplus taken away from people who live in such misery and degradation nevertheless provided and still provides the material foundation for Indian culture and civilisation.

The uniform appearance of passive village distress hides a considerable differentiation. The bulk of the producers are peasants with small holdings. A few are self-sufficient. Some may rise to be powerful in the sense of a Kulak class, which is, in fact, being strengthened by current land legislation. Mostly, the richer holdings are possessed by people who are not peasants and do not labour on the land. The great landlords are generally absentees; their titles to land derive as a rule from the feudal period. Many of them shook off feudal obligations to become bourgeois landholders with the advent of the British. However, the British registered all land titles and fixed taxes in cash. This means that no village can today be self-contained. Even the most secluded must sell something, not only to buy the little cloth and household goods required but to pay some tax or rent. Even otherwise, the village could not be completely self-sufficient. In most of India clothing is not a physical necessity, though it has become a social need. Salt, however, has always been indispensable; metals in some quantity had to be available before regular agriculture could be practised. These two necessities are not produced in most villages, but have to be acquired from the outside. In spite of its timeless appearance, the village too, is tied to commodity production, now in the framework of a bourgeois economy.

Nevertheless, it does remain true that the Indian village is nearly self-contained. Only when overpopulation forces people from the Konkan or Malabār to labour in distant big cities and to send money back home does the urban control make itself directly felt. Otherwise, the contact is

FIG. 1. Ploughing, breaking up clods, sowing and trampling grain into the furrows. The cereal is probably wheat. From a nineteenth-century Persian MS in the Indian Office Library (Oriental Volume No. 71). The locality is Kaśmīr, but operations in other parts of India will differ primarily in costume of the peasants.

primarily through touring officials, who rarely trouble themselves about the village except when taxes are in arrears. Nowadays, the vote-catching politicians come once every five years, just before elections. This economy has clearly very low commodity production per inhabitant. A commodity is an article or object of use which passes into the hands of the ultimate consumer by exchange. Whatever a man produces for himself or his family or other kinship group and is then consumed within the small group or is taken away without payment by landlord or overlord is not a commodity. Some production requires specialised technical knowledge. Though the Indian village uses very little metal, the villager does need

FIG. 2. Rice cultivations. Note the seed-beds from which rice seedlings are transplanted into prepared plots ankle-deep in mud. The irrigation ditches are also shown. The ploughing is done before the land is flooded, or Indian water-buffaloes have to be harnessed in place of oxen. The roots of the seedlings would normally be dipped in some fertiliser before transplanting. The empty seed-beds are then planted to beans, automatically rotating the crops. From the same source as Fig. 1.

pots, usually of earthenware. This means that a potter must be available. Similarly, a blacksmith to repair tools and forge ploughshares, a carpenter for building houses and making the simple ploughs, etc. The priest must serve whatever ritual needs the village feels. He is generally a brahmin, though that is not obligatory for certain lower cults. Certain occupations such as that of barber, or skinner of dead beasts, are low; yet the barber's tasks and leather goods are essential. This necessitates the presence in the village of a barber and a leather worker; of different castes, naturally. Normally, each such profession forms a caste, the Indian substitute for the medieval guild. The great problem of the apparently self-contained

19

FIG. 3. Market gardening, or kitchen gardening. The man dips water out of a pit well with a *shadduf*, counterweighted beam on which a pot is hung; the woman sees to it that the carrots and other vegetables are properly watered by the trenches. From the same source as Fig. 1.

Indian rural economy was to obtain the services of such indispensable artisans for every village even though they were separated from the bulk of the peasant villagers and from each other by caste. The normal villager could not work at these various trades, while the workers could not intermarry except within the same caste profession. One artisan household of each type was the most that an average village could afford. At the same time transport was difficult and the density of commodity production (*i.e.* commodity production per head) was low. A settlement of carpenters or blacksmiths as commodity producers serving many other villages was impossible except at certain brief periods of early Indian history. Regular payment for the artisans was therefore a problem that could not be solved by a barter economy merely on the basis of exchange for value produced, with an irregular demand. How were the artisans to be induced to serve the villages? The solution of this problem, clever in its own way, was the backbone of the sluggish Indian village economy, particularly in the feudal period. The remnants of the system are still to be seen in the countryside, though cash payment steadily

20

displaces the old method. Transport is easier, so that a journeyman barber or blacksmith is common. Tins and metal pots have reduced the number of potters, who work oftener than not on the basis of production for sale against cash. However, the potter carries out certain ritual tasks which may date from prehistoric urn burial and have been augmented to make him virtually the priest to certain lower castes. The invention of the clay-plaster in bone-setting is due to the Indian potter, just as plastic surgery to restore noses mutilated in war or by disease was a discovery of the rather despised barber. Both were practised extensively in the eighteenth century; the low caste status of the practitioners and contempt for science on the part of their betters prevented full development as in the West.

The differentiation within the village is by caste, even beyond that between artisan and peasant or priest. When there are forests close by one may still see people like the Kāthkaris of the Western Ghāts, or the Mundas and Orāons of Bihār who are barely out of the food-gathering stage. Such marginal tribesmen are dying out because of disease, drunkenness, the disappearance of forests, the advance of civilisation and of moneylenders. If these people practice cultivation, it is often mere slash-and-burn on shifting plots. If they provide irregular labour at harvest-time, along with the poorest of the peasants who have regular landholdings, they are paid less and generally in kind. As a rule they have also the right of gleaning after the harvest whether they have helped in the work or not. Some hunting, eating insects, rats and mice, snakes, and even monkeys (which horrifies most other Indians), the chaff and leavings of peasant cultivation supplement their diet. They still practice witchcraft on a deadlier level than the peasants; at least, Indian newspapers announce every few years the arrest and trial of tribal men and women in a group, on suspicion of ritual murder (human sacrifice). Their primitive tribal gods have something in common with the lower village gods. Often they pay worship to the gods of a village and the village recognises their deities, too. The country festivals that draw many villagers from a distance can often be traced back to a primitive tribal origin, though the actual tribe may have vanished. The names of local village cults also prove such primitive beginning. Often a peasant caste bears the same name as some aboriginal tribe in the same region. The two groups no longer intermarry, for the peasant has become a superior being; in fact, the difference in food supply, ampler and more regular diet, changes the physique and even facial index in a few genera-tions. Nevertheless, some traces of common origin remain and are ad-mitted; sometimes by a common annual worship, particularly of mother goddesses with peculiar names not known in other villages. The peasant, however, also worships other higher gods which look primitive enough

21

but go a step above the local gods. There may be a 'guardian of the fields', generally a cobra with a relief image who has divine status. The 'Elders' are commemorated by a slab with a human couple in relief. They are normally worshipped in a corner of the plot when the land has been held for generations by farmers in the direct line descended from that couple. The Buffalo Demon (*Mhasobā*) is a farmers' god common to whole regions, though duplicated by each farmer. Other small deities have to be propitiated at ploughing, sowing, harvest, threshing. *Vetāl* is a cacodemon, prince of goblins, but also a god. Still higher come the brahmin gods Śiva, Vishnu, the incarnations of Vishnu such as Rama and Krishna, and their consort goddesses. Sometimes the primitive local god or goddess is identified with one of the deities found in brahmin literature. The older gods were not smashed, but adopted or adjusted. Brahminism thus gave some unity to what would have been social fragments without a common bond. The process was of crucial importance in the history of India, first in developing the country from tribe to society and then holding it back, bogged down in the filthy swamp of superstition.

The difficulty in studying Indian history through village tradition is the lack of a chronology. Events that happened fifty years ago and traditions formed 1,500 years ago are on much the same level to the villager, because he lives from season to season. The four *yugas*, periodic ages of mankind that remain in Indian myth, reflect the four major changes of season accurately. They are supposed to end with a universal deluge, after which the cycle begins again. This is roughly what happens in the countryside after every monsoon. Every year is much the same as the others, the difference being that some have a good harvest, others famine or pestilence. Records are not kept, the peasant being almost entirely illiterate. Even when he has had some schooling, the way of life is such that literacy is of no use to the villager, who slowly lapses into ignorance..No books, newspapers, or any such reading matter penetrates the average village. Special care has thus to be used in separating the elements of a village tradition. On the other hand, it shows how very ancient observances can survive with little change of outward form to this day. Often the feudal baron or the brahmin priest himself took over these local customs as his own, perhaps giving them a little surface varnish. History as we have defined it is to be seen displayed in full detail in the villages of India—provided one has the vision and insight required to read that history.

1.6. Recapitulation

The foregoing says first that the dominant class in India and India's urban life bears the stamp of the foreigner who imposed the bourgeois mode of production. Secondly the countryside at large and Indian religious institutions carry the indelible mark of their primitive origins because primitive modes of life have been and are still possible in many parts of India. The first of these two statements is generally admitted, though patriotism leads many to depreciate the role of foreign invaders in modern Indian history. The second statement infuriates most Indians of the middle class, who feel their country ridiculed or their own dignity insulted. Primitive cultures are neither ridiculous nor undignified till debased by contact with vicious by-products of the feudal or bourgeois mode. India's development was in its own way more 'civilised' than in other countries. The older cults and forms were not demolished by force but assimilated. Superstition reduced the need for violence. Much more brutality would have been necessary had Indian history developed along the same lines as that of Europe or the Americas.

This shows that the course of Indian history presents some highly distinctive features. It will be necessary to examine these in outline, just to prevent later misunderstanding. So far as annals, king lists, chronicles, dates of important battles, biographies of rulers and cultural figures go, there is no Indian history worth reading. Any work where the casual reader may find such detailed personal or episodic history for ancient India should be enjoyed as romantic fiction (like some Indian railway time-tables!), but not believed. At the other extreme there is also the possibility of some misunderstanding. It is understood that human society offered the following modes of production in order: primitive communism, the patriarchal mode (Abraham in the Old Testament) and/or the Asiatic mode (undefined), the slave society of classical Greece and Rome, feudalism, the bourgeois mode; and for some countries socialism. Indian history does not fit precisely into this rigid framework either. First, as has been pointed out, not all parts of the country were simultaneously in the same stage. At every stage, in almost every part of the country, a great deal of the superstructure survived, along with the productive and formal mechanism of several previous stages; there always remained some people who could and did cling stubbornly to the older mode. However, we need concentrate only upon each particular mode as it became dominant to the extent that it was bound to prevail over most of the country. Secondly, it is impossible to find slavery in the classical European sense in India at any period. Some Indians were not free, from the earliest times till the middle of the present century; a report publicised as these lines were written maintains that certain tribal people are still being sold in the open market like beasts in Kerala. But the importance of chattel slavery in the relations of production and as a supply of labour for production was negligible. The place of the slave whose surplus product could be expropriated was taken by the members of the lowest or *śūdra* caste in older days. During the feudal period, purchased or kidnapped slaves became more important as enabling the ruler or baron to become less dependent upon his followers. This was hardly classical slavery, seeing that royal slaves were always regarded by the barons as dangerous to feudal rule. Moreover, any slave of this sort could own unlimited property and soar as high as any other person in feudal society. For example, the ablest and best of the earlier emperors of Delhi and the capable founder of the Bāhamani dynasty of Ahmadnagar all rose from slavery. Indian feudalism, too, has therefore its own peculiar features (but then feudalism in England differed from that in Rumania). Penal servitude, house slaves, purchased entertainers of all sorts, and harem slaves were known before, during, and after feudalism; but the treatment of all except at times the first group was better than that of paid workers, as they had cost money. This situation provides a strong contrast with classical European slavery, as with European feudalism under which slavery withered away. Slavery in Brazil did not precede feudalism. Slavery came in the U.S.A. without any feudalism at all, with the bourgeoisie for the development of cotton plantations; it was abolished a hundred years ago after a bloody civil war which still echoes in the southern states of the most advanced capitalist democracy in the world.

This brief sketch of Indian cultural history has no doctrinaire purpose. I had to adopt a certain definition and procedure because the futility of any other was proved by rather painful experience. The chapters that follow have necessarily an intimate connection with the present state of Indian society, not only with the past.

'The function of the historian is neither to love the past nor to emancipate himself from the past, but to master and understand it as the key to the understanding of the present. Great history is written precisely when the historian's vision of the past is illuminated by insight into the problems of the present . . . Learning from history is never simply a one-way process. To learn about the present in the light of the past also means to learn about the past in the light of the present. The function of history is to promote a profounder understanding of both past and present through the interrelation between them.'

The technical capacity of the present author may not be adequate to the task of writing such a history. The reader may find the result unsatisfactory for some other reason, but at least he knows what to expect. In the main this brief work will consider the following developments: Primitive society and tribal life. The civilisation of the Indus Valley. The Aryan invasion that put an end to this civilisation, but made eastern settlement possible. The opening up of the Gangetic basin with the aid of the caste system, iron implements, and the plough. The rise of Magadha and of Buddhism. The Mauryan conquest of the whole country, with an imperial state based on food production in agrarian villages. The collapse of empire, the development of kingdoms in the Deccan and settlement of the coastal strip. The long process of emergent feudalism and the decline of Buddhism. This brings us into the Muslim period and the Indian Middle Ages, to the end of what may reasonably be called ancient Indian culture.

Note. The reader who wishes to go through the scholarly criticism and endless discussions that precede any attempt at writing a valid history of India may find some interest in the following works of mine; which are to be regarded as footnotes to the present work: (1) *An Introduction to the Study of Indian History* (Bombay, 1956), (2) *Myth and Reality* (Bombay, 1962); (3) *Exasperating Essays* (Poona, 1957). Besides the papers referred to in these three books, the following might also help grasp the technical difficulties involved: 'Dhenukākata' (*Journal of the Asiatic Society*, Bombay, Vol. 30, 1957, pp. 50–71); 'The text of the Arthaśāstra' (*Journal of the American Oriental Society*, Vol. 78, 1958, pp. 169–73); 'Indian Feudal Trade charters' (*Journal for the Economic and Social History of the Orient*, Leiden, 1959, Vol. 2, pp. 281–93); 'Primitive Communism' (*New Age*, Delhi, Vol. 8, Feb. 1959, pp. 26–39); 'The Use of Combined Methods in Indology' (*Indo-Iranian Journal*, Vol. 6, 1963, pp. 177–202); 'The Autochthonous Element in the Mahābhārata' (*Journal of American Oriental Society;* to appear shortly); 'The Beginning of the Iron Age in India' (*JESHO*, Vol. 6, 1964). In addition, I should like to recommend A. L. Basham: *The Wonder That Was India* (2nd edn., London, 1964); L. Petech: *Indien bis zur Mitte des 6. Jahrhunderts* (Propyläen Weltgeschichte/Eine Universalgeschichte, 1962), L. Renou, J. Filliozat and others: *L'Inde classique* (Paris, Vol. 1, 1947; Vol. 2, 1953). These histories have been written from other points of view than my own by masters of the subject. For chronology, two studies by L. de la Vallée Poussin: *L'Inde aux temps des Mauryas et des Barbares, Grecs, Scythes, Parthes, et Yuë-tchi* (Paris, 1930) and *Dynasties et Histoire de l'Inde depuis Kanishka jusqu'aux invasions musulmanes* (Paris, 1935) are specially recommended. Two rather specialised monographs ought to be better known than they are: J. Gernet: *Les Aspects économiques du Bouddhisme dans la société Chinoise du Ve au VIe siecle* (Saigon, 1956); and Wilhelm Rau: *Staat und Gesellschaft in alten Indien nach den Brāhmana-Texten Dargestellt* (Wiesbaden, 1957). The quotation in the final section of this chapter is from E. H. Carr's *What is History?* (London, 1962), pp. 20, 31, 62.

Primitive Life and Prehistory

2.1. *The Golden Age*

LEGENDS of man's fall from a pristine state of perfection are found in the myths of many different lands and people. So also in India. Modern Hindus speak of the present as the dark age (*kali yuga*) of mankind. It was supposedly preceded by three nobler periods. The first and best was the golden 'Age of Truth' (*satya yuga* or *krita yuga*). Men knew neither illness nor want. They toiled not, neither did they spin, for this good earth bore in plenty of her own accord. Peaceful, innocent, simple, virtuous, each man lived for thousands of years. Then human greed developed; men began to accumulate private property, to hoard acquisitions. These sinful activities led successfully to the *treta*, *dvāpara* and *kali* ages, each worse than the preceding. Life spans became shorter; war, disease, poverty, and hunger afflicted mankind because of its lapse from purity. The Buddhist and Jain religious books contain similar versions. The brahmin record, being the most recent, branched out with a further theory of endless cycles (*manvantara*). The present dark (*kali*) age is to end in a universal deluge. After the total destruction of all life by the flood, the earth will emerge from the waters and a new golden age begin again, followed in time by the three other ages of progressive decay, to end in another flood. Thus it was in the past, so shall it be in future cycles. This depressing view of pointless historical repetition is simply a projection of the dull seasonal life of the Indian village, as said before. The October harvest is followed by cool weather with a season of health and plenty. Then comes progressive scarcity, ending in a period when bitter toil under bad conditions is needed just to prepare the parched fields for sowing. Finally, the terrific monsoon rain floods all the land; after which the seasonal cycle repeats itself for another year of the same type.

In spite of the widespread myth, there was no original golden age of mankind outside the imagination of later poets and priests. We know this first by interpreting historical records directly where they exist, say from 2500 B.C., in a few places outside India. Beyond that archaeology has to help decipher the past. When the archaeologist digs in a spot where the earth has not been disturbed seriously in recent times, he finds a deposit in uneven layers (strata) clearly separated from each other. The older strata are the lower ones, so that the order in time is clear. Many of these strata contain evidence of human activity. This evidence may be in the form of bodily remains such as bones, a skull, or even a single tooth which can tell a great deal about the type of human being who grew it. The bones of the animals man hunted are often found with his own; so also of the animals he tamed: dog, cattle, sheep, horse. It is possible by comparing the layers to say that the dog was tamed long before the horse; cattle and sheep at some intermediate period. Pottery, tools of stone, metal objects are all in the class of things made by man, which are therefore called artifacts. If the climate is dry, as in Egypt, wooden implements, bones and ivory weapons, basketwork, fibres such as wool and linen woven into cloth, cereal grains, pictures or writing on papyrus are preserved, so that we can tell approximately the order in which man learned to produce these various things. Cultivated grains—though not classed as artifacts—are as much a product of human activity as pottery. All of them were developed over thousands of years by careful selection and repeated sowing of the fattest natural grass seeds. If human activity ceased, all cultivated varieties would vanish or be replaced by the hardier wild prototypes in a few plant generations. The stratified record is a historical sequence; any later disturbance such as a pit dug through the upper layers can be recognised and set aside by the trained expert. Comparison of finds in various places tells us how far a given type of tool, pottery, cereal, etc., was spread. Finally, modern technique allows a fairly good system of dates to be assigned by measurement of fluorine content, radioactivity of charcoal and bone, geomagnetic observations, seasonal variations in the growth of tree rings (dendrochronology), and the like. The past thus reconstructed goes back (with many gaps) for several hundred years till we reach barely human types such as Java man, Peking man, and the pre-human African Proconsul skull. This takes us from archaeology into geology; from a study of history to that of the evolution of mammals, vertebrates, and other forms of life.

But throughout all this, nowhere is any evidence found of a lost golden age, a state of pristine glory. Man did not progress uniformly or steadily; but he did progress on the whole, from a fairly inefficient animal to a tool-making and tool-using creature who dominated the whole planet by his numbers and by the varied forms of his activity, and has now only to learn to control himself. Human bones dug up after several tens of thousands of years show that it was a spectacular achievement for any Old Stone Age man to reach as much as forty years of age; far from being healthier, he suffered even more than we do from parasites and crippling illness that shortened his life. The golden age, if any, lies in the future, not in the past.

2.2. Prehistory and Primitive Life

The archaeologist's finds do not tell by themselves how the men of some particular period actually lived. To reconstruct that way of life (the whole 'culture') needs comparative study of many different primitive tribes still surviving in out-of-the-way places of this world. Then it gradually becomes clear how a given set of tools was made and used, how the people who made them in the remote past must have lived. Something can even be said of the social organisation—when social organisation came into being—but with less certainty. The very fact that a primitive tribe in Australia or the interior of Brazil can be studied means that the tribesmen have had some contact with the outside world and eventually with civilisation. This has to be allowed for, because there is no contact without change. Secondly, no human group can remain in a fixed state for long. Either they evolve to some more efficient form or decay by atrophy. The prehistoric people we want to study have vanished from the face of the earth. Some groups left descendants who advanced to modern civilisation, others just disappeared. The few that remain in the remote corners have developed some ideas, mental attitudes, superstitions, ritual customs, observances that prevent them from trying newer forms of life. Most contemporary savage groups have a social structure which is rigid enough to discourage any innovation, though it is not the same social structure for all. No materialist can afford to neglect the effect of ideas upon social development.

The archaeological record over such parts of the world as have been extensively dug up shows roughly the following sequence: Lowest, hence earliest are crude bits of chipped stone. These were used as tools, along with pieces of wood and bone that have generally perished. This Old Stone Age (Palaeolithic) made several very slow advances over a hundred thousand years or more in the technique of stone-tool chipping. It was ultimately succeeded by the age of polished stone tools (Neolithic). In between the two came what was called the Mesolithic Age, a term not now in fashion; its extent and duration are indeterminate. These underlying strata, bearing tools only of stone (and presumably of bone, wood, and horn) were covered in time by other layers with remains of metal tools and metal weapons. The first widely used metal was copper, which can be reduced from its ores by a kiln not more efficient than that needed for pottery; pottery is to be found along with stone tools in the Late Stone Age. Copper is too soft to be useful without working, and then too brittle unless properly alloyed with some metal such as tin, which gives bronze. Since tin is not widespread, the Bronze Age implies considerable exploration. Trade over long distances was in full swing by 3000 B.C. or even earlier. Bronze was at best rather rare and remained in the possession of a few. This meant differentiation of society into classes. The Bronze Age saw considerable fighting and raids over large distances for control of metal ores and of good sources of water. In the second millennium B.C. (2000–1000 B.C.) there were numerous tribes on the move, with an ample but mobile food supply (usually cattle), who wandered the Eurasian continent. The older river-valley agrarian cultures of Egypt and Mesopotamia had developed city-states, monarchies, temple priesthoods and warfare a good thousand years earlier. Such development was local and exceptional.

The present age is archaeologically that of iron, the metal which is cheap enough and widespread enough to make agriculture a universal possibility. Some agriculture did emerge in the Late Stone Age, so that we can speak of a 'neolithic revolution' in the means of production. But this was restricted to certain favoured places where it was not necessary to clear away heavy forests: Mesopotamia (Iraq), Egypt, the Indus valley, highland plains in Iran, Turkey, and Palestine, and parts of the Danube valley loess corridor; perhaps some loess areas in China. Iron, though softer than bronze when first prepared, did enable forests to be cleared and the plough to be used in heavier soils. It was the first metal that was available to many, not the monopoly of a tight warrior class. The first farmers who could build towns go back to 7000–8000 B.C. at Catal Hüyük (Turkey) and Jericho (Palestine); but their technique of producing food could not be widely applied to the neighbouring terrain. Their farming, unlike that in Egypt and Iraq, remained a supplement to food-gathering and herding till iron became available in quantity towards the end of the second millennium B.C. The first good processes of iron manufacture seem to have been a closely guarded monopoly of the Hittites in what is now Turkey. Iron was so rare even in 1350 B.C. that the Pharaoh Tutankhamen was buried in a solid gold coffin, in a tomb full of copper, gold, bronze, ivory, and other precious objects, but with an iron amulet bound below his skull. The discovery of cheap iron did not mean happiness for the majority. The small isolated farming communities of Asia Minor had often been swept away even in the Bronze Age by raiders. Only when abundant manpower (often slaves or helots bound to the soil) was available did the use of iron mean more food—with more oppression. There remained (almost to this day) a few isolated tribal people, away from trade routes, who stubbornly persisted in Stone Age techniques of food-gathering rather than change to production. They dropped out of the advance to civilisation. The casual use of stone continued from prehistory well into history. Many Saxons of King Harold's army were armed with stone axes at the battle of Hastings in A.D. 1066, though England had entered the Iron Age long before Julius Caesar's invasion of the island in 54 B.C.

It is not easy to characterise food-gathering society as a whole. The modern romanticist school believed that primitive man must be a noble savage, a child of nature uncorrupted by civilisation, free from vices and cupidity. This fiction of a 'natural' earthly paradise began with a letter of Christopher Columbus to Queen Isabella of Castille. The explorer, having failed to reach the golden cities of India, was anxious to show that he had at any rate discovered something extraordinary—Caribbean man in the natural state. European imagination thus stirred up found something not in the Bible (after the Garden of Eden) nor the utopias of the Greek-Latin classics rediscovered by the Renaissance. The social theories of Rousseau and the devastating satire of Voltaire against the society of his day gained strength from this discovery of Natural Man. Some people even now talk of primitive communism as if it were an ideal state of society in which all shared alike and satisfied their simple needs by co-operation. Carried to its extremes, this is again the legend of the 'Golden Age' in pinkish modern garb.

Early food-gathering society was severely restricted. Its special character was determined in each locality and period by the scanty and uncertain food supply. A careful archaeologist like Grahame Clark estimates the Upper Paleolithic population of England and Wales as perhaps 250 human beings in ten small bands; in the Mesolithic, 4500 for Great Britain as a whole, 20,000 in the Neolithic at any one time, and less than double this number in the second millennium B.C., when the Bronze Age and food production were well under way. It is not possible to give corresponding estimates for India, so poor is the necessary archaeological evidence at present. However, it would be surprising if the Stone Age population exceeded one per ten square miles over any extensive region of the Indian sub-continent. Even where nature is kind, it is not uniformly bountiful at all seasons; there may be several consecutive years of scarcity.

A large total population and fixed settlements are out of the question without some form of food storage. The preservation of food comes comparatively late in food-gathering life. It needs salt obtained from some distance for meat and dried fish; also containers such as baskets, leather bags, pottery. Not all food can be preserved. The best forms for storage are nuts, grain, and some roots. Most of these are not digestible without cooking, which implies control of fire and some pottery or utensils. Long before advancing to this stage man had already developed particular ways of social life, because he had already lived as a tool-using animal for many thousands of years.

Two features are obvious. If food cannot be preserved, it must be eaten fairly soon. This means sharing any surplus, or most humans would starve; but many animal groups also share their surplus. In primitive human groups which go beyond the stage of utter scarcity the sharing eventually became a social obligation, say the need to give feasts on special occasions. It does not mean that every person had equal right to the share of all food gathered. Secondly, food-gatherers rarely collect or kill more than they can use; there is no greedy accumulation or slaughter of game for pure sport, letting the meat rot. To this extent the legend of the 'Golden Age' has some truth. However, most of primitive man's energies were absorbed in the search for food. The largest food-sharing unit, always limited in size by the environment, tended to concentrate upon some one type of food, say an animal, fish, bird, insect, fruit, or tuber. This meant not just specialisation but overspecialisation. The human unit regarded itself not only as a kinship group but as of the same substance as its principal or favoured food. Other human groups specialising in some other food object were not in the kinship and at first not even considered as human. We may call this special food the totem, though at a much later stage inanimate objects or parts of an animal could be group-classifying totems also. The particular aptitude for gathering the totem food was associated with special ritual. Sacrifice of some sort (including human sacrifice) and other ceremonies were meant, however blindly, to secure the increase of the (special) food supply, hence of the particular semi-parasitic human group that ate it. These ceremonies are important to us because they contain the seeds of modern human cultural activities. The dance, perhaps with some people imitating the animal, others the hunters, was ritual as well as practice for work in the field, a drill in the technique of the hunt, as it were. The ballet and the drama would develop from this after many millennia. Pictures of wild animals drawn with remarkable faithfulness in the Ice Age (French and Spanish caves) now count as masterpieces of art. Nevertheless, the original pictures could not have had art as their main purpose. They were

drawn with the aid of dim tallow lamps or torches in pitch-dark sub-
terranean caverns where daylight never penetrated. The pictures often
overlap and spoil each other. Excellent animal sculpture was used for
ritual target practice, as shown by the holes made by spears and arrows;
these sculptures are also underground, in the very womb of Mother Earth.
Pairs of coupling animals carved or moulded on the cave walls show that all
such artistic expressions were part of what are called fertility rites, the
exclusive secret of the particular group. Animals, too, may form exclusive
communities within the same species because of restricted food supply.
For example, gopher groups in the U.S. midwestern prairies do not
tolerate a strange gopher in their territory, but live at peace among themselves. They have a peculiar 'rite', the 'kiss' which serves for recognition
within the group. The human groups we are considering must have had
similar reserved though shifting territories. Each group communicated its
limited ideas by means of a special set of sounds, which could hardly be
classified in modern linguistic varieties, as far as we can collect any evidence on primitive life. Because underlying causes later discovered by
scientific analysis were still hidden, primitive man dared not deviate from
accepted ritual.

The great step of bringing the groups nearer to each other was literally
in the relations of production, namely by exchange. Free barter is not
known to primitive societies in their earlier stages, such as (for example)
could be found at the turn of the nineteenth–twentieth centuries in the
Trobriand Islands. Outside the sharing kinship group, barter appears as an
exchange of gifts. The gift is not made to just anyone, but to persons with
specific relationship, often called 'trade friends'. The gift cannot be asked
for or refused, nor paid by haggling about the equivalent. But such a gift
does oblige the recipient to give something of his own back at some later
time when he has a surplus. No accounts are kept, yet there is a general
sense of equivalence over a period of time. He who does not eventually
return what is tacitly recognised by both sides as an equivalent loses his
social standing in some way. According to the accepted reconstruction, the
first exchanges between totem groups led also to the exchange of persons,
i.e. to some form of 'marriage' relationship. It also led to a better diet, a
wider range of food, and improved techniques of tool-making or tool-using
and pottery. Finally, the language of the combined groups was enriched.
All known primitive languages have a needlessly complicated grammar, a
feature also shared by Sanskrit, Greek, and Finnish. General concepts are
less common than special terms; 'animal', 'tree', etc., as general categories
are absent, but there is a word for every particular species and type of
animal and plant. The word 'colour', as is known, originally means 'red',

the colour of blood. Language itself thus develops from communication and exchange. Man is then on his way not only to the control and then the production of food but also to becoming a thinking animal. There is a genetic advantage in marriage-exchange. Small human groups often become inbred and physically stunted or mentally retarded. Intermarriage ('hybridisation') increases the vigour of the offspring to a level above that of both parents. The sudden appearance of the superbly built Cro-Magnon man in Late Ice Age Europe could have been due to such cross-breeding between stunted inbred parent stocks. It should be understood that race is not a valid concept at this stage of human development. The use of the word 'race' in common parlance is rarely valid at any stage. The extant races developed later from large populations that grew out of pools of common groups; the development of language was sharper.

The advantages were not the result of experiment, planning, or reasoned action. Those groups that adopted the new scheme of exchange increased in numbers and efficiency; the rest were driven to extinction. The first step, a dialectical inversion, was the banning (tabu) for each group of its special food, the totem. The tabu would be broken only at special seasonal ceremonies or in connection with the cult of the dead. With the tabu on totem food came a tabu on sexual intercourse within the totem. Thus tribes were formed out of several totemic clans. No member of a clan was normally permitted to partake of the clan-totem food or to cohabit within the totem clan; nor could he 'marry' outside the tribe. Often, he could not accept food prepared by individuals not of his own tribe. Members of the clan retained special cults from which all other clans were excluded. There were also similar cults common to the whole tribe, as was the tribal language. Once formed, this tribal organisation beyond the small clan provided a model that has left its mark on most human societies.

2.3. Prehistoric Man in India

So far the statements have been general. The picture has been restored from conjecture and reasoning based upon reports of observations all over the world. Nothing specific has been said about India, simply because the data are much too meagre. There is no reason to believe that early developments in India took any course materially different from the foregoing. If prehistoric changes occurred as suggested above, many features of rural and tribal Indian society as well as old Sanskrit texts would be logically explained; if not there would be no reasonable explanation.

Two special characteristics of Indian prehistory must be noted. The last Ice Age was neither so hard nor so extensive over the Indian sub-continent as over Europe. Hereafter, India is taken as a geographical unit also including Pākistān with a part of Afghanistan and at times of Burma. No political claims or motives should be imputed to this extension. Whereas there was an Ice Age in the north, the south and south-east escaped altogether. There is every likelihood that the eastern parts of India proper were penetrated by prehistoric people from Yunnan and Burma. The movement may even have continued well into historic times. The stone tools of this eastern region show common materials and technique. Secondly, food-gathering apart from hunting or fishing remained much easier over most of India and had a far greater range than in Europe or elsewhere on the Eurasian continent. Where half a dozen cereals, peas and beans make up almost the entire variety of European staple foods, even a region of average fertility like Mahārāshtra has over forty kinds of indigenous staples, most of which are cultivated but can also be found wild. All are suitable for storing. These include rice and wheat, millets, sorghum, barley; with a considerable variety of vegetable proteins, and seeds like sesamum that produce edible oil. Pepper and spices give good taste as well as vitamins. A balanced diet is possible without killing any living creatures, especially as milk, butter, curds and cheese, fruit and vegetables can be had without taking animal life. This simple fact was later to revolutionise Indian theology and religion with the doctrine of non-killing (*ahimsā*). At the same time, it makes the historian's task more difficult than elsewhere. People could and did survive in the food-gathering stage when their immediate neighbours had become food-producers centuries earlier. Peasants and tribal people, especially in out-of-the-way places in the jungle, normally know over a hundred other natural products beyond the staples, which may be gathered without cultivation: fruits, nuts, roots, tubers, honey, mushrooms, leaf vegetables, etc. With the older mode there would always remain older beliefs and ways of life. India is a country of tremendous survivals for this very reason. It becomes difficult to say precisely when a given stage passed and another took over. The process of acculturation was mutual. Not only did advanced immigrants influence aboriginals in every part of India but the newcomers (before the intolerant Muslims) generally took over some indigenous and even aboriginal beliefs and customs. To constitute a proper society, a set of human beings must be in some productive relationship which involves the creation and transfer of surplus. In India the formation of such a society and of its culture was—because of the ease and survival of food-gathering—based to a considerable extent on religion and superstition. This reduced the amount of violence (force) necessary, as compared with Europe or America.

We have now two main tasks: To say whatever is known about prehistoric man in India; and to trace primitive survivals as the contribution of prehistory to modern Indian society.

The great difficulty in tracing prehistoric man in India is the problem of dating. Prehistory survived late in the south when the north was already developing historical empires. The few Indian cave paintings discovered show battle scenes of feudal times in the top layers. How old the pictures underneath might be is anyone's guess. Prehistoric tool-making man in India as in the Soan valley (W. Pākistān) generally used the Levallois technique in flaking his stone tools. This is not the oldest method of tool manufacture, but roughly the second oldest. The date may be (at a rough guess) 50000 to 100000 B.C. Hand axes of this type can be traced over the whole Eurasian continent. Nothing can, so far, be said of any corresponding movement of human beings. By 7000 B.C., however, large deposits of much smaller stone tools (microliths) are found from Europe to Palestine. Their continuity through caves inhabited by prehistoric man in Iran and Afghanistan makes it likely that the Indian specimens are not much later. There is no reason to believe that such little stone tools originated in India to spread out into the rest of Eurasia.

Microliths are first found with larger stone hand axes and scrapers, perhaps as waste products of manufacture. The Mesolithic Age showed a remarkable development in many parts of the world in that microliths are then found in considerable deposits without any larger tools at all (the age of polished stone tools, Neolithic or Late Stone Age came later). This happens for example at Jericho, in the pre-pottery B layer. The absence of pottery is also significant. In India such purely microlithic pre-pottery 'cultures' have also been traced, as for example from the sand dunes (teri) of the south-east coast. These Teri cultures are roughly dated at 4000 B.C. or earlier. A thousand years is as close an approximation as can be made by known methods for such dating. No radiocarbon or other tests have so far been possible. These microlithic people left their deposits of beautiful little chalcedony flakes and cores along narrow tracks all through the western peninsula. The most productive microlith sites are by minor streams with fishing-pools in ancient times, though the pools are now generally silted up because of modern deforestation and erosion. The same erosion of the soil exposes the stone-tool deposit on the banks while showing the absence of occupation strata. These users of microliths were not in the crudest stage of food-gathering. Their tools are too small to be used as we find them. From comparison with the practice of African Bushmen, it is obvious that the Indian pieces of chalcedony, beautifully faceted and sharpened by chipping or cutting fine teeth in the edge, were part of compound tools. The chips were set in handles of wood, horn, or

35

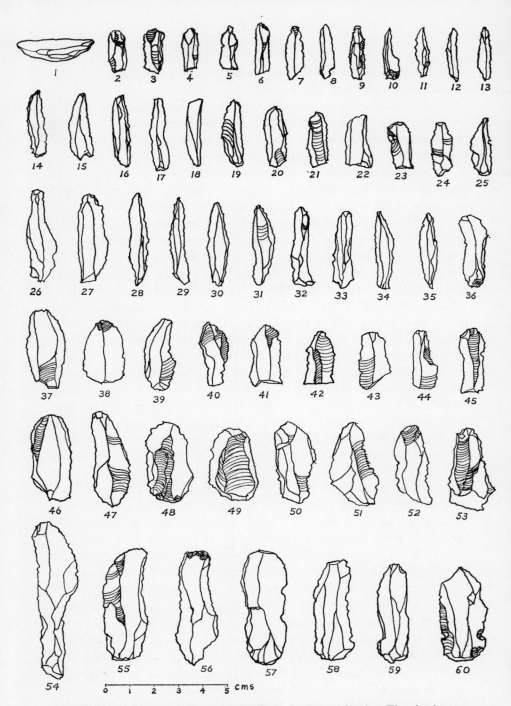

FIG. 4. Pre-pottery microliths from Deulgão, in Poona district. The site is on a tributary to the Bhīmā river by an ancient fishing-pool, still in use. The material for the flakes is almost exclusively chalcedony, and many of the pieces formed compound tools, set into wood, bone, or horn hafts for arrows, knives, sickles and the like. The finer pieces are awls for stitching leather or hide bags, for food storage in the absence of pottery. The date might be 4000 B.C. or earlier, at a rough guess.

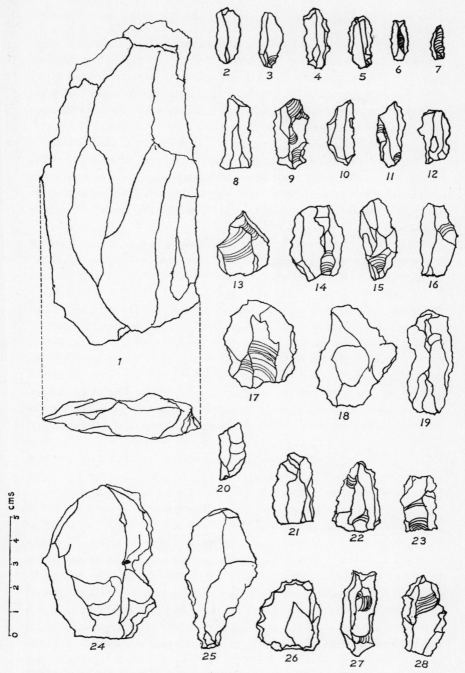

Fig. 5. Highland microliths, found near Poona, mostly in association with mega-lithic rock-engravings and hillside terraces. Though of rougher fabric, these seem to be later than those in the preceding illustration; the hides on which they were used were thicker. The users were early cattle-raisers, of whom successive waves came into the territory. The male gods were definitely associated with the final waves.

bone by means of tree-gum or some such adhesive. This is also proved by discoloration on some facets, away from the cutting edge. Thus could be made javelins, barbed harpoons, arrows, knives, sickles, etc. Some types of small flints are known, in fact, to be sickle-teeth, which means that grain collection was already in progress, whether the grain was planted or natural grasses cut for their seed. These tools are ideally suited for skinning animals, 'tanning' their hides by scraping off the flesh and breaking the fibres under the skin; suited also for splitting basket-maker's withes or preparing fish for the pot. A good number of narrow, sharp-pointed flakes are needles or awls for stitching the hides, presumably with sinew. In other words, the first steps towards food storage in baskets and leather bags had already been taken long before pottery.

Along with these purely microlithic people were others (perhaps branches of the same groups) who left large stone piles, the megaliths. In Karnātak, Āndhra and granite-based country, these megaliths were found to belong to the Iron Age. In Mahārāshtra (based on Deccan trap), the megaliths seem to be much older, but later than the best microliths. Many of the rock piles in the western Deccan might be due primarily to nature; but prehistoric man left his mark upon them in the form of deep engravings. The grooves were made entirely by rubbing, or at least finished by rubbing. The amount of labour expended is shown by the depth of grooves, which is at times as much as 4 centimetres. The stone is hard enough even to turn the edges of modern steel tools. In some cases, rocks weighing more than three tons have been shifted and placed upon others. It follows that the megalith people had enough time and enough regular food surplus to produce monuments that needed a great deal of hard and continued physical work. There are so many thousands of these rock piles and rock engravings discovered so far that the work must have gone on year after year, century after century. The purpose is not clear. The grooves rarely make any special design beyond the simplest circles or ovals; never any recognisable human or animal figures or trees. Often they are just meandering grooves made by human agency, not by nature. It is a fair guess that these megalithic people had some cattle. The microliths found in their piles of boulders are decidedly thicker as a rule than those by the fishing-pools or camp sites. There is often a clear demarcation line between the territory of the two types. Sometimes each type is found on one bank of the stream exclusively, with the megaliths always close to the rougher microliths. But this does not hold for the whole length of any known stream. The implication is that the rock engravers and megalith builders had to deal with thicker hides, hence possessed cattle. The 'thin-microlith' people could have processed only thin skins: deer, sheep, goats, hare, along with the dressing of fish and birds. What the relations were between those two human groups is not clear. There is no evidence of any early conflict. The terrain does not permit stratified deposits except in a few unusual places. That is, the heaviest deposit of soil today is not only washed down from higher levels and levelled by ploughing but also lies in places where there must have been swamps and thick jungles in prehistory. These would generally be the localities where prehistoric man would find no exposed stone for tools nor sites favourable for camping. The older camp sites have now very little soil, owing not only to erosion but also to the original need for dry spots away from thick vegetation and dangerous wild life. There was no question of permanent occupation; no stratified deposit is possible in most of these situations.

These two cultures are of special interest for their continuity into history. We shall show that the western Deccan developed agriculture very rapidly in the sixth century B.C., with the local Iron Age; but not earlier. There was no Copper Age worth the mention in the Deccan. An occasional site with a bronze tool but long-interrupted occupation is found as at Maheśvar (early in the second millennium B.C.). There had been several waves of the megalithic people, perhaps moving slowly over long periods up and down the river valleys (Bhimā, Krishnā, Tungabhadrā, Godāvāri), part from their short-term seasonal movements for better grazing and water. The seasonal oscillation is called 'booly' or 'transhumance', its total range being limited compared to the long-range migration. It is obvious that both the microlithic and the megalithic people had movements of both types. When the monsoon sets in, the constant damp will rot the hooves of sheep. Game will move downriver, towards the drier east. After the monsoon months, it is easier to move back where the grass and forest have been renewed after the rain. The westward movement would also bring primitive man nearer to the salt of the coast. A few prehistoric sites on the coast are known from excavations—presumably salt camps. The high Deccan scarp which rises sheer to 500 metres or more and lies only 50 kilometres or less from the coast is broken by a few passes. These passes were to tie down the later trade routes. On the coast, as on the plateau, an occasional stone ring is found which was used to weight digging sticks. This implies primitive agriculture of some kind, not so productive as cultivation with a plough, and probably the work of women only. Thus we have cattle, salt, access to the coast, stone tools, control of fire, with a maximum variety of natural products (game as well as vegetable) on the mountain range near the coast. The stage was set for history in the Deccan, which would begin when the aborigines learned to extract iron from 'red earth' by fire. That

39

the ultimate stimulus and technique came from the north will be shown later. It is not known, however, whether the earliest cattlemen had something to do with the north as well. Their tracks go across the peninsula, up and down the main river valleys of the south. The last waves re-used megalithic cult spots as their own, where the gods are still worshipped by modern villagers; but the pastoral (*gavali*) people who brought the present gods did not build the original megaliths, only re-used megalithic material with engraved rocks for their cults or burial cairns. Their male god, later become Mhasobā or some equivalent, had originally no consort and was for a while in conflict with the earlier mother goddess of the food-gatherers. The two groups soon fused, however, and the deities were accordingly married. Sometimes, one can find the goddess crushing the buffalo-demon Mhasobā in some rude shrine while 400 metres away she is married to the same Mhasobā with slightly changed name. The brahminical reflection of this is Pārvati as consort of Śiva, but crushing Mahishāsura; and on occasion she reverts to type by trampling upon Śiva as well. It is significant that the three-faced prototype of Śiva on an Indus valley seal wears buffalo horns as part of his headdress.

The prehistoric survivals which affect both the means of production and the religious superstructure have only been pointed out in recent years. For no other country is the peculiar survival and expansion of prehistory even during the course of long historical development so clearly discernible. This is the special historical and social character of India. The course of evolution has left its clear, indelible mark upon the complex Indian society of today.

2.4. *Primitive Survivals in the Means of Production*

How is the development of prehistoric man into a civilised human being to be traced in India? One method tried is anthropometry, the measurement of physical character such as height, weight, size and shape of skull, length and breadth of nose, colour of skin, eyes, and hair, etc. This method gives no results worth the mention. Prehistory yields only a few human bones. Anthropometric characters (including facial type) change in a few generations of decidedly better or decidedly worse way of life. All surviving primitive people in India seem at first to be slight and physically underdeveloped when allowance is made for admixture from the surrounding population. But they do not otherwise belong to one common physical type. There is every reason to believe that such primitive types are generally unstable. Better diet and regular work on the fields change stature and physique after some generations. Statistical analysis of such Indian data as are known shows that the head measurements and face (nasal index) also change with the height.

Linguistic research is even less fruitful for this stage. The dozen or so main languages and some 753 dialects of varying importance used in India are often grouped into three classes: (1) The Indo-Aryan group, in north and west: Panjābi, Hindi (including Rājasthān and Bihār varieties), Bengāli, Gujarāti, Marāthī, Oriyā; (2) Dravidian, in the south: Telugu, Tāmil, Malayālam, Kanarese, Tulu; (3) the 'Austro-Asiatic' group into which most primitive languages of India are quite arbitrarily thrust: Mundāri, Orāon, Santāli, etc. The theory was that these primitive people were pushed into odd corners of the jungle by Dravidians, whom the Aryans in turn drove southwards. The Aryan invasion is historic and well attested. The rest is extremely dubious conjecture. One skull of Dravidian type found in Soviet Central Asia, in strata of the third millennium B.C., was rare in that environment. The Brāhui language in the north-west is a solitary Dravidian 'island' among speakers of Aryan languages. The Brāhui-speaking group may have reached their place in historic times, for Dravidians in considerable number went northwards as late as the eleventh century A.D. The linguistic analysis pays no attention to the influence of the way of livelihood upon language. All primitive Indian languages do not belong to a single group, as dispassionate research has shown. In Assam, where every valley has several tribes with different speech, the number of languages or major dialects rises to over 175, mostly primitive tribal idioms which cannot be related to Mundāri or indeed even to any one linguistic group. Nor can the Assam people be regarded as having been pushed back by the Dravidians. This is generally ignored with the explanation that Assam is not India proper; primitive man in India (we are told) must have been thrust into the jungle by the Dravidians, who took over the fertile lands. As a matter of fact, this fertile land was obviously covered with dense forest or swamp before the Iron Age. Primitive man would live best in the thinner marginal jungle, not in territory now bearing the deeper, cultivated soil; that is, the best localities for the food-gatherers were approximately where they are found today. The first cattle-breeders and food-producers had no need to push anyone back. Finally, though the Dravidians are on the whole darker than the Aryan-speaking people, there is no chance of correlating language and race; the Brāhuis are not of Dravidian race, so far as I am aware of the results of modern anthropology.

This leaves us simply the instrument and relations of production, of which the former can be compared with prehistoric finds. There are no tribesmen left in India who make stone arrowheads, hand axes, or microliths

41

for general use which could then have been compared to the prehistoric. Kāthakari tribesmen of the Western Ghāts do say that their ancestors some generations ago made stone arrowheads of the crudest sort. None of their modern descendants can make such arrowheads now, or show any that belonged to their ancestors. In the Andamān islands, the aborigines in contact with the British began to strike flakes out of bottle glass because the glass sherds were sharper than any stone. Metal soon became the common tool material everywhere. I know of only one exceptional survival of the use of microliths. The Dhangar (shepherd) caste in the Deccan and Central India still use freshly made chips of chalcedony for castrating rams and he-goats. These are microliths in the strict sense of the word, though very crude. The prehistoric technique was far more delicate, but prehistoric microliths are not recognised as artifacts or tools by modern Dhangars. The reason for this survival of flint knives is that the wounds made by freshly chipped stone are not readily infected, as would be those made with unsterilised metal knives. The stone fragment is discarded after a single operation. (The Jews retained the use of flint knives for circumcision even when metal was in general use; the practical reason was presumably the lower incidence of infection. However, ritual tends always to be conservative; the ancient Romans retained stone axes and bronze knives for their sacrifices, when iron and steel were in common use.)

The Dhangars are mostly nomadic sheep-herders. The unit (*vādi*) of a dozen people and about 350 sheep moves constantly for the greater part of the year to come back to a temporary residence for the four rainy months. If this place should be at a spot where the precipitation is still too heavy, they again move eastwards after the monsoon begins. The men tend and graze the sheep, while the women go directly with their few pots, fleece tents, and the children, loaded on pack ponies, to the next camp site. The Dhangars have now become an adjunct of farming. Their main source of food is not the meat of the sheep or produce gathered from the jungle, but the grain (or money) given by the farmers on whose land they pen the sheep by agreement for two or three nights. The sheep droppings fertilise the land and increase the yield. The route of the drover's round, which may cover as much as 400 miles in the eight dry months, has obviously changed from the original pasturage booly track to farmland. The original Dhangar language, whatever it was, has also changed into that of the surrounding peasantry, Marāthi or Hindi. The Dhangars supplement their livelihood by selling an occasional sheep and by sale of the wool clip. A few used to weave rough blankets from the wool. All these activities now relate them to the general society within which they move. Hence they have become a Hindu caste just below the peasant farmers. It is possible to restore their original seasonal movements by studying the places most convenient for grazing and for rainy-season settlement. The remarkable fact then appears that the best of these older Dhangar tracks, roughly the left-bank margin of the Karhā valley (which was never under dense forest), goes back into prehistory and is a firm base for the fine Deccan microlithic culture. In other words, the Dhangar way of life has its roots in pre-history. They now cremate as well as bury their dead; burial was their former general custom—a normal course of development in India. Two of their special gods (Birobā and Khandobā) can be traced back to well before the fourth century A.D., though the principal worshippers of these gods are now other Hindu castes. One place (Vir) of special annual worship has clear relics of human sacrifice made to the god (and perhaps to the cult of the founder) when the settlement was founded, probably in the early centuries A.D. The peasants of the modern settlement are not Dhangars, having changed their caste with the transition to agriculture; but the main founder and principal devotee of the god was a Dhangar according to the strong, uncontested tradition.

We could as well have investigated castes or groups other than the Dhangars, say the Bhils. Originally a pre-Aryan people, presumbably not Dravidians, they have now become semi-tribal peasants farming the poorest land, though still known as good archers, hunters, fishermen, and food-gatherers. They took at some intermediate stage to the pastoral life, their agriculture being a recent development. As a result, the Bhil language is now a dialect of Gujarāti close to that of the Gujars from whom they learned to keep cattle. This is a normal phenomenon: when two cultures are in contact the stronger form of production often imposes its language upon the other. The Bhils are themselves supposed to have had a similar effect upon their dependants, the Nahāl tribesmen who once had a distinct language of their own. The specially interesting feature of the tribal Bhils is that they would and did fight at need throughout historic times, though never regularly organised as warriors. Some seem to have become kings near Mālavā about the first century B.C.; the royal house soon disappeared. The Gond tribesmen are as a whole still in the primitive stage, but a few of these chiefs became Gond *rājās* under feudalism. These baronial Gonds still exist, regarding themselves as separate from and superior to the rest. The primitive Todās of the Nilgiris have become a sort of tourists' and professional anthropologists' attraction. Most primitive of all, the Chenchus have lost their original language (though still primarily gatherers) and now speak a form of Telugu, the language of the peasants who furnish the productive environment. In other words, all such study proves that primitive societies are heavily affected by contact with those

43

whose means of production are more efficient. The immediate problem of Nāgaland lies in that some Nāgas have acquired a modern bourgeois education while the bulk of their fellows refuse to become the passive substratum of helpless peasants that characterises India past and present. The Nāga demand for a separate state (just granted) or complete independence was based on the remnants of tribal unity that come from the (former) absence of plough agriculture and bourgeois property-holding; and upon a long tradition of armed resistance to the encroachment of food-producing society.

What most observers miss is the *reciprocal* influence of tribesmen on the Indian peasant and even on the upper classes. Tribal cultivation is generally a shifting affair. A limited area is burned out, or the bush chopped down and burnt. Some seed are scattered in the ashes. Occasionally, the seeds are put in holes made by a pointed digging-stick (dibbler; Marāthī: *thombā*). The fertility of the soil is rapidly exhausted. After two years at most, new plots must be cleared and the old fallowed to grow new bushes and trees for six to ten years. This type of food production is actually practised by most tribes all over the country: Gāvadā on the west coast, Ho, Orāon, Santāl, Koltā, etc. The land cannot support as many people as with regular agriculture, but then plough culture demands more labour: levelling the ground, terracing the hillside, removal of stones, clearing of forest and stumps, the regular use of manure for fertiliser. All this means the ownership of plough beasts and implements. It often means individual ownership of the land by division into fixed plots, which eventually leads to class differences when the population increases owing to the better food supply. Nevertheless, even in many farming villages (say in Mahārāshtra, from which I take most of my examples because of familiarity) the peasant also supplements his plough culture with primitive slash-and-burn methods. These are naturally restricted to the village wastelands, usually high up on the hill, where terracing is not possible because of the hard basalt underbed and the steep slope. The seed-beds of rice (paddy, which has to be transplanted) are also prepared by a method that clearly derives from the slash-and-burn cultivation. In these beds are put leaves from the forest, with manure, earth, and chaff. The cake is allowed to dry till the leaves will burn, dampened so that it will not burn too fast, and then ignited. It smoulders; the chemicals needed for the young seedlings are baked into the soil. The rice seeds are planted on this prepared bed in the first rain. When the transplantation takes place these beds are left empty. On that small plot of land the peasant then plants the legumes (pulses, beans) without which rice cannot furnish him a balanced diet. This procedure led very naturally to the dicovery of crop rotation, so fundamental to efficient agriculture.

Some of the planting is still done by some Indian peasants and many tribesmen on the hillsides, with the *thombā* digging-sticks. This differs from the prehistoric in that no stone ring now weighs the digging-stick down. The modern stick is chest-high in place of the primitive ell-long tool; therefore heavier and thicker, with a steel point; but the primitive origins of the *thombā* are unmistakable. The seeds planted are of the lowest quality of staples such as *nāchani* (*Eleusine coracana*), *vari* (*Coix barbata*), *sāmvā* (*Panicum frumentaceum*), which are sometimes found wild. No ploughing is necessary or even possible on the steep hillsides where this method is used, but such cultivation requires extensive fallowing for about eight out of ten years. On small but level plots the hoe or long-handled pick is used in place of the plough. Where the soil is poor the cultivation is done by women to supplement the men's heavier agriculture. In the most primitive tribes the use of the digging-stick and hoe, i.e. all agriculture, is a monopoly of the women, as hunting is of the men. The fishermen have now become a set of specialised castes. Nevertheless, tribesmen and many peasants fish without nets, driving the fish into shallows or towards specially constructed brush dams and scooping them up with bare hands. I have seen incredibly dense microlith deposits left by their prehistoric ancestors on the banks of the same pools. Similarly for pottery. Though archaeology shows excellent pottery made on the fast wheel as long as five thousand years ago in the Indus region, prehistoric archaeology in the Deccan also shows cruder pottery made without the wheel. Such pots of all sizes are being made today, by exactly the same methods, on the slow-turning disc (*śevtā*) or without any disc at all. The remarkable feature is that this potter's disc is to be handled only by the women. The men finish the rough pot by paddling it down, with a wooden paddle used on the outside while a fist-sized stone 'anvil' is held in the other hand inside the pot. The sides can thus be made thinner and firmer before baking and the pot looks much better afterwards as regards finish and shape. The 'anvils' are found in excavation of strata two to three thousand years old. Pottery-making must have been the sole prerogative of the women, though the fast potter's wheel is and apparently always has been a men's apparatus.

2.5. Primitive Survivals in the Superstructure

If so much of primitive and prehistoric technique survived, it would be surprising to find no corresponding survival in form of social organisation, customs and beliefs, i.e. the relations of production. In fact, there are such survivals in plenty. For example, richer Indian kitchens may use oil or electricity for fuel, but they will also use (except in Āndhra and the south-east) the saddle quern and muller, which is a Stone Age appliance. There is a difference in shape; the modern kitchen quern is flat and wider than the muller. Its main use today is to grind or pulp coconut, spices, and soft condiments for the curry and vegetable dishes with which rice is eaten. Nothing harder than sea-salt is now ground on this type of quern. However, prehistory has left its imprint on the users. First, it is noticeable that the upper-class women who use it for cooking normally grip the muller stone on top. The lower-caste women generally grip it at the ends, which means less efficiency because the degree of rolling is restricted. If, however, the quern is shaped as in prehistory, with the muller stone wider than the bed-plate and the bed-plate sloping upward away from the user, the shape and the end grip are both more suitable for grinding hard stuff such as grain than the top grip with a flat modern quern. This indicates that the lower castes are closer to the days when the quern was actually used for making flour out of grain. All castes now use the much more efficient rotary quern or machine milling for flour manufacture, but the difference in using the saddle quern signifies the later transition to food production of the lower castes. Precisely these lower castes are now the workers and peasants, the primary food-producers. The class difference is also due to their later entrance on the stage of food production. This is clearly a very important historical and sociological phenomenon. The upper castes came from the north or were earlier influenced by northern food-producers, who first introduced real agriculture into the Deccan and had begun to use the rotary quern earlier. There is a second archaic heritage associated with the saddle quern, a peculiar ceremony not in the 'Hindu' (brahmin) books and indeed not reduced to writing at all. It is attended only by the women, which betrays its primitive and prehistoric origin. On the tenth (sometimes sixth or twelfth) day after the birth of the child the hard, smooth, cylindrical muller stone is passed around the cradle by the senior lady present, and deposited in the cradle. This is supposed to ensure that the child will grow up as free of blemish and as enduring as the stone. The stone is dressed in an infant's cape (kuñci), but also with a necklace or garland like a mother goddess. Some red and at times yellow pigment is put on the stone. The symbolism is never simple in such ceremonies. The stone represents at once the child and the mother goddess or good fairy which would bless the child. But the male priests remain unaware of the ceremony, which is practised by all castes, brahmins as well as the lower, and has undoubtedly been acquired from some portion of the primitive population, probably after the northern immigration. This is one example of reciprocal acculturation. Modern field investigators are almost always men to whom the aboriginal or lower-caste women would not talk of their special rites, if indeed they talked at all to the queer strangers. Otherwise we should have learned much more about such customs. It would also have been possible in some cases to discover the earlier language of the tribal group, which survives in women's parlance and ritual oftener than in those of the men. In general Indian women retain archaisms where the men show a cosmopolitan polish due to more frequent contact with people outside the tribe or caste group.

Better-known religious observances can also be traced back into the primitive or prehistoric past. The *holi* spring festival, an obscene and nowadays rather depraved saturnalia, has dancing around a great bonfire as its central feature. This may be followed by fire-walking by a select few on the embers, but is always followed the next day by a great deal of vociferous public obscenity; in out-of-the-way places by sexual licence and promiscuity as well. In prehistory the diet was poor, life hard, procreation none to easy. The obscenity was then necessary as a stimulus. The depravity is a modern transformation due to better diet with heavier peasant labour, resulting in a totally changed sexual appetite and attitude to sex. Some features of the *holi* festival seem to go back to a prehistoric matriarchal stage. In some places one man (called the *kolina*) has to wear woman's clothing and join the dancers about the *holi* fire. The chief participant at the great annual *Karagā* festival at Bangalore has to dress as a woman before officiating. So also the priest of the quail-snaring Pārdhis in western India for the Pārdhi fertility chants and ordeal by boiling oil. These rites and festivals have been taken over by men, though originally a women's monopoly. Similarly, groves sacred to the mother goddess are mentioned in brahmin myth and legend. Such groves still exist in villages away from the road; but women are now generally forbidden entry except in the few cases where the priesthood has remained in primitive hands, not transferred to immigrant settled cultivators. Originally, the ban was on the entry of men. When society changed from matriarchal to patriarchal, the priesthood and ritual were correspondingly transformed.

The intelligent study of village gods can also tell us a great deal. Most of the deities are simple bits of stone coated with red pigment, red lead in oil, ochre, or cheaper scarlet colouring matter. The colour is a substitute for blood. Indeed, blood sacrifices are still made on a few particular occasions to most of these gods and goddesses. When the village becomes richer through agriculture and the brahmin priest enters, these worships are identified with a few standard cults such as of the monkey god Hanumān, the elephant-headed Ganeśa, or Vetāl, prince of goblins. The deities are then represented by sculptured images which never completely shed their primitive features, but eventually rise in the scale to lose their red pigment and blood sacrifices. This progress of civilisation can easily be traced step by step. In some cases the prehistoric god (more often goddess) is still worshipped on or near the original cult spot, though there is usually no way of telling whether the name has survived unchanged. One striking exception is the Buddha's birthplace, where the goddess has survived under the same name (Lummini-Rummini) for over 2,500 years. At Junnar it can be said that the goddess Manmodi was present before the Buddhist caves were carved out at the beginning of the Christian era, and returned without change of name after Buddhism faded away a thousand years later. Many a time the god is identified, when worship becomes widespread and popular, with Śiva or Vishnu; a goddess with Pārvati, Lakshmi, or some such brahminised deity. The most interesting are the goddesses that have a strong, highly localised cult, but whose name has no known etymology: Mengāi, Māndhrāi, Songjāi, Udālāi, Kumbhaljā, Jhanjhani, etc. The termination *āi* means mother. Such names often represent some vanished tribe or clan group. The goddess Bolhai near Pernem is still worshipped at a prehistoric megalith (though the opulent feudal princely family of the Gaekwars built and endowed a fine temple a mile away, thereby wrecking a rich megalithic site). The name was old in the twelfth century A.D. and may perhaps be of Kanarese origin. There is no question, however, of a universal mother goddess. If the local cult spreads, it is generally possible to trace this spread to migration. Bolhāi's senior worshippers, now inhabiting a single village sixty kilometres away, all have the surname Vāji ('horse'). The goddess is supposed to have gone with some brigands (*cora*), which is a sure indication that she had been the patroness of an untamed tribe for a long time. There have been so many movements and changes in the population of this region that her megalith need not have been in continuous worship since prehistory. The memory always remained that certain types of places and stones were associated with the supernatural, the gods or demons. Both gods and demons are paid worship, for safety. The following often happens: Some peasant may have a dream in which a goddess (more rarely the Vetāl demon god, or the ghost of a dead relative) appeared. If there is already a shrine to that particular spirit or deity, he generally offers some sacrifice (nowadays, a coconut or a fowl; in great need, a goat) to escape further nightmares. A ghost is further propitiated by a funerary stele. But sometimes a goddess appears in the dream on some new spot. If the crop is unusually good that year, a cult is founded on that spot and continued by the peasant's family. The 'image' is often a simple stone (*tāndalā*—'shaped like a grain of rice') coated with red pigment. Or there may be installed a crude relief that looks five thousand years older than its date of fabrication. The family then maintains the new worship, which might spread to an entire hamlet if the deity 'saves' the whole community from disaster at some time of peril, famine, or epidemic. Remarkably enough, such new cults lie oftener than not on the site of some prehistoric predecessor, with microliths or megalithic engravings. I recently pointed out a neglected megalith to some friends who worship Vetāl in the scanty forest close to Poona. They immediately revived the lost cult in their own way with flowers and red pigment after more than twenty to thirty centuries of total oblivion. The modern name of the now flourishing cult is Nandi, from a fancied resemblance of the graven stone to Śiva's bull.

It is easy to point out many more primitive survivals in Indian life. A woman in her courses may not be touched by any male; even accidental contact means that the male must purify himself by a bath and have his clothes washed at once. The woman has to remain in isolation during her period. This menstrual tabu is being destroyed by modern city life. The Gondhalis are a professional caste of celebrants who specialise in a long-continued tumultuous dance to their own music and song, for special rustic ceremonies. The name can be traced to the aboriginal Gonds, from whom the performance seems to have been derived before A.D. 1100. The connection is now forgotten. The custom of swinging people by iron or steel hooks suspended from a horizontal ladder (bagād) on top of a post survives in many villages. The privilege of being swung is reserved for a few leading families. The hook is passed under a sash or belt; till the last century (and even now in a very few villages) the hook was actually passed through the muscles of the loin. This looks like an Iron Age custom, and so it may be. But it can be traced farther back in some localities as a substitute for still earlier human sacrifice. The chosen victim—also a privilege jealously reserved for members of a special clan or two—was treated as a god for a brief period, then beheaded and the head placed on a particular slab before the permanent god.

All such work remains the study of superstitions, an exercise in psychology and sociology. The study of the more recondite gods and cults can be taken somewhat deeper. The higher gods have one or more wives, children—sometimes half-animal like Ganeśa—with attendants who may be goblins. The gods ride different animals or birds, once tribal totems. The divine family and entourage is an historical phenomenon marking the emergence of a unified society out of different tribal elements which were formerly not united. To justify such combination, the brahmin books (purānas; which claim immemorial antiquity but were written or re-written to order generally between the sixth and the twelfth centuries A.D.) record specially fabricated myths. Then comes a higher stage of deep theology and a feudal court of the gods. This is in turn superseded by some philosophical interpretation, mysticism, and perhaps social reform. Such are the principal stages of characteristic Indian religious thought; the element of consistency and logic is unfortunately all too rare in such 'thinking', which never faces reality or gives a clear record of simple facts. The process of combining originally different gods is not continuous; it was repeated in parallel cycles all over the country as divers local cults were assimilated along with their followers. The organisation of the gods followed that of contemporary human society in a cruder way.

The people who were absorbed along with these cults managed to retain their identity and to some extent their previous clannish aloofness. This was accomplished by caste and always encouraged by unemployed brahmins, who would then serve as priests for the group. The caste group would not normally take cooked food from or with other castes, nor inter-marry with them. In fact kinship is at times described as exchange-intercourse in 'bread and daughters' (*roti-beti vyavahār*). This is a precise equivalent of primitive exchange of surplus food within the marriage-kinship group. (The most securely binding form of marriage in ancient Rome was the *confarreatio*, literally, exchange and breaking of bread by the couple. The binding power of commensality is also shown by 'companion', from *con* = with and *panis* = bread, as again in the etymology of the modern French *copain* for crony.) What holds caste together in theory is the top position of the brahmin, from whose hands anyone may take food, but whose daughters are to marry only brahmins. The bond of production varied, but there was a bond. *Caste is class on a primitive level of production.* In many cases the bond is simply of peasant families, all related, joining in general agriculture. But many castes were the equivalent of medieval guilds following specialised professions such as basket-makers, herb-vendors (Vaidū), diggers (Vaddars), fishermen. Some of these still try to remain in the Middle Ages with the rest of isolated village life. The tribal origins of many such castes is known: e.g. Kaivarta in Bihār and Bengal for 'fisher-man', Bhoi in Mahārāshtra. Totemic features also manifest themselves. Clan villages like that of the Vāji mentioned above are paralleled by others where every original inhabitant has the same surname: Crocodile (*Magar*), wolf (*Lāndge*), peacock (*More*), the sacred pipal tree (*Pimple*) speak for themselves. Whatever the origin, some totemic observances still remain. For example, the Mores cannot eat peacock flesh; the Pimples will not eat off the leaves of their totem tree and at one time would not cut its branches for firewood, though the lack of fuel has erased this tabu. The late-Vedic brahmin clan name Paippalāda ('eater of *pipal* figs') was formed in the same way.

The historical picture is of a slow expansion of food-producing society in a virtually limitless environment very thinly populated by food-gatherers. The productive society naturally bred much faster, and hence covered more and more virgin territory. Contact between producers and gatherers, whether by fighting or by some form of exchange, could not be avoided as the food-producers extended operations. Each marginal food-gathering group was numerically very small, but there was an endless variety of different tribes. Where agriculture will support as many as a hundred people per square kilometre, the most efficient hunting and food-gathering would not support even one person, and the richest pastoral life less than three on a rough calculation. Moreover, good agriculture is possible, with irrigation and fertilisers, over a much wider range of terrain than is food-gathering. The first food production on a large scale in India (actually Pākistān) was in the valley of the Indus river, namely West Panjāb and Sind. The dates would be 3000–1750 B.C. This could not spread beyond the particular type of land. Then came the real expansion to the east for 1,800 kilometres into the Gangetic basin; this required totally different techniques of food production, accompanied by a new social organisation —caste. That expansion took another thousand years, say to 700 B.C. Such a diffusion would not have been feasible under primitive conditions without an early stage of the caste system under which the fruits of labour could be expropriated without slavery.

The next major thrust, into the peninsula proper, was backed by the highly developed northern society with its advanced techniques; in particular, a recently acquired knowledge of metals. The new territory was far more varied and therefore not to be settled in the same way as the northern. Hence the further development and new function of caste, where the brahmin would write *purānas* to make aboriginal rites respectable, while the savage chiefs of the tribe would turn into kings and nobles ruling over the tribe. This was really the formation of new classes under external stimulus, whereas the older northern caste system had first developed as a class structure from within the tribe. Finally, with feudalism, caste performed an administrative function, still keeping the primary producer at work without the use of too much force. Peasants of villages in newly settled land normally belonged to the same kinship group, as noted above, within a caste that had been a tribe. Land was held by this group. No stranger could enter the community except by consent of the first settlers. A person expelled by the group had literally no place in society, hence the term out-caste. Each such group retained its particular laws and customs. The king, his officials, and their brahmin advisers adjusted disputes between members of different groups, paying the fullest attention to local usage and law. Disputes within the group were mostly settled by caste or village councils (*sabhā*), as they still are where modern forms of individual property and money have not destroyed the older tradition. Caste division and brahmin cunning kept the country superstitious, helpless in the face of foreign aggression. Nevertheless caste did protect the poor at times even under feudal oppression. The only form of protest possible for a disarmed peasantry was mass refusal to cultivate their overtaxed land. While there still remained unsettled land or uncleared forest, they could just go elsewhere. With saturation of cultivable land in the later stages of feudalism, this mass 'desertion' (Mārathī: *gāmvai*; in Greek, *anachoresis*) would have been difficult without external support from their equals. They could always claim such necessary assistance from other members of the caste. This was the classic Indian type of peasant strike. Caste, which had long become the worst form of superstitition, developed into a set of political groupings during the late nineteenth century. This may continue to persist under the new bourgeois-democratic forms and threatens at times to become a source of dangerous tensions. Caste division was encouraged and used systematically by the British to keep India divided. The question: 'How long will this modern baseless and debased caste system survive?' is bound up with the intensity of the latest mode of production in India. Caste is no longer recognised at law. It is not even recorded in the Census, on the principle of reform by hiding one's own head ostrich-like in the sand. However, city life, crowded accommodation, modern transport by rail, bus, and boat, the packing together of workmen of all castes into one factory, and the overwhelming power of money in a cash economy destroys the main feature of caste: hierarchical isolation by groups. The brahmin priest is out of place in mechanised life; machines run by scientific laws that do not justify a caste hierarchy.

CHAPTER THREE

The First Cities

3.1. The Discovery of the Indus Culture

THE two previous chapters dealt with the nature of acculturation in India. The Indian peasants now forming the vast majority of the country's population and the few remaining tribesmen exercised reciprocal influence through the ages. The zigzag, though on the whole steady, development of the peasantry by inner growth because of the better food supply and externally out of the withering away of tribal life can be traced without much difficulty. The outlines are clear, though not always the precise order or date in each region. The question remains of the origin and development of city life. After all, civilisation means the formation of urban, civic life as a leading feature of the life of a whole country. Though modern Indian cities owe their position to a foreign mode of production, there were cities in India long before the machine age and before the feudal period. How did they develop out of prehistory?

The accepted view till a generation ago was that the first Indian cities of any importance appeared only during the first millennium B.C. These were supposedly built by the descendants of pastoral nomads, the Aryans, who entered India as invading Bronze Age tribesmen from the north-west. From about 1500 B.C. to a little after 1000 B.C. they fought among themselves and with a few aborigines in the Panjāb. Then came civic life and civilisation, rather slowly, in the Gangetic basin. The first really great Indian city in the older view seemed to have been Patnā. But this was mostly conjectured from the oldest Sanskrit books, hymns, and stories, which were all on the level of myth and legend. In 1925 archaeologists announced a spectacular discovery of immense urban ruins of which no

53

mention was to be traced in the ancient literature. The principal remains were of two cities, each perhaps a mile square in its third-millennium hey-day. Both were in the basin of the Indus and both had been on important rivers. The southern, now a deserted mound known as Mohenjo-dāro in Sind, had been on the Indus proper. The upper, Harappā in west Panjāb, was once on the Rāvi, a major tributary of the Indus. The rivers have formed new channels, as happened so often in historic times, because they flow through deep alluvium. The city houses had been many-storied, palatial, solidly built of well-baked bricks and supplied with such amenities as excellent bathrooms and lavatories. The pottery was very good in quality, mass-produced on the fast wheel, though not too well decorated. Gold, silver, jewels, and other evidence of lost wealth came to light. The layout was unique, originally in rectangular blocks about 200 × 400 yards, with wide main streets and good minor lanes. Nowhere else was civic organisation of such complexity and excellence to be found so carefully planned at so early a date. The Egyptian cities were architecturally insig-nificant compared to the mountainous tombs of their rulers, and to the great temples. Sumeria, Akkad, Babylon had brick-built cities nearer to the Indus type, but they just grew. The streets in all these cases, as in Rome, London, Paris, and for that matter in later Indian towns followed irregular country paths. The Indus cities show town planning of a truly amazing nature. Besides the straight streets meeting at right-angles, there was a superb drainage system for carrying away rain-water and cesspools for clearing the sewage. No Indian city possessed anything of the sort till modern times; far too many still lack these amenities. There were enor-mous granaries, too large to be in private possession. They were accom-panied by small tenement houses in regular blocks which must have accommodated the special class of workers or slaves who pounded and stored the grain. There was evidence of considerable trade, some of it across the ocean.

This meant that all earlier ideas of ancient Indian history had to be re-oriented. India's cultural development had not been in a straight, logical sequence, but showed a great set-back and unexplained reversion to pastoral barbarism. A large city like Harappā implies the existence of supporting territory which produced enough surplus food. The city normally becomes the seat of power. That is, the existence of one or more cities means the presence of a state. Some people had to produce a food surplus which was then taken away by others who did not produce but who might plan, direct, or control operations. This merely says that no cities could exist in antiquity without class division and division of labour, based upon the rule of a few over many. But then why should such a city vanish without successors or trace? Its ruin should mean the rise of some other cities under its direct influence or in rivalry. In Iraq, those who conquered the cities continued in occupation. The great Babylonian king and lawgiver Hammurabi (seventeenth century B.C.) came from such conquerors, originally barbarians. Similarly in Egypt. This expected continuity of urban culture was missing in India.

It is clear from comparison of other finds in Mesopotamian excavations that there was trade in the third millennium between these cities and their counterparts abroad. The duration of the Indus urban culture may roughly be taken as 3000–2000 B.C. Its end came soon after 1750 B.C. at the latest. There was a long period of gradual decay before the end, but the actual termination was abrupt. At Mohenjo-dāro, the city was set on fire, the inhabitants slaughtered, and occupation after the massacre was negligible. The corresponding evidence at Harappā is poor, because the top layers have been devastated. The material (mostly bricks) was taken away for modern structures, but to a far greater extent as the cheapest available railway ballast. With the evidence of a violent end, it became possible to interpret as reality the figurative old Sanskrit texts, where enemies are spoken of as having been ruthlessly smashed in battle, their treasures looted, and cities burnt down. Thus, what had been understood as the Bronze Age, pastoral second-millennium beginning of ancient Indian culture really meant the victory of barbarism over a far older and decidedly superior urban culture. The normally expected course of historical progress had received a powerful setback rather than fresh impetus.

This leaves the historian with a peculiar problem. None of the Indus records have been deciphered. Besides, these records are merely brief legends on seals of seal-impressions, plus a few scratches on potsherds. The alphabet is unknown and as yet unread. Even had it been read, the information yielded would have been a few personal names, perhaps names of trading organisations and of a god or two. All ancient history rests upon the tallying of archaeological finds with written documents, inscriptions, and the like. Here the Indus archaeology is extensive, but no relevant document has been read till the very end. Not a single personality or episode can be associated with any particular find. We do not even know what language the people spoke. On the other hand, the barbarian invaders who smashed this millennial culture beyond recovery left virtually no known archaeological deposit. The old Sanskrit records thus remain without firm meaning in crucial details because some important words cannot be related to specific places or objects; some terms cannot even be understood. There remains a clear gap of over 600 years between the end of the Indus civilisation and the earliest possible beginning of the new,

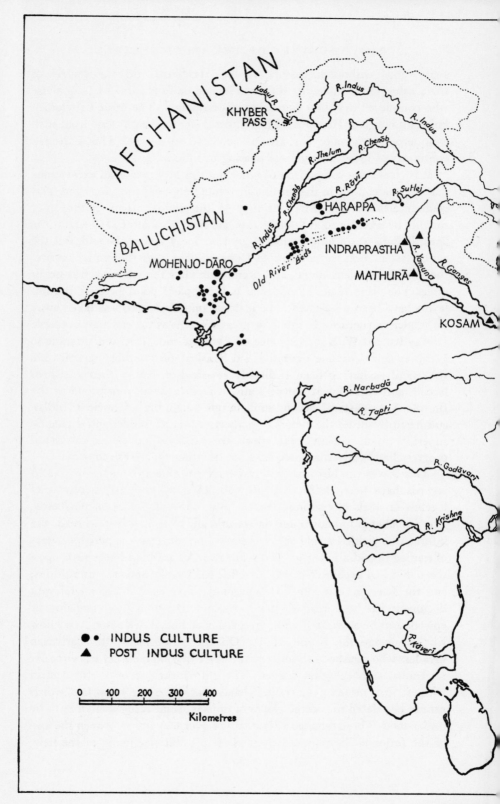

The Indus

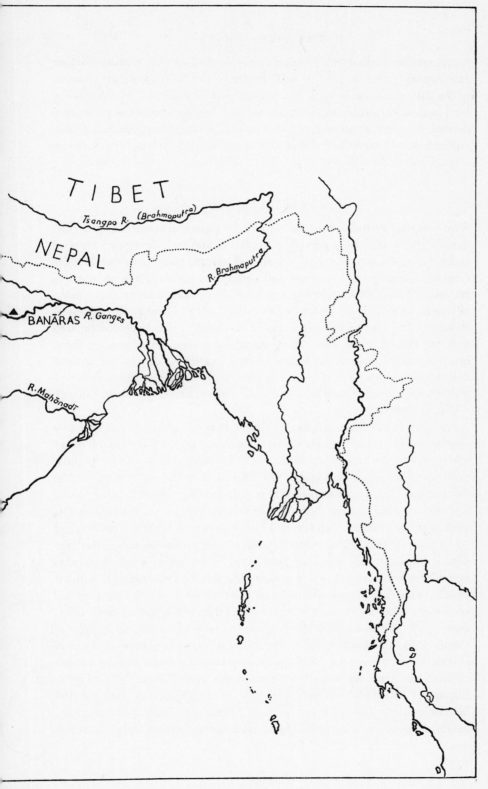

TIBET

Tsangpo R. (Brahmaputra)

NEPAL

▲
BANĀRAS R. Ganges

R. Brahmaputra

R. Mahānadī

Culture.

much smaller Indian cities which bring us into history without further interruption. The destroyers and the destroyed functioned in a corner of the sub-continent, actually in what is now west Pākistān. The rest of the land was very thinly occupied by food-gatherers who went their own several ways in tiny Stone Age tribal units. The beginning of India's main cultural development and the possibility of writing Indian history of the second and third millennium B.C. have both been seriously damaged.

3.2. Production in the Indus Culture

The essential feature of the Indus culture passes unremarked as a rule, namely that it could not spread to the fertile and well-developed parts of India. Its range was vast but of a special nature, about a thousand miles from the north to the sea-coast, and perhaps as far along the sea-coast to the west. The trade outposts or small colonies of this culture have gradually been located, thinly scattered from the gulf of Cambay in Gujarāt to Sutkagen Dor on the Makran coast. The entire region is arid compared with the rest of India. The climate might have been better in older days, but not much better. The difference could easily be due to the greater deforestation in modern times. Why should the first great urban development on the sub-continent have taken place along a river that flows through a virtual desert?

The answer is fairly simple. The river is necessary for water and as a source of fish, a main food. Later, it becomes a handy means of heavy transport by boat over long distances. This enables the primitive population to increase at the first stage. The alluvial desert is just as important in its own way. It means that the early population is confined to a strip along the river. Food-gathering beyond a certain stage and range is impossible, the forest being at best thin scrub. This disadvantage is greatly outweighed by two advantages. First, protection against wild animals, dangerous reptiles and insects is less necessary than in the dense Indian jungle. Secondly, agriculture becomes not only necessary but also becomes feasible without clearing away a heavy growth of forest. Fire would do for the clearing and even stone tools are enough, whereas the real Indian monsoon-fed wilderness cannot be brought under cultivation without an ample supply of metal—iron. The alluvial soil is fertile beyond compare provided the land is watered regularly. All this is quite easy to prove. The world's ancient civilisations grew up along just such rivers: the Nile and the Tigris-Euphrates complex, both in a very dry environment. The Danube pre-historic cultures and the early seats of Chinese civilisation had something nearly as good as a surrounding alluvial desert, namely loess corridors (with thin forest) which provided a reasonably fertile base for agriculture. The rivers Amazon and Mississippi, though the greatest of all streams, did not develop civilisations in prehistory. The Amazon forest is too dense to clear with profit even today. The sod of the U.S. midwest was too thick for cultivation to be possible before the advent of the heavy steel plough. Correspondingly India's sacred river Ganges had no significant urban settlements near or on its banks till towards the first millennium B.C., when even the memory of the Indus valley people had faded away.

The Indus valley culture belongs to the Bronze Age. Though excellent chert flakes continued to be used as knives and household tools, the best tools used at Harappā and Mohenjo-dāro were of bronze, sturdy and serviceable; not copper, but real bronze, an alloy of copper and tin with traces of other metals. The copper ore came from Rājasthān and was available in sufficient quantity for export of the metal to the west. The conclusion is reached from Babylonian and earlier records. The great trade depot for exchange between the Indus region and Iraq was the island of Bahrein in the Persian Gulf. This was the Tilmūn of Mesopotamian legend. Here the deathless, legendary Sumerian Noah Ziusudda spent his days after surviving the deluge and was sought out by the hero Gilgamesh in search of the secret of immortality. The cuneiform clay tablets that speak of trade through Bahrein conducted by a special class of merchants, the *alik Tilmūn*, have been amply confirmed by modern excavation, though about 100,000 grave mounds still remain unopened. Certain round button seals found in the Indus cities and in Mesopotamia seem to have originated in Bahrein. Later, the merchants traded under the special protection and partnership of the Assyrian king, who took a major share of the profits, but must also have been their greatest customer. The Indus region seems to have been called Meluhha by the Mesopotamians. All mention of Meluhha ceases by about 1750 B.C., which means that trade contacts were then interrupted, presumably by invaders. There was some other intermediate trade centre, Magān or Makkān, not properly identified, probably on the coast between Bahrein and India.

Besides copper, the Indians exported peacocks, ivory and ivory articles such as combs (still made to much the same pattern today in India as in the Indus culture and indispensable for combing lice out of the hair), apes, pearls ('fish-eyes'), and cotton textiles. In return, they received silver and other commodities whose exact nature is still unknown. There must have been a small but active settlement of Indian traders in Mesopotamia even then, to account for Indian seals and other objects found in Iraq excavations. The reciprocal settlement seems to have been absent or less prominent in India. The few seals of Mesopotamia inspiration found in the Indus valley show purely local technique. The route of communication was by sea, the boats sailing along the deadly inhospitable coast by an ingenious system of navigation. If driven out of sight of the land, the crew released a crow, which would fly towards the nearest point of the coast. This is precisely the method followed by Noah in the Bible, when he first released a crow from the Ark to find out in which direction the land lay, and then a homing pigeon to make sure that the land was fertile. A seal dug up at Fara in Iraq shows just such a boat with the compass-bird. It is known from Indian stories that the 'direction-finding' crow was so used. A *Jātaka* story tells of traders making precisely this kind of a sea-voyage to Babylon (Bāveru). The fact that the crow was unknown in Mesopotamia may help to explain why there is no evidence of reciprocal trading.

The exports mentioned come in the class of luxuries. The food was produced at home. Wheat, rice, barley still grow in the region as they did in the remote antiquity which we are discussing. Fish have always been plentiful in the Indus river system. The soil of the river basin is remarkably fertile to this day. The Indus seals portray two types of cattle, the fine humpbacked and characteristically Indian 'zebu' specimens as well as a flat-backed 'urus' type now extinct in India. The rhinoceros, elephant, ram, and many composite animals partly one or the other are shown, too. The argument that the region had more rain and that many wild animals then moved about is not valid. The rhinoceros was known and hunted in the Panjāb even in the sixteenth century. The Himālayan elephant became extinct in feudal times. But the first was of no importance in the Indus economy and the second probably had not been tamed. The water-buffalo, now so common in India, occurs only on a few seals; it is shown on one seal tossing one or more hunters, so was probably not tamed at the time. The seals, however, had a different purpose from the portrayal of animal life or life in general of their day. One has a three-faced god surrounded by animals, a prototype of the later Śiva, lord of beasts (*paśupati*). A few other seals show such divine figures. One shows a ship with sail, oars, and steering-sweep or rudder. Two portray an archaic and characteristically Indian form of a hero strangling a tiger with each hand, taken over from the Sumerian Gilgamesh strangling lions. Enkidu, the bull-man who was the companion of Gilgamesh in so many Mesopotamian exploits, is also recognisable on an Indus seal. This incidentally proves Indo-Mesopotamian contact. The seals thus had some religious significance. They are stamp seals, not cylinder seals (as in Mesopotamia) to be rolled on clay. The purpose of such seals was to protect packages of goods or filled vases. In Mesopotamia, as in China, they were also used as signatures on documents; but no such signed documents, whether clay tablets or any other kind, have

been found in the Indus cities. The bundles or jars of goods were covered'
corded, and the knots plastered with clay that was then sealed. Today,
this would only provide testimony that the bundle has not been tampered
with, if the seals be intact. In antiquity, the seal must have imposed some
sort of a tabu which protected the merchandise. In fact, many of the seal
impressions found in India do not bear the marks of cords, knots, or reeds
on the reverse, hence were not stamped on to any parcel. There were
special cultic seals in Sumeria (differing from business seals only in being
larger) which were used in religious ceremonies. All these seals are descended from the small engraved pebbles of about the same size which served

FIG. 6. Artist's 'sketch sheet' of a bison, of the late French Ice Age, found at La
Laugerie Basse. Paintings of animals drawn to much larger scale in selected underground caverns, reproducing the sketches in precise detail, have also been discovered in places a couple of hundred kilometres away from the 'sketches' and
from each other. It is only a step from such graven pebbles to the stamp-seals of
the Indus valley.

European Ice Age artists as 'sketch sheets' from which they would repro-
duce exactly, though on a much larger scale, the bison or other animals
painted in dark caves. The act of duplication had some particular ritual
purpose and significance. Though society later used the decorative seal
image for other purposes than worship or a fertility rite, the original magic
implication was not lost till the first millennium B.C.

   The most important feature of the Indus valley culture has to be reconstructed: their particular method of cultivating grain. This can be restored
only by comparison with the two parallel river cultures of Egypt and
Mesopotamia. In the Indus basin there were just the two magnificent
cities of Mohenjo-dāro and Harappā. All other settlements or their ruins
are tiny in comparison. Such minor settlements are decidedly fewer than

one would expect. In Egypt the narrow river valley between the first Nile cataract and the swampy delta of the mouths of the Nile supported the densest known population of antiquity. Less than 10,000 square miles of land cultivated by the most primitive methods along 750 miles of the river's length sustained a population of 7,000,000 souls in Roman times. In addition, the surplus fed the city of Rome and was traded to other parts of the Mediterranean as well. The Nile valley does not exceed 30 miles in width between barren stone cliffs; the cultivable soil is never more than 10 miles or so of alluvial deposit. But the deposit is renewed every year by the terrific annual flood of the Nile, with virtually no rain in Egypt proper to supplement it. In Mesopotamia the agriculture of the late third millennium was based on canal irrigation. In a smaller area and one not more fertile A than that covered by the Indus basin there were over a dozen prominent cities and several lesser ones. Each city with its hinterland constituted an independent state with its own manufacture and trade, often at war with the others. Why were there just two large Indus cities, without the grandiose monuments of the Pharaohs or the numerous city mounds of Mesopotamia?

The answer seems to be that the Indus people did not practise canal irrigation nor did they have the heavy plough. These two modern features make agriculture in Sind and the Panjāb what it is today. With flood irrigation alone, not much can be cultivated, though the yield on the soil where the floods have deposited rich silt is excellent without deep ploughing. Thus the harrow can be recognised as a common Indus ideograph symbol (sometimes interpreted as the hand with fingers), while there is no plough symbol. The land now contains only five great rivers, hence the name Panjāb,' land of the five waters'. In antiquity, there were seven major rivers; two, namely the Ghaggar and Sarsūti, have dried up. The natural flooding of the Indus river continues to this day. The flood-irrigated lands are still the most productive, though the deposit is shallower and less fertile than in Egypt. The Indus people seem to have increased the flooded area, not by canals but by dams that impeded the flow. These dams were at times seasonal. The surplus grain from the harvest could be sent up or down the principal rivers to the two main capital cities, where the granaries took care of the processing and distribution. This surplus supported the trader and navigator, the people who lived in palatial houses or poorer quarters, the artisans who manufactured articles for use at home and sale overseas and the lowly humans who kept the city habitable. The surplus apparently remained constant from almost the very beginning of the cities to nearly the end. No new cities, no well-advertised changes of dynasty as in Egypt, no real, massive expansion into the equally fertile but forested plain of the Ganges mark the Indus culture.

3.3. Special Features of the Indus Civilisation

The problem now is to make some reasonable guess about the methods by which the surplus was taken from those who grew it. To this end it is essential to note just what sets the Indus cities apart from developments in Egypt and Mesopotamia of the third millennium B.C. Explaining these differences would then be one method of reconstruction of the Indus society.

The first point has been mentioned: the lack of great changes. The twin cities seem to have sprung up fully planned. Both have the identical layout as far as can be ascertained. Neither changed till near the very end of the period. The pottery, the tool types, and the seals remained the same. The alphabet also was static; this is in strong contrast to India in the historical period, where the form of the letters varied so much from one century to the next that the script offers a fairly good method—sometimes the only known method—of dating manuscripts or inscriptions. The ground level of the cities rose steadily. At Mohenjo-dāro the lower stories of a house might be filled up to rise above periodic floods; fresh stories were then raised on top. Some houses decayed naturally, to be rebuilt on top of the levelled debris. The street level also rose. Nevertheless, the street plan remained fixed, the houses were raised still higher on the same walls or the same room plan with very little change. The wells were built up so high on the original brick lining that they look like factory chimneys as the excavation goes to deeper levels. Only towards the end are there signs of decline and disorder. Some of the upper-level houses, crudely built of poorer materials, encroached upon the street plan; which means that the particular quarter of the city was then ruined. Pottery kilns appeared within city limits, as they never had at any earlier stage. Brick kilns have nowhere been found; the bricks during the cities' millennium of prosperity were made at a distance, wherever fuel was handy, and carted or floated down to the metropolis. The timber came from the Himālayas, down the great rivers. The last houses re-used some of this older material with unbaked mud bricks dried in the sun. During the Indus millennium, Egypt had a dozen complete dynasties; Sumer had been conquered by Akkad; Sargon the Great founded an empire which collapsed under his successors. Every Mesopotamian city showed significant variation in its structure during this period, as the Indian did not.

Secondly, the Indus cities have no public monuments or display in the sense of the two parallel cultures, with one possible exception. There is no great meeting-place, though a 70-metre-long hall at Mohenjo-dāro with pillared aisle or portico may have been for public use. There are no known

*NO Art
No Wareheve?*

(inscriptions, no obelisks or statues, no public decrees of any sort. Some of the richer houses have walls 7 feet thick, of well-burnt brick, which means that the houses rose to several stories. None dominates the rest as the palace or temple complex did in the other contemporary riparian civilisations. (The street front as far as can be seen was of blank, undecorated walls. Mosaics, frescoes, glazed tiles, specially moulded bricks with figures, stucco work, and even decorated doorways were lacking.) The entrance to the house was normally through a side lane, with door narrow enough to be easily secured. That is, the wealth within these houses was not connected with the great display one associates with temples or the vainglory of military conquests. At the same time, the accumulated treasures were not secure enough against unsocial elements or brigands. Whatever authority ruled the city had not reliable police arrangements.

This brings up the third special feature, the curiously weak mechanism of violence. The weapons found at Mohenjo-daro are weak as compared with the excellent tools. The spears are thin, without a rib; the spearhead would have crumpled up at the first good thrust. There are no swords at all. The sturdy knives and celts are tools, not weapons. The archer becomes an ideogram symbol, but there were no bronze arrowheads, only stone. Whatever authority controlled the people did so without much force. At one side of each of the cities there appears a 'citadel' mound, fortified at Harappā in later times. Earlier it was simply an unfortified building complex on a 10-metre-high artificial platform, with ramps leading up the sides that would make ceremonial uses easy, but ruin defence.

The lack of change on the Indus was not due to mere sloth or conservatism but to much deeper causes. It was a deliberate refusal to learn when innovation would have greatly improved matters. The merchants surely knew about canal irrigation in Babylon and Sumeria. No canals are discernible in any of the air photographs of the Indus region, apart from modern irrigation works. The simple open-cast bronze celt continued in use as a tool, though the axe and adze with a socket or a hole for the wooden shaft were certainly within the technical capacity of Indus craftsmen. The only specimens of the latter types are found in the top layers and belong unquestionably to invaders from the north-west whose graves (outside India) have such tools; so also with more efficient weapons such as swords, all foreign to the Indus culture.

The sudden completion, say within a century or so, of cities which had no predecessors, which began from a dead start, points to a stimulus that came from the outside. The enduring changeless stability shows that the form evolved was suitable to local conditions; the evolution itself was much too rapid for gradual rise out of the prehistoric villages whose ruins one finds in Baluchistan, to the west and north-west of the Indus region. Pottery of a type similar to the Baluch lies just below Harappā city, but not in the city. The immigrant city-builders did not invade in large numbers. The Indus construction and general technique is special and peculiarly characteristic, not borrowed from some other large-scale urban culture such as Sumeria. At the same time a couple of archaic (Gilgamesh-Enkidu) Sumerian types of seals made by local Indus technique have been noted above. For that matter the Sumerians were also not indigenous to the Tigris-Euphrates river banks; they came originally from some mountainous area. Their principal temples were erected on mud-brick platforms 70 feet or more high, called *ziggurats*, which were really artificial mountains. The primitive pottery found below the lowest Mesopotamian urban layers (Hassuna) sometimes goes back to the fifth-millennium farmers of the Iranian plateau, say Jarmo. Similarly in Egypt. The first formation of strong Egyptian kingdoms seems also to have been due to people who came from outside. The extraordinary find of a prehistoric knife-handle in Egypt (Gebel-el-Arak) showing an athlete strangling two lions again resembles the Gilgamesh type. Though the period is very early in Nilotic urban development, there is a difference in that the lion-killer here is gowned as no Egyptians ever were. The Sumerian and the Indian lion-stranglers were stark naked. Such foreign motives in art are clear indications that the seeds of the great cultures came from outside. The three river-basin cultures we have compared nevertheless expanded into quite distinct civilisations because of favourable though totally different local conditions.

The best explanation would seem to be as follows. The people who touched off these mighty river cultures came from some restricted but developed locality or localities; restricted, in that there could have been no room in each case for expansion in the original, unknown homeland; developed, because each of the three great ancient civilisations shows knowledge of agriculture, brick-making, construction and proper grouping of houses, and some military technique. The last was needed for two reasons. Sometimes, access to water had to be fought for. In the great alluvial valleys of rivers flowing through a desert the mere presence of agriculture would not suffice to turn food-gatherers into farmer-peasants. This problem of conversion had to be faced repeatedly in later Indian stages, too. The food-producers would always breed much more rapidly than the gatherers and encroach upon more and more territory. This naturally led to armed conflict between the two. At some point the discovery was inevitably made that the need for more labour could be rapidly satisfied by force of arms, i.e. by taking slaves.

Possible origins, or at least prototypes of the seminal cultures are found at Catal Hüyük in Anatolia and Jericho in Palestine as early as the seventh millennium B.C. At the former site there was a small town, compactly put together with access barred to intruders by pulling up a series of ladders; pottery was just developing out of basketwork. Stone images were made and worshipped. Jericho had a remarkable fortified tower of stone blocks even in its pre-pottery microlithic days. This tower was necessary to defend its spring, the only source of water in an otherwise dry region. Neither of these two places need have been the immediate source of the Nilotic, Mesopotamian, or Indus civilisation. There is nothing so far to show any direct connection. The gap in time and space will take a long time to fill by archaeological methods. However, the existence of such early farming communities on a small scale in localities unsuitable for continued development into large city-states was the indispensable seed for later growth into the magnificent riparian cultures.

3.4. The Social Structure

Before trying to say something about the kind of society that inhabited the Indus cities, one more special feature common to both must be noted. Adjacent to the finest group of houses, but clearly separated from the rich dwellings on a 10-metre-high mud-brick platform, is the 'citadel' mound. The mound in each case is of the same size and rectangular shape. The Harappā mound has been ruined by use as a brick quarry in modern times, while part of the Mohenjo-dāro complex is still covered by a Buddhist *stūpa* monument of about the second century A.D. Assuming that the plan and layout was the same for the buildings on the mound, it is clear that the original use of the buildings was public, but not military. The fortifications came later. The Mohenjo-dāro group still has a many-roomed and originally several-storied building around an open courtyard which contains a rectangular tank about 23 × 39 feet and 8 feet deep. The bricks are very well laid, with a waterproof intermediate layer of pitch in the tank wall. At each end a flight of steps originally covered by wooden planks leads to the bottom of the tank. A finely built drain allowed the water to be emptied, probably for cleaning the tank. The 'bath' was filled with water drawn laboriously from a well in one of the rooms adjoining the courtyard. The remaining rooms have doors that do not face each other; some have flights of steps leading to one or more upper stories. This 'Great Bath' cannot have been for mere cleanliness, for every house had excellent bathrooms and good wells and the Indus flowed past the citadel mound. The purpose was surely for some elaborate ritual considered vital by the inhabitants.

The original purpose can be ascertained fairly well by comparing

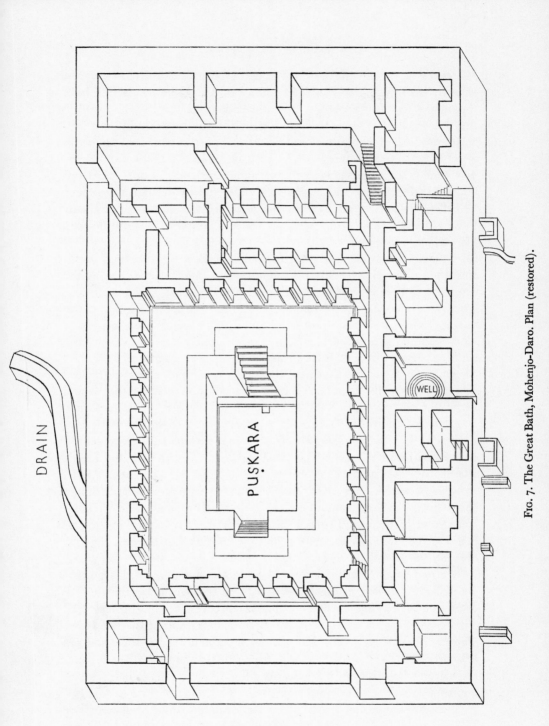

DRAIN

PUSKARA

WELL

FIG. 7. The Great Bath, Mohenjo-Daro. Plan (restored).

67

references to ritual tanks in later though archaic Indian literature. The name in Sanskrit is *pushkara*, 'lotus-pond'. Such artificial ponds were built throughout the historic period: first independently, later to adjoin temples; they are so constructed even now. A natural lotus-pond would not serve, apparently. Apart from ritual baths and ritual purification, such *pushkaras* were needed in early times for consecration of Indian kings and priests. The Indian king was 'sprinkled', not 'anointed' as in Europe. Moreover, the steps (the modern Indian *ghāt*) are characteristic of pilgrimage spots. The name *tirtha* for a place of pilgrimage implies that water had originally to be crossed by fording. These two features connect the Mohenjo-daro 'Great Bath' quite well with later Indian holy tanks. But in the very oldest references there is described a third function of the *pushkara* which associates it with primitive fertility rites. These lotus-ponds were generally the resort of a special class of water-deities or water-witches, the *apsaras*. The *apsarases* are described as irresistibly beautiful women who would entice men to consort with them and eventually lead the heroes to destruction. These bathing beauties were also accomplished in song and dance. The demi-goddesses had individual names and each was associated with some particular locality. Several ancient Indian dynasties were supposed to have descended from the temporary union of some particular *apsaras* with a hero. The *apsaras* could not marry a husband and settle down to permanent, normal family life. This would explain the use of the peculiarly constructed rooms at the 'Great Bath'. It was part of the ritual for men not only to bathe in the sacred water but also to cohabit with the female attendant representatives of the mother goddess to whom the citadel complex belonged. This is not far-fetched. The temples of Ishtar in Sumer and Babylon had similar practices in which girls of the leading families had also to participate. The goddess Ishtar was herself eternal virgin and harlot at the same time, mother goddess but not wife to any god. She was also the goddess of the river. The citadel mound was, in fact, the Indus counterpart of the Mesopotamian *ziggurat*. Confirmation of the mother-goddess is furnished by small but terrifying terra-cotta figurines which show women wearing a heavy bird-mask that covers the head completely. These are found in the ruins of pre-Indus villages and of the two cities. They were not merely toys or dolls, but representations of some goddess who presided over birth and death. She needed no larger statues, because the hierodules performed all necessary ritual duties on her behalf without the image.

The situation in Egypt and Mesopotamia has now to be compared. The Egyptian Pharaoh was in theory a divine ruler, absolute master of the land. Actually he could reign only with the support of a numerous class of armed nobles and a still larger class of priests. His rule performed an essential function in the narrow river valley. All raw materials needed besides food had to be imported with a considerable and at times military effort: timber, ores or metal, and the like. After import they had to be apportioned. Individual villages would not have been able to do this, for the division of tasks and of materials had to be directed without dispute. The direction and allocation—and, when necessary, a war of aggression—was the Pharaoh's basic function. Hence the lavish scale on which everything connected with the Pharaoh's rule and memory was constructed, *e.g.* the pyramids. That there is nothing comparable in the Indus basin leads us to exclude the dynastic rule of divine warlords. It has already been remarked that no palace can be identified, while Indus weapons found were exceptionally few and feeble. No monuments to glorious conquerors exist at Mohenjo-dāro or Harappā. The two great cities have been regarded by some distinguished British archaeologists as the northern and southern capitals of an empire; not only on the analogy of Egypt but perhaps because of the feeling that anything so advanced in India could have resulted only from strong imperial rule (like the British). This opinion needs no further comment.

Mesopotamian culture was closer to the Indus civilisation. Unlike the Egyptians, they had no need of foreign conquest for economic survival, nor was a strong central authority so necessary for internal distribution. Trade played a more important part in Mesopotamian economy (both to the east and west, as well as along the African coast). However, whereas the Mesopotamian city had a number of temples, each owning land and participating in trade, the Indus city had only the one *ziggurat* mound, with no evidence of any other powerful or fashionable cult spot for the general public, whatever the nature of family or household cults. The Mesopotamian merchants were prominent, with ample property in land, slaves, animals, and goods; but their houses are not on the lavish Indus scale and had miserable sanitary arrangements. We know a good deal about their inheritance laws, contracts, debts, and mortgages. No Indus records have survived. Of course, it is a puzzle why the Indus merchants did not adopt writing upon clay tablets from the Iraq counterparts with whom they traded. Why did they not take over the better foreign tools? Why not use canal irrigation and deep ploughing for agriculture? Some of them must have seen the heavy crops thus yielded on the Euphrates. The answer would be that the Indus merchant could not profit from any of these improvements. It follows that the land as a whole must have been the property of and directly administered by the great temple and its priesthood. Once established, they would insist in the way of most ancient priesthoods upon preventing all innovation. For them, change was not necessary; for the merchants, change was not profitable. In Mesopotamia there was a strong secular ruler, the *ishakku*, who led the city's army in war and eventually became a divine or semi-divine king. He did not interfere too much with the temple administration of his own city, but he did whatever he liked in captured cities. In the Indus region there is no evidence for this type of king either. Kingship was not indispensable. The food surplus was yielded up by the primary producers without the use of much armed force. Religion, not prowess or violence, was the essential ideological force of the Indus society. This can be said repeatedly of Indian society at several later stages; the historical pattern was for peaceful religious stagnation to alternate with violent periods of war, invasion, conquest, or anarchy. On the Indus the stagnation was long and steady.

The merchants could pile up their wealth behind the massive walls of palatial houses, but there was no one house which can be taken as the palace proper, none that greatly exceeds all others in size and importance. This means that the Indus merchants' taxes were light and net profits decidedly heavier in comparison with Iraq. No king imposed himself upon them as a senior partner who grabbed most of the profit. On the other hand, they had inefficient police protection, or none, and so had individually to guard themselves and their treasures by the peculiarly depressing type of heavy, blank architecture we have noted. Even before the end, evidence of robbers or brigands operating inside the cities is available in the excavated ruins. The merchants' records might have been on cloth, palm-leaf, or some such perishable material; but with restricted local transactions, they did not need many records, because memory would serve. This, too, remained a feature of later, pre-feudal Indian society, where contracts made by simple word of mouth were fully honoured, to the astonishment of foreign observers.

The grain would be collected and distributed by the great temple. The granaries belonged to the citadel mound, being part of the complex or close to it. The work of processing the grain was done by people who lived in adjacent quarters built to a uniform but rather mean pattern. These might have been temple slaves, of the sort known in Mesopotamia as *qallu* (*gallu*). To what extent the temple participated in the processes of manufacture is not known, but the participation must have been full, to judge by foreign parallels. It is notable, however, that the merchants' seals do not show any female deity. The totem animals are male without exception. The very few human figures, where identifiable, seem also to be male. One possible implication is that the traders developed their own secondary cults in which the mother goddess had no direct share. This would then be true of the profits of the trade as well, in contrast to revenue from the land.

This is about as far as we can go in the reconstruction. The system obviously did not expand. The Indus colonies in the north and on the coast are petty and few. The main urban population even decreased at the end of the third millennium. How much of the Indus culture survived the final destruction of the cities is the logical question. Certainly, a great deal that was connected with craftsmanship and trade did survive. The later Indian standards of weight and apparently measure (this part is not so clear) often went back directly to those at Mohenjo-dāro and Harappā. Certain myths and legends must have survived as well, as for example the Indian story of the flood, a universal deluge on the Sumerian-Babylonian and Biblical model. The story appears in later—not the earlier—Sanskrit records, and is one of the many symptoms of progressive assimilation of old and new, of Aryan and pre-Aryan, which sometimes reverses the expected sequence in Indian literature and legal practice. It is noticeable that dynasty after dynasty ruled in Egypt without any profound change in the basic fabric and pattern of Egyptian life. Such changes as are apparent only manifest themselves at the level of Pharaoh's court because of sudden access to new ores in foreign lands or control over a large number of foreign slaves taken prisoners in war. The life of the common people remained much the same. Some of the invaders even in Egypt were Aryans. The language and cults changed in Mesopotamia with successive invaders, but the cities remained. At most, the centre of gravity would go from one city to the other, whether Sumerian, Babylonian, Assyrian, or Persian ruled. Only when the irrigation system was allowed to fall into disrepair did the civilisation ultimately collapse with reversion of food-producing land to desert. The complete ruin of the Indus cities could have been due to just one cause, the wiping out of their system of agriculture. Inasmuch as there were no canals, this means two things. First, the rivers may have changed course, as happened so often. This would ruin the city as a port and make the maintenance of a food supply difficult. Secondly, the conquerors were not primarily agriculturists. They shattered the dams by which flood irrigation was made to deposit silt on a wider expanse of land. This signalled the end of cereal production, and so of the cities which had already begun to decay from long stagnation. The really viable society had to grow again, as a combination of new and old.

CHAPTER FOUR

The Aryans

4.1. *The Aryan Peoples*

THE word *ārya* in Sanskrit, and from that language in most Indian tongues, means 'free-born', or 'of noble character', or a member of the three higher castes. The word, like so many others, changed its meaning through the centuries. Though used in later days as the equivalent of the formal term of respect 'Sir', it designated some special tribe or tribes as an ethnic group at the earliest stage. Most histories of India begin with these ancient Aryans. Some writers still maintain that the Indus people must have been Aryans, from the prejudice that every peak of Indian cultural achievement must have been Aryan. The hideous racial implication given to 'Aryan' by the late Nazi régime and its official philosophy has increased the confusion. There is, naturally, some doubt as to whether there were really any Aryans at all, and if so what sort of people they may have been.

The outstanding Aryan feature, the one characteristic that justifies the name for a large group of people, is a common family of languages. These important languages spread right across the Eurasian continent. Sanskrit, Latin, Greek were the classical Aryan languages. From Latin developed the Romance language group (Italian, Spanish, French, Rumanian, etc.) in southern Europe. In addition, the Teutonic (German, English, Swedish, etc.), the Slavic (Russian, Polish, etc.) are also sub-groups of the Aryan linguistic group. This is proved by comparison of words for many different objects as against the same terms in non-Aryan languages. Finnish, Hungarian, and Basque in Europe do not belong to the Aryan languages. Hebrew and Arabic, though they may be derived from ancient cultures going back to Sumeria, are Semitic languages, not Aryan. A third considerable non-Aryan set is the Sino-Mongolian, which covers Chinese, Japanese, Tibetan, Mongolian, and many others; this group is culturally and historically most important, though not for India as such. The Indo-Aryan languages are descended from Sanskrit. The earlier tongues thus derived were Pāli, called also Māgadhi from being spoken in Magadha, and various others generically called Prakrits. From them came the modern Hindi, Panjābi, Bengāli, Marāthi, etc. However, there is a considerable and culturally important group of non-Aryan tongues in India of which the Dravidian languages include Tāmil, Telugu, Kanarese, Malayālam, and Tulu; besides these there are the numerous but small tribal idioms which tell us a great deal about the primitive stages of Indian speech. They were sometimes grouped together as 'Austric', but the term is now recognised as meaningless, in view of the differences between Mundāri, Orāon, Todā, etc. The main question is: Does the community of language or a common origin for the group of languages justify the conclusion that there was an Aryan race or an Aryan people?

It is difficult to believe that blond Scandinavians and dark Bengalis belong to the same race, however loosely defined the term 'race' may be. Some excellent European linguists therefore concluded about a century ago that it was as ridiculous to speak of an Aryan race as of a 'brachycephalic grammar'. Aryan was to be taken as a linguistic term, with no reference to ethnic unity. For all that, there actually were people in antiquity who called themselves Aryans and were called Aryans by others. The Achaemenid emperor Darius I (died 486 B.C.) speaks of himself as 'an Achaemenid (*Hakhāmanišiya*), Persian (*Pārsa*), son of a Persian, an Aryan of Aryan descent' in his inscriptions. Therefore the Aryans were once an historic assemblage of human beings including both the Achaemenid clan and the Persian tribe. The oldest Indian documents, the sacred *Vedas*, speak of the Aryans as the people who venerated the gods worshipped in those Vedas. By going back step by step from dated inscriptions and records, it is possible to arrange all Indian written material, including the Vedas, in some sort of chronological order. The later books refer to or copy the earlier. Archaisms of language prove priority in time. In this way, the *Rigveda* turns out to be the very first, followed by the *Yajurveda* (in two branches, the White and the Black), the *Sāma-veda*, and much later by the *Atharva-veda* which concentrates more upon witchcraft. A reasonable guess is that the greater part of the Rigveda was prepared, or at least refers to events that took place, about 1500–1200 B.C., in the Panjāb. However, the Aryans of the Vedas, just like other Aryans outside India, fought each other as regularly as they battled with non-Aryans and pre-Aryans. So it is reasonable to conclude that only some of the people who spoke Aryan

73

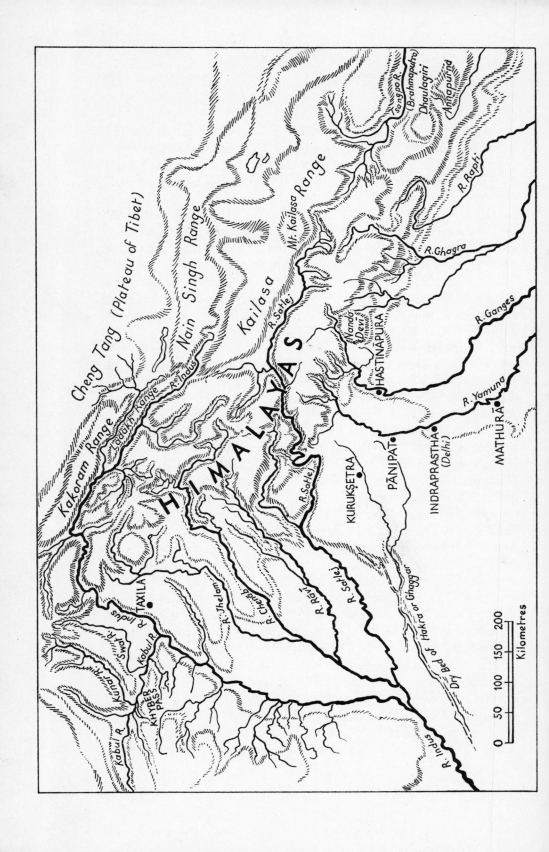

Cheng Tang (Plateau of Tibet)

Nain Singh Range

Kailasa

Mt. Kailasa Range

Kakoram Range

Ladakh Range

R. Indus

R. Satlej

R. Ghagra

R. Ganges

Sanpo R.

Brahmaputra

Dhaulagiri

Annapurna

R. Rapti

H I M A L A Y A S

Nanda Devi

HASTINĀPURA

R. Yamuna

KURUKṢETRA

PĀNIPAT

INDRAPRASTHA (Delhi)

MATHURĀ

R. Satlej

R. Satlej

Kunar R.

Swat R.

Kabul R.

Kabul R.

Indus R.

R. Indus

TAXILA

KHYBER PASS

R. Jhelam

R. Chenab

R. Rāvī

R. Satlej

Dry Bed of Hakrā or Ghaggar

R. Indus

200

150

100

50

0

Kilometres

tongues called themselves Aryans. There were Aryan contingents (by that name) in the army of Xerxes, son of Darius, and it is known that the Medes who preceded the Persians formerly bore the name 'Aryans'. Irān is derived from *āryānām*, '(the country) of the Aryans'. Though Greeks, Persians, and the Indians of the Panjāb spoke Aryan languages, Alexander's contemporary historians used 'Aryan' to refer only to special tribes bearing that name, settled on the right bank of the Indus at the time.

What kind of people were the original speakers of the primitive Aryan language? As pointed out before, primitive languages have separate terms for every kind of bird, beast, fowl, and plant rather than generic words like 'tree', 'animal', 'fish', etc. Philologists have compared the common root words for 'tree', for example, in many Aryan languages, omitting the strictly local words. The original Aryan tree then seems to have been the birch, which grows in northern Europe and along the Himālayas, but not in warmer climates. The fish was apparently the salmon. This type of analysis can be extended. The general distribution of plants (apart from cultivated and widely travelled varieties), wild animals, birds, and fish over the earth's surface is fairly well fixed and known. Some allowance has to be made for domestic varieties that human beings might have carried from one place to another. For example, tea came in historical times from China along with the word for tea. We cannot conclude that tea was an Aryan word or drink, or that Chinese is an Aryan language, or that China was the Aryan homeland. Eliminating such ambiguities, the conclusion is that the original Aryans were familiar with and probably originated in the northern regions of Eurasia.

However, linguistic analysis is of limited range and value. The Aryan kinship terminology is startlingly uniform. Father, mother, brother, father-in-law, widow, etc., are named by very similar words in the languages mentioned. We might conclude that the original social organisation was the same and that the people were really one. At the same time, though there is a common Aryan word for 'foot', there is none for 'hand'. The word 'daughter' can, through Sanskrit, be given the meaning 'she who milks'; and the same word for daughter is widespread in the Aryan languages. This led some European scholars to construct a charming picture of Aryan domestic life. Unfortunately, there is no common word for 'milk'. There are common words for 'cow' and 'horse' in the older Aryan languages, so that we know the animals that formed the mainstay of their economy; but the method cannot be carried too far without ridiculous conclusions. It is to be used only when nothing else offers.

4.2. *The Aryan Way of Life*

It may be stated as a general principle that a language cannot impose itself upon a large number of people who had a different speech, unless accompanied by a superior form of production. The Aryans could not have been a vast horde of invaders, because the land from which they came could not support a greater population than most of the civilised and cultivated regions they invaded. How did they impose themselves and their languages upon others? What was their main contribution to culture in the wider sense of the word? It is possible to say a great deal about the Aryans who afflicted India. The name Aryan is definitely justified for the Indo-Iranian people from the second millennium B.C. onwards by documentary and linguistic evidence. Archaeology tells us that these particular Aryans were a warrior-nomadic people in the second millennium. Their main source of food and measure of wealth was cattle, which they pastured across vast stretches of the continent. The horse, harnessed rather inefficiently to the chariot, gave them speed in tactical manoeuvre and superiority in battle. The structure of the Aryan tribes was patriarchal, the male being the dominant figure and holder of property in the tribe. The Aryan gods are overwhelmingly male too, but some goddesses were taken over from older times or older people.

When talking of Aryan culture, the sense must be made clear. The Aryans were not civilised as compared with the great third-millennium urban cultures which they attacked and often ruined. There is no characteristically Aryan pottery or special Aryan tools which would describe Aryan culture in the archaeologist's sense. What gave these people their importance in world history was precisely their unequalled mobility due to the movable food supply in cattle, the horse-chariot for war, and ox-carts for heavy transport. Their chief achievement was the brutal demolition of barriers between the small, closed, and often decaying peasant communities that characterised the third millennium, away from the great riparian civilisations. The Aryans took for their own whatever local technique suited them, and moved on. The devastation left in their wake was often irreparable for the people overrun. Nevertheless, the difference between Aryan and Egyptian (and later Assyrian) invasions was fundamental. When the Egyptian Pharaoh had gained his loot, tribute, control of copper ore, or slaves for work on his projects, he went back. Unless wiped out completely, life in the locality invaded continued in much the old way. But after the Aryans had passed over the old settlements, many of them too far out of the way and not worth the Pharaoh's while to invade, human society and human history began again—if at all—on a totally different level. The old isolation in small farming units and closed tribal communities was thereafter impossible. Techniques which had been closely guarded local secrets, often bound up with senseless ritual, became general knowledge. Aryans and pre-Aryans combined as a rule into new communities, by regrouping, often with a new, Aryan language.

Two main Aryan waves started from Central Asia in the second millennium, the first about the beginning and the second towards the end. Both affected India, and probably Europe, too. Neither was a deliberate, planned, or directed movement. The pasture of the particular homeland (approximately modern Uzbekistān) was insufficient to support the cattle and their owners, perhaps because of a long dry spell. The migration was not always in a fixed direction. Some of those who penetrated into India recoiled, either because they were beaten back or were otherwise dissatisfied with conditions in new territory. This is shown by the characteristic Indian humped bull on some Hittite seals late in the second millennium. The Hittite language had an Aryan base; the word *khatti* which means Hittite may possibly be connected with Sanskrit *kshatriya* and Pāli *khattiyo*. The Hittites settled down to rule over a conquered peasant population in Anatolia. Contact between them and India was neither continuous nor very strong. The intercourse, however interrupted and brief, was important in that the knowledge of iron which the Hittites show before any other people (no matter which older community had taught the secret to the Hittites themselves) could thus reach India through the second wave of Aryans.

The immediate foreign Aryan group related to India was in Persia. The Persians and Medes had an Aryan speech close to Sanskrit. About 1400 B.C., Mitannian records show that people worshipping Indo-Aryan gods in an Aryan language were settled near Lake Urmiyeh in Irān. The same gods Indra, Varuna, Mitra, etc., were worshipped by Persians till Zoroaster swept them away in the late sixth century B.C. Only the Indo-Aryan god of fire (Agni) remained in common worship for both. The Sanskrit word *deva* for 'god' became the Iranian term for 'demon'. However, the Avesta mentions the land of the seven rivers (Panjāb; two of the rivers later dried up) as a recognised (Aryan) territory. Some of the Indo-Iranian heroes came from the shores of the Caspian, in what is now Gilan and Mazanderan. The Iranian records speak of the *var* of King Yima, a rectangular place into which neither death nor the winter cold could penetrate till someone sinned; in fact, a limited form of the 'Golden Age', as it were. Then good King Yima saved his people from general punishment for the broken tabu by taking death upon himself, to become the first mortal. In India, Yama of the Rigveda was also the first mortal, the old ancestral

77

death-god, and still remains a god of the dead. Originally, the dead Indo-Aryan went to join his ancestors in the protection of Yama; later, Yama presided over the tortures of the dead in the underworld while other gods ruled in heaven. Rectangular enclosures discovered by Soviet archaeologists in Uzbekistan have the exact traditional dimensions of the *var* of Yima in Iranian religious books. The prehistoric builders lived in small rooms in the stone walls while the cattle were penned in the central open space in times of trouble. Yima and his protected domain was a prehistoric reality before the great Indo-Aryan migration. The *var* would reappear in Greek myth as the Augean stables cleansed by Herakles.

The Rigvedic hymns were properly edited, written down, and commented in South India during the second half of the fourteenth century. The text had till then been memorised syllable by syllable (as a few scholars in India still do to this day), but not generally committed to writing. It follows that not all Vedic tradition survived. Rigvedic action lay in the Panjāb. The line of priests who maintained the tradition had lost all contact with that region for many centuries, so that the names of localities often conveyed no meaning. Many important words even apart from names of places, rivers and people are still difficult to interpret, for the language has changed. The historical value of the Veda is rather small in comparison with that of the Old Testament of the Bible, which was always presented as history by people who retained contact with their particular land. The archaeology of Palestine, much more advanced and more scientifically conducted than in India, provides ample confirmation of many Biblical events. The Aryans, on the other hand, were always on the move. The names of rivers and mountains often travelled with them. The Sarasvati river, sacred in the Vedas, was once the Helmand in Afghanistān (Harahvaiti in old Persian, Araqattu in Assyrian); then a river in the eastern Panjāb which dried up after the *Rigveda*, probably by the first millennium.

Taking the Rigveda as it stands, for lack of anything better, we have at least confirmation of the negative action, the ruin of the Indus cities. The principal Vedic god is Agni, the god of fire; more hymns are dedicated to him than to any other. Next in importance comes Indra, who resembles a human war leader of just such violent, patriarchal, bronze-age barbarians as the Aryans of the first wave patently were. In fact, it still remains an open question whether Indra is not a deified ancestral war leader who had actually led the Aryans in the field, or perhaps a succession of such active human chiefs. Many a time Indra is invited to drink the powerful intoxicant *soma* (a very heady drink not properly identified) and to lead his Aryan followers to victory. Indra smashed the enemies of the Aryans, looted the 'treasure-houses of the godless'. The demons he killed are

named: Śambara, Pipru, Arśasānas, Śushna (who may be a personifica-
tion of the drought), and Namuci among others; many of these names
sound un-Aryan. It is always difficult to separate Vedic myth from possible
historic reality; rhetorical praise may or may not represent some military
success on the battlefield. Were the women in Namuci's 'army' human
or mother goddesses? Did the demon have two wives or does he represent
the local god of two rivers seen so often on Mesopotamian seals? The
Aryans had destroyed other urban cultures before coming to India. Indra
wiped out the remnants of the Varaśikhas at Hariyūpiyā on behalf of
Abhyāvartin Cāyamāna, an Aryan chief. The tribe destroyed was that of
the Vricivats, whose front line of 130 panoplied warriors was shattered
like an earthen pot by Indra on the Yavyāvati (Rāvi) river, the whole
opposing army being ripped apart 'like old clothes'; the rest fled in terror.
Such vigorous language describes some actual fight at Harappā, whether
between two Aryan groups or between Aryans and non-Aryans. It is
tempting to believe that cemetery H at Harappā, which comes later than
pre-Aryan urban culture, represents Aryan burials in its top layer. Similarly, we are tempted to discover Mohenjo-dāro in the city Nārmini, but no
details can be extracted from the Rigveda except perhaps that the city was
destroyed by fire. The pre-Aryans did have many stockades and fortified
places, some seasonal ('for the autumn'), others strong enough to be called
'brazen'. The enemies were dark (*krishna*, black) and short-nosed
(*anāsas* = noseless). Some of the teeming strong-places shattered by
Indra are figuratively described as 'pregnant with black embryos'.

One feat for which Indra is praised again and again is the 'freeing of the
rivers'. During the nineteenth century, when nature-myths were made to
account for everything including the Homeric destruction of Troy, this
was interpreted as bringing down the rain. Indra was the rain god who
released the waters pent up in the clouds. However, the Vedic rain god is
Parjanya. The rivers Indra freed had been 'brought to a standstill' by
'artificial barriers'. The demon Vritra 'lay like a great snake across the
hill-slope'. When this demon was smashed by the Indra, 'the stones rolled
away like wagon wheels', the waters 'flowed over the demon's inert body'.
This can hardly mean anything except the destruction of a dam, for all the
figures of speech. The word *vritra* as analysed by good philologists means
'obstacle' or 'barrier', but not 'demon' as such. Indra was called *vritrahan*,
Vritra-killer, for this spectacular feat. The same word was transferred as
verethraghna in Iranian to the supreme Zoroastrian god of light Ahura-
Mazda. The myth and metaphors give a clear account of the methods whereby the Indus agriculture was ultimately ruined. At the same time, Indra
confined the (unidentified) river Vibāli, which had been flooding over its

banks, to its proper channel. Flood-irrigation by special dams, sometimes temporary, had been the Indus practice, as noted. This would have made the land too swampy for Aryan cattle herds, while the blocked rivers made grazing over long reaches impossible. With the dams vanished the possibility of an enduring Aryan occupation of the Indus cities, the annual rainfall being low.

The main non-Aryan people specifically named, though not very often, were the Panis. Wealthy, treacherous, covetous, unable to stand up to Indra in battle—such is their general description. A late though famous Rigvedic hymn contains a dialogue between these Panis and the dog-goddess Saramā ('mother goddess of the lake') sent as messenger by Indra. The exchange of words was not merely chanted but obviously meant to be acted out, therefore the ceremonial commemoration of some important historical event. Commentaries generally declare that the Panis had stolen and hidden Indra's cattle. Saramā was supposed to be the herald demanding their return to Indra's followers, the 'gods' (deva). Actually the hymn says nothing about stolen cattle, but is a direct, blunt demand for tribute in cattle, which the Panis scornfully reject. They are then warned of dire consequences. This sounds very much like the standard Aryan procedure for invasion. The name Pani does not seem to be Aryan, but the word left important derivatives in Sanskrit and through Sanskrit in later Indian languages. Trader, modern baniā, comes from the Sanskrit vanik, which in turn has no known origin except in Pani. Coin is pana in Sanskrit; trade goods and commodities in general are panya. The earliest weight standards for Indian coins are exactly those of a definite class of weights at Mohenjo-dāro, not standards prevalent in Persia or Mesopotamia. It would seem that some Indus people survived Aryan rapacity to continue the old traditions of trade and manufacture.

The Rigveda says nothing of fixed settlements (let alone brick-built cities) or of reading, writing, art, architecture. Music was restricted to chants for ritual. Technology amounted mostly to the construction of chariots, tools, and weapons of war; it belonged primarily to the god Tvashtri and his followers, both seemingly of Indus origin. However, there was no caste or class differentiation within the tribe at this stage; the craftsmen were still free members of the tribe, not degraded in caste status as they would become at the next stage when the tribes began to dissolve. Weaving was a speciality of the women, though male seers might 'weave' a hymn as if it were a patterned garment on the loom. The centre of men's communal life was the sabhā; the word denoted both the tribal assembly and its mote hall. Apart from tribal council meetings, the sabhā was used also for relaxation by the men, and only by men. This tribal 'long house' was the scene of a favourite activity, gambling. The gambler with his one incurable passion and complete disregard for home and family appears in a late though famous hymn of the oldest Veda. There is occasional mention of chariot races, female dancers, male fist-fighters. The Aryans were manifestly barbarians on a lower level of culture than the urban people they destroyed.

4.3. Eastward Progress

Later Rigvedic military feats seem historical, as they are ascribed to human beings, heroes, or kings, not to the god Indra. The best known episode of the kind is the victory of King Sudās (pronounced Sudāh) over the Ten-Kings confederacy. Sudās, called descendant of Pijavana, is also stated to be the son of Divodāsa. The termination *dāsa* is curious. In later Sanskrit, the name Divodāsa may be translated 'servant of heaven', but originally *dāsa* or Dasyu applies to a hostile non-Aryan people. They had the special colour (*varna*, later to mean caste also) namely black (*krishna*) which distinguished them from the Aryans, and hence can only refer to their darker complexion, as contrasted with the lighter skin-colour of the newcomers. Only after repeated conquest does the word *dāsa* come to mean slave or helot (just as 'slave' and 'helot' both derive from ethnic names), a member of the śūdra caste, servant; or in the form Dasyu, 'robber' or 'brigand'. That so early a name of an Aryan king should end in *dāsa* means that there was some recombination between Aryans and non-Aryans soon after 1500 B.C. The tribe over which Sudās was chief is given as the Bhāratas, or perhaps a special branch of the Bhāratas called the Tritsus. The modern official name Bhārat for India means 'land of the Bhāratas'. These Bhāratas were definitely Aryans. Obviously, racial purity meant nothing to the early Aryans; adoption of the autochthones was always possible and practised.

The names of Sudās's opponents are also given. Tribe and chief then, as for a long time afterwards, bore the same designation, especially to outsiders. The hostile names in this case are more than ten. Again, it is certain that some of these Ten were also Aryans. Paktha is conjectured to be related to the modern Pakhtoon or Pathān in Afghanistān and Pākistān. They speak Pashto, an Indo-Iranian Aryan language. The Rigvedic origin of these people seems plausible because Herodotos does mention such an Indian tribe, the Paktyans. Alina means 'bee', Matsya 'fish', both clearly totemic names. Of the former nothing is known; but Matsya tribesmen in historic times were settled near modern Bharatpūr, well to the east of the Rigvedic battlefield. For that matter, the grammarian Patānjali, writing in the north-west Panjāb early in the second century B.C., gives 'eastern Bhāratas' as an example of redundancy: 'for there are no Bhāratas except in the East'. In general, the eastward movement is clear from these and other citations. Another of the Ten opponents, Śigru, bears the name of the drumstick tree (*Moringa pterygosperma*; but some translate as 'horse-radish'); a brahmin clan (*gotra*) derived from that name is known in a Kushāna inscription at Mathurā, though not to be found in the clan-lists now extant. The totemic nature of such tribal names is not in doubt. Most surprising of all, however, is the name Bhrigu among Sudās's enemies, obviously then a tribe. The word is philologically related to 'Phrygian'. A chariot made by the Bhrigus for Indra is mentioned in another place with special appreciation. However, the only survival of this name from classical Sanskrit down to the present day designates nothing more than one of the principal exogamous brahmin clan groups, still powerful and important. They came late into the brahmin fold but climbed fast.

The cause of the Ten-Kings battle was that the Ten tried to divert the river Parushni. This is a stretch of the modern Rāvi which, however, changed its course several times. Diversion of the waters of the Indus system is still a cause for angry recriminations between India and Pākistān. The 'greasy-voiced' Pūrus, though enemies of Sudās, were not only Aryans but closely related to the Bhāratas. Later tradition even makes the Bhāratas a branch of the Pūrus. The same clan priests in the Rigveda impartially call down curses and blessings upon the Pūrus in diverse hymns, which shows that the differences between them and the Bhāratas were not permanent. The quarrel was of another sort than that between Aryan and non-Aryan. The Pūrus remained in the Harappā region and expanded their rule over the Panjāb in later times. It was they who put up the strongest fight against Alexander in 327 B.C. The modern Panjābi surname Pūri may possibly originate with the Pūru tribe.

The priest who sings of victory over the Ten Kings has the clan name Vasishtha ('most excellent'), still one of the traditional 'seven' major brahmin exogamous groups. The original priest had been Viśvāmitra of the Kuśika ('owl') clan. The priestly function was not as yet specialised to any one caste in the Rigveda, and in fact the only caste difference in the earliest Veda was of colour between light-skinned Aryans and their darker enemies. As in ancient Greece or Rome, the cults of family, clan, or tribe could be and had to be maintained by any male member of the group called upon for the duty, whether by seniority, election, or custom. Though the various specialised priestly offices at a fire sacrifice are listed, there is no brahmin caste as such with a monopoly of the priesthood. Vasishtha, however, was a new type of priest. He was begotten of the seed of two

Vedic gods Mitra and Varuna, once the sun and the sky god respectively. His mother is not mentioned. On the contrary, he was—in one and the same account—'born of the mind of Urvaśi' (an *apsaras* or water goddess); born also of a jar which received the combined semen of the two gods; and discovered 'clad in the lightning' in a *pushkara*. This apparently confused narrative is really quite consistent and straightforward. It means that Vasishtha came of the human representatives of a pre-Aryan mother goddess and as such had no father. Going over to the patriarchal Aryans required some respectable father and at the same time a denial of the non-Aryan mother. Agastya, founder of another major brahmin clan group still extant, was similarly born of a jar. The jar represents the womb and thereby the mother goddess. The seven main brahmin clan progenitors may go back to hoary Sumerian or Indus antiquity as the 'seven sages'; their names do not tally in the various lists given by brahmin scriptures. Viśvāmitra is an eighth, the only genuine Aryan of the lot. The adoption of such 'jar-born' seers into the high Aryan priesthood was a fundamental innovation. By such recombination of Aryan and autochthone, a new class of specialists developed which would eventually claim monopoly of all Aryan ritual—the brahmin caste. What we possess of the ancient sacred books has been preserved by this caste, rewritten by this caste, and gives a naturally over-inflated view of their importance. Nevertheless, they did perform one task whereof the value is rarely brought out: the assimilation of otherwise hostile groups, along with their many new cults, into one society worshipping common gods.

There is Rigvedic evidence for the germination of a new professional brahmin priesthood that could serve more than one master at need, Aryan or not. A sage Vaśa Aśvya thanks the Dāsa kings Balbūtha and Taruksha and calls down manifold blessings upon their tribes for various gifts, which included a hundred camels. The camel is rare in ancient Indian tradition and was not tamed even outside India till about 1200 B.C., which dates the hymn in a loose way. The names Balbūtha and Taruksha do not have an Aryan ring and are not elsewhere known in Sanskrit works. All this suggests also that some of the Asura titans mentioned in the Veda might have been historical Assyrians, of whom King Tiglath-Pileser III invaded and conquered Aryan territory as far as the Helmand river. The Aryan seer of another hymn thanks none other than 'Bribu, chief of the Panis', for his patronage.

The Aryans who moved eastward differed from the first invaders of India. A new sort of tribal slave, the *dāsa*, was available for extra labour. A highly specialised priesthood had been formed by grouping of old and new, of pre-Aryan and Aryan. Archaeologically, this period is still blank. The only material object the hymns describe carefully enough for reconstruction is the chariot. It is too much to expect that Vedic chariots will actually one day be dug up. There was no special Aryan pottery, though the northern (painted) grey ware would soon assume this position; no particular Aryan or Indo-Aryan technique is to be identified by the archaeologist even at the close of the second millennium. It is a fair guess that some of the peculiar Vedic gods not known elsewhere had been adopted from the pre-Aryans: the dawn-goddess Ushas, the craftsman-god Tvashtri who is credited with fashioning Indra's weapons; and the obscure Vishnu who was later to find a great future in India, whatever his past had been. Of these Ushas had had a famous brush with Indra on the Beās river, which ended in her ox-cart being smashed and the goddess's flight. Later, Indra and a hero Trita killed Tvashtri's son, the three-headed priest-demon Tvāshtra, who has much the same name as the father. The hymn that described the killing is assigned to the authorship of the beheaded Tvāshtra himself, which means that he could not be destroyed, just as Ushas could not. His three heads became birds, of which two at least are known brahmin clan totems. Moreover, Tvāshtra is explicitly named high up in the line of Upanishad teachers. Deeper analysis of these legends would take us much too far from the main problem, though the killing of a three-headed demon is found in Iranian myth as well and Ushas is related to the Greek Eos. But the brahmins, at the very least, recognised some kinship with the enemies of Indra and with the originally hostile gods they worshipped even in the Vedas.

4.4. Aryans after the Rigveda

Not all Aryans moved to the east, nor was the advance steady. It was not a simple matter of more Aryans entering India to push their predecessors farther ahead. As has been said, the Pūrus maintained themselves in the Panjāb till the end of the fourth century B.C., though they had to send out colonies and branches; their original territory could support only a limited number of pastoral tribesmen. The southward expansion was restricted by desert. To the east, near the Yamunā, lay increasingly heavy jungle which could not profitably be cleared without iron, except for a narrow strip on the low watershed between the Panjāb and the Gangetic basin and another along the Himālayan foothills where fire could clear the shallow soil fairly well. Copper might be available from Rājasthān, but iron ores lie much farther away, at least the ores of grade high enough to be worked at profit. Mere knowledge of metallurgy and metals would not suffice; the main problem was to get at the mineral deposits. Therefore the Aryan tribes had to break up into small units, about most of which nothing—not even the name—is known. A few survive only in casual references in Greek or Indian books.

The Yajurveda helps us draw some conclusions for the period 1000–800 B.C.; the attached book, the *Satapatha Brāhmana*, extends the information to, say, 600 B.C. No firm dates are known; we can only guess at the endless social and tribal variety. Some of the Panjāb tribes of Alexander's time still divided the grain among the tribal households according to need and burned the surplus rather than barter it in trade. Others had developed into rich, aggressive kingdoms. In the early seventh century A.D., the Chinese pilgrim Hsiuan-tsang was shocked to see a considerable population on the lower-middle Indus, still in the pastoral stage with crude tribal group-marriage customs. These people were probably descended from the post-Vedic Abhiras, but they serve at least to prove that the Aryan manner of life remained possible in a few special localities till the historic middle ages. General statements cannot be made for the state of the country as a whole at any one time. We can at best look for such basic changes as would eventually sweep over the entire land.

Even a cursory reading shows that the pastoral life formed the basis of Yajurvedic society, as of its ritual. Nevertheless, the growing importance of agriculture and of metals is made very clear in a prayer (still recited) that would not have fitted into the earliest Rigvedic frame: 'May for me . . . milk, sap, clarified butter, honey, eating and drinking at the common table (*sagdhi* and *sapiti*), ploughing, rains, conquest, victory, wealth, riches, prosperity . . . low-grade grain (*kuyava*) food, freedom from hunger, rice, barley, sesame, kidney beans, vetches, wheat, lentils, millet, *Pancium miliaceum*, *Pancium frumentaceum*, and wild rice (prosper through the sacrifice). May for me the stone, clay, hills, mountains, sand, trees, gold, bronze, lead, tin, iron, copper, fire, water, roots, plants, what grows on ploughed land, what grows on unploughed land, tame and wild cattle prosper through the sacrifice (*yajña*)'. This may be dated at about 800 B.C., and shows that the Aryans had begun to face new problems of production in the Iron Age where their Rigvedic Bronze Age ancestors had been content to loot a richer civilisation and then take their chance of discovering fresh pastures.

The future lay with people within and beyond the eastern portion of the vanished Indus culture's range. The Aryans had little difficulty in penetrating to within 50 miles of the Yamunā river. The thinner forest of the region could be burnt down. But the social organisation necessary for settling the land cleared by fire went beyond the simple tribe. The lowest caste—for caste had developed within the tribe—was now called *sūdra*, possibly from a tribal name (e.g. the Oxydrakoi on the lower Indus who fought against Alexander). These were helots who belonged to the tribe or clan group as a whole in much the same manner as the tribal cattle, without the membership rights of the tribe proper as granted to the three upper castes. These three higher castes were properly recognised as Aryan and full members of the tribe: *kshatriya* (warrior and ruler), *brāhmana* (brahmin priest), *vaiśya* (the settler who produced all the food surplus by agriculture and cattle-breeding). The word *varna* came to mean one of these four class castes, which constituted a class structure within such of the tribes as had reached advanced forms of property-holding and indulged in trade exchange on a sufficiently large scale. This was not true of every single Aryan tribe, many of whom continued undifferentiated while others had only the *ārya-śūdra* (free v. helot) division. That the śūdra was not bought and sold as in ancient Greece and Rome was due to no kindness on the part of the Indo-Aryans. It was simply that commodity production and private property had not developed far enough. That the cattle were held in common with some sort of group ownership is easily proved. The word *gotra*, literally 'cowpen', also means the exogamous clan unit. It is known that the cattle of a *gotra* had some special mark, brand, or ear notch to distinguish them from the others. The form of property imposed its name upon the social unit that owned it, and has left us a rule in later canon law to the effect that the property of a man who dies without immediate heirs passes to the *gotra*.

The existence of the śūdra caste had a peculiar effect upon later Indian society. Chattel slavery in the sense of classical European (specifically Graeco-Roman) antiquity was never to be of any size or importance in the means and relations of production in India. The expropriable surplus could always be produced by the śūdra. The development of caste foreshadowed a general class society beyond the exclusiveness of a tribe. A few of the brahmins had begun to officiate for more than one clan or tribe, which implied some type of relationship between several groups. A few brahmins at the other end of the economic scale had begun to advance into the dense forest to the east, in fairly small groups with their own cattle; sometimes even as individuals with no property and no arms for defence or hunting. Their harmlessness was obvious, and they were of the utmost importance in coming to terms with the food-gathering *Nāga* savages of the forest, whom they often joined, or with whom they lived on friendly terms. Their sole protection was their poverty and manifestly innocuous nature. The traders, on the other hand, were convoyed at need by armed kshatriyas who would protect them against the aborigines (*nishāda*). These kshatriyas grew into mercenary groups ready to fight in anyone's service for hire.

The sacred books deal overwhelmingly with *yajña* blood sacrifices. Such collective sacrifices were made to other Vedic gods besides Agni, though always in the presence of the sacred fire. The duration and complication of the ceremony began steadily to increase. The number and variety of animals sacrificed seems incredible today. The highest ranking sacrificial 'beasts' were man, bull, stallion; but almost every beast and bird was killed at these *yajñas*, according to the Yajurveda and Brāhmanas. Such monstrous preoccupation with unlimited ritual killing proves that the society had begun to exhaust its means of subsistence. The prayer cited earlier shows that increase of cattle, food, and prosperity were the main purpose of the sacrifice, and further, that all of these could also be secured by aggression. The sacrifices were considered indispensable for victory in war, as for the war chief's success in general. The horse sacrifice, for example, was no longer the simple killing and eating of an animal so important to the Aryan economy. The chief queen had to couple with the slaughtered stallion in a rather revolting fertility rite, probably a substitute for some earlier sacrifice of the king or his surrogate. The horse was allowed to wander at will for a year before the killing; any obstruction to his free progress by another tribe was taken as challenge to battle. The constant fighting and round of sacrifices increased the brahmin's sacrificial fees and kept the kshatriyas occupied. The *yajña* already had a deeper, recognised, social purpose. Without mincing words, the ritual books say: 'Like a vaiśya . . . tributary to another, to be eaten up by another, to be oppressed at will . . . Like a śūdra . . . the servant of another, to be removed at will, to be slain at will.' These two lower castes, the primary producers, were to be enclosed between the two upper castes during the sacrificial procession of the whole tribe, 'to make them submissive'. After this the basic class nature of caste need hardly be doubted, though it was still class on a primitive level of production. The first taxes were called *bali* because they were gifts brought to the chief at the sacrifice by members of the tribe or clan. There was a particular official known only at this transitional period, the 'king's apportioner' (*bhāga-dugha*). His job seems to have been the proper sharing out of the *bali* gifts among the tribal king's immediate followers, and perhaps assessment of taxes as well.

There were very few cities as yet worth the name. In times of peril the whole tribe or clan might gather together behind some stockade where the chief normally dwelt. The shortage of metals and constant changes in the course of any Panjāb river would make large or permanent settlement difficult. The lowest unit was the *grāma*. Later to mean 'village', it was at this time only a kinship group (*sajāta*), generally on the move with its cattle and śūdras, led by its own *grāmani* who ranked as an officer of the tribe responsible to the chief. The *grāma* in summer would take its human beings and cattle to good pasture near the water. In the rains they would move back to higher ground above the normal reach of floods, to cultivate some grain. There was always trouble when two *grāmas* even of the same tribe came together on the march. This is shown by the new word *samgrāma*, literally 'the meeting of *grāmas*', which is Sanskrit for 'battle'. The various *grāmas* of a tribal kingdom (*rāshtra*) would gather together only for the common sacrifices or to oppose some common enemy. The king over such people was normally the first among a whole set of tribal oligarchs who held the chieftainship as often by rotation or election as by hereditary privilege. The word *rājanya*, 'fit to rule', is used equally for 'prince', 'king', or kshatriya in general. Royal prerogative was seriously restricted by tribal custom and tribal law. However, constant fighting increased the king's powers and tended to restrict kingship to one family. Possible rivals, whether princes, former chiefs, or strong oligarchs, had increasingly often to be restrained in some way or driven out (*aparuddha*) to preserve internal peace. This forced exile, which corresponds precisely to the ostracism of ancient Athens, led inevitably to intrigue and further weakening of tribal bonds. A regular class-based state mechanism, which would dispense altogether with tribal unity as its main driving force, was about to come into existence.

4.5. The Urban Revival

The society described above can hardly be called civilised. Brahmin theory still regards the Vedas as supreme among all Indian writings; Indian culture would not have been worth writing about if the Vedas had retained that position in practice. Some new form of social life without the shortages and the never-ending conflicts of Vedic society was essential for the development of a higher culture. The intolerable exaggeration of *yajña* fire sacrifices and the social philosophy which that implies led to a dead end. The main story of the new society belongs to the next chapter, but we may survey the preliminaries here. Briefly, city life as such is a new development in northern India, of the first quarter of the first millennium B.C. Urban routine, trade, and the careful accounting implied by the accurately weighed silver coinage from about 700 B.C. would not have been possible without literacy; just what the alphabet was and to what extent it was used remains to be determined. There definitely were illiterate Aryan tribes over the greater part of the Panjāb; but the presumption is strong that the later Brāhmi alphabet was known, at least in rudimentary form, in the new cities. For the rest, when the Buddha admonished the son of a 'householder' as to well-bred behaviour in a city like Rājagriha, it has to be remembered that even in the seventh century there could not have been more than two really large cities. The rest were towns where everyone knew each other, or villages where there would hardly be a street to loiter in. What now seems only normal civil manners was something new to a society which had yet to abandon the tribal 'men's house' for assembly (santhāgāra) as its principal focus of social life.

The first cities after the final ruin of Harappā (occupied for some time after the conquest) and Mohenjo-dāro (suddenly and permanently ruined by the irruption) were built at the eastern margin of the Indus range, and beyond. Their scale was decidedly humbler, but they were cities that implied heavier stress upon agriculture than in a pastoral economy, which still remained important. Already, the Yajurveda speaks of ploughs drawn by twelve-ox teams; such ploughs are in use to this day, indispensable for driving deep furrows and turning over heavy soil which otherwise will not yield well or retain its fertility. The strong plough could be made of wood trimmed down by bronze tools, but the ploughshare in east Panjāb, particularly on stony soil near the watershed, had to be of iron. Where did the iron come from? Were there no new sources of the copper needed in increasing quantities for swords and other tools which were still of bronze?

The metals began to come in significant quantity from the east from about 800 B.C. India's finest deposits of iron and copper ores lie at the eastern end of the Gangetic basin, in south-east Bihār (Dhālbhūm, Mānbhum, Singhbhūm districts). To this day, however, the jungle and the rains are heavy in these regions, while clearing the forest will not permit of such profitable agriculture as in the Gangetic basin proper. So, quite primitive tribal life still persists there, in spite of adjacent blast furnaces and metalworks. We know that the copper of the region was tapped. Slag and clinker deposits of unknown date are found where the copper ore lies, and hoards of copper objects of about 800 B.C. are found all over the Gangetic plain. Some are fashioned as harpoons, shouldered celts, semi-human figures, etc. The largest bar celts, about 2 feet long with a crude chisel-end, are too unwieldy to have been tools. These objects clearly form traders' hoards. They were not made by the aborigines themselves, because copper refining means controlled fire, hence good kilns. Such kilns would also produce excellent pottery, and it is believed that they were, in fact, first derived from pottery kilns. But the only pottery found with these copper hoards is remarkably crude, badly fired, ochre-washed ware that goes to pieces even in the digging. Therefore settlements of the Indus people and of the Aryans (who had begun generally to use the painted grey ware of the north) are excluded. The conclusion is that the traders were Aryans on the move. But the same ochre-washed low-grade pottery lies below the painted grey ware and just above natural soil at the new Aryan sites like Hastināpura. Clearly not all Aryans settled down to cattle-raising in the Panjāb. There were certainly people in the second millennium, particularly in the second major Aryan wave, with all the hardihood and daring needed for pioneers. They were good fighters with some knowledge of metallurgy, especially of iron, which had become common by the beginning of the first millennium all over that part of Asia through which these Aryans had to each India. The Gangetic riparian jungle was still too thick for agrarian settlement. The main Aryan settlements therefore extended eastwards in a chain, a thin line along the Himālayan foothills to southern Nepal, and then swung south through the Campāran district of Bihār to the great river. The land was cleared by burning over, which would not have been possible nearer the Ganges. This method, which limited the original expansion to the foothills west of the Gandak river, is explained in a famous passage of the *Śatapatha Brāhmana*. The date should be earlier than 700 B.C. But the turn through Campāran to the south was meant only to reach the ores, which lay beyond the hills of Rājgir, the one early Aryan settlement south of the great river.

It is clear that the first cities with full continuity into history lie on the river route, in spite of the difficulty of settling alluvial regions: Indraprastha (Delhi) and Hastināpura in Kuru-land, Kosambi (Sanskrit, Kauśāmbi) on the Yamunā and Banāras (Vārānasi, Kāsi) on the Ganges became famous. Their foundation at the beginning of the first millennium can be explained only on the basis of still earlier navigation on these powerful rivers that flowed swiftly through impenetrable forest and swamp. A tag verse in the Rigveda makes Dirghatamas, brahmin son of Ucathya and Mamatā, a river pilot in his old age. Ships with a hundred oars and voyages on water three days from the nearest land receive passing mention in the oldest Veda, so that the Aryans knew how to manage boats. The sole possible explanation is that the sea was reached and the ores found by these daring pioneers of unknown name early in the first millennium; otherwise there is no reason or explanation for the eighth-century pre-embankment deposits at Banāras fort, on the Ganges. Once the ores were found, it was easy to extend the chain of foothill settlements to the river by a land route going as far as the jungle allowed land clearing to proceed. The hypothesis is not so wild as it might seem. The river itself would supply fish in inexhaustible measure, while the forests on the banks provided game. All that was needed was the intrepid spirit of enterprise.

There is some connection between the Agastya clan and Aryan penetration south of the Vindhyas, but this still belongs to the realm of myth, tempting though it may be to relate it to the southern megaliths. The megaliths at Brahmagiri in Mysore state are related to the ash mounds left by neolithic cattle-keepers in Raichūr district. The stone tools and the pottery sequences prove this. The ash mounds are dated by radiocarbon to a little before the end of the third millennium. Their grey ware as well as the occasional piece of bronze found with pottery of a different type in sporadic second-millennium deposits on the Narmadā have led some anti-quarians to suggest Iranian contacts. If so, the mechanism of this early diffusion remains a puzzle. Was there a peaceful wave of 'proto-Aryans' which percolated through the Indus region when the urban culture was at its zenith? Did the Aryans take to marauding only when a later wave had learned the use of bronze weapons in warfare? The early first-millennium exploration of the Ganges, on the other hand, is demonstrable by archae-ology. The 'northern intrusion' stratum in Raichūr and Mysore is decidedly later and ushers in the iron age. In contrast, the 'chalcolithic' deposits at Pandu Rajar Dhibi (on the Ajai River, West Bengal) show a lack of continuity. Like the parallel finds on the Narmadā, these can only denote sporadic, transient settlements of second millennium explorers, presumably Aryans, where Atranjikhera was permanent.

4.6. The Epic Period

Of these small early cities, two in Kuru-land (Delhi-Meerut) were to leave an indelible mark upon Indian tradition, though Banāras eventually be-came the centre of sanctity that it still remains for brahminism. The divide between the Panjāb and Uttar Pradesh was strategically important in historic times. Delhi is at present the capital of India, as it has been for some centuries. Several decisive battles fought through the ages at Pānipat in Kuru-land settled the fate of the whole northern area of the country. The subject of the great Indian epic, the *Mahābhārata*, is a battle of exter-mination in Kuru territory. If such a battle really took place, it could only have been about 850 B.C., counting the traditional number of dynastic names down to historical kings. The actual scale of the supposed incident must then have been minuscule, but its literary importance was as great as that of the Trojan war in Greek. The original settlement at Hastināpura in Kuru-land was due to a small branch of the old Vedic Pūru tribe. The painted grey ware of Hastināpura II should be taken as Pūru-Kuru cera-mics, not as Aryan pottery in general. A second branch, called the Pāndavas ('sons of Pandu') cleared Indraprastha (probably the Purāna Qilā suburb of Delhi) by the traditional method of burning down the forest. The clearing was conceived as a grand sacrifice to the fire-god Agni. Every living creature that tried to escape from the ring of fire was slaughtered and the new territory settled for plough farming. The two neighbouring and related kingdoms then fought a battle of mutual annihilation. This was later represented as having been fought by millions for mastery of the whole world (which meant India). Production at that date, however, could not have supported any large armies, let alone enabled the supposed regional kingdoms to send large, regularly equipped contingents over long distances to Delhi. Actually, a small tribal kingdom still ruled by a Kuru chief survived in Kuru-land till the fifth century, but was completely extinguished soon after. There was no question of Kuru dominion at any time over the whole country, except in the imagination of later bards. Parikshit, a descendant of the Kurus, was supposed to have been crowned at Taxila in imperial style; but Taxila (Takshaśilā) was hardly more than a village before the fourth century, by which time it enters history without any Parikshit. The fourth chief in line of descent after the *Mahābhārata* war was driven out of Hastināpura by a flood—for which there is some archaeological evidence. He moved the Pūru-Kuru capital down the river to Kosambi.

The development of the *Mahābhārata* as a poem was the most important feature of this fictitious great war. The work began, like the Iliad, as a lament over the end of the nobler line. The victors, however, still ruled, so the lays were naturally changed fairly soon to a somewhat ironic song of their victory (*jaya*), a name still found attached to the work. The singing of any episode was usually prefaced (as in other countries at the time) by a sacred (here Vedic, as in Greece a Homeric) hymn. If there were a patron for the performance, his genealogy would be recited with a panegyric. The hymns made it easier for the brahmins to gain control of the tradition. Professional bards (*sūta*) were the original poets and singers when brahminism had not separated its priest caste greatly from the other Aryans. The brahmin redaction, which is all that now remains, took its present form between 200 B.C. and A.D. 200 as a collection of over 80,000 verses, with a few prose passages. The prologue states clearly that an earlier version in 24,000 stanzas was then still current, though now lost beyond recovery. The new editors added every conceivable sort of legend and myth to attract varied audiences. Many episodes that have nothing to do with the war as such appear nevertheless as tales within the tale, narrated by various characters. The inflation was made more natural by adding a frame-story. King Janamejaya III performed a great *yajña* sacrifice for the total destruction of the Nāgas, cobra demons who could take on snake or human form at will and one of whom had killed Janamejaya's father Parikshit II. The war stories and other narratives were then the revolving tales that had to be told at such sacrifices of long duration. That is, the

Mahābhārata as it now stands is not primarily the account of a great war but of the great *yajña*. The process of *Mahābhārata* inflation did not end by any means in A.D. 200, but continued down to the nineteenth century. Comparing different versions in different parts of the country, it was possible to restore approximately a critical archetype that may be as old as the late third century A.D. There is no question of restoring anything nearer to the original lays.

Most of the later additions are religious in character, dealing with something different from the Vedic ritual and religion. The brahmins thereby regained an important position in society after Buddhism had deflated their ancient prestige. The most brilliant of these additions is the *Bhagavad-Gītā*, a discourse supposedly uttered by the god Krishna just before the fighting. The god himself was new; his supreme godhead would not be admitted for centuries afterwards. The Sanskrit used is of about the third century A.D. But the major function of the *Mahābhārata* at the first stage of its redaction as a unitary brahminised epic was performed by its frame story, long before Krishna had any status as a god. The frame story is, in fact, much more important than has been realised. Janamejaya's sacrifice, which has there taken precedence over the actual war, had to be abandoned unconsummated, according to the narrative. This odd result was achieved by the brilliance of young Āstika, son of a brahmin father and Nāga mother. Moreover, Janamejaya's chief priest Somaśravas was also of the same mixed parentage. By strict brahmin rule, the children of a brahmin father by a mother of any other caste can never count as brahmins. Therefore, if the brahmins who edited the over-inflated epic could proclaim ancestry so far beyond the Aryan pale, without shame, the Nāgas were in some way a very respectable people, not demons nor a low caste. Āstika's line was the Yāyāvara ('wanderer') clan. A family by that name existed as late as the ninth century A.D. and produced the famous Sanskrit poet-dramatist Rājaśekhara, who was not a brahmin, or at least married a non-brahmin wife of the Marāthā or Rajpūt feudal Cāhamāna clan.

Who, then, were these Nāgas, snake demons and yet human at the same time; evil enough to be destroyed by a specially powerful fire sacrifice, and yet whose females could bear legitimate, highly respectable children to brahmins? The answer can be worked out from extant sources. Apparently, 'Nāga' became a generic term for forest aborigines, not necessarily connected or interrelated, who had a cobra (*nāga*) totem or worshipped the cobra as so many Indian aborigines (and not only aborigines) still do. These particular Nāgas were in the adjacent jungle at the time Kuru-land was first settled by Aryans. Food-gathering was much easier in the Gangetic forest than in the open, semi-desert river basins or the foothills of the

Panjāb. The same dense forest made it impossible to conquer the Nāgas or to reduce them otherwise to the status of tribal slaves, as had been possible with *dāsa* and *śūdra* to the west. As long as they remained free food-gatherers they were never degraded to the rank of a low caste. The Vedas themselves show that there were poor brahmins not sheltered by any Aryan tribe, who would go in peace into the wilderness to live as they could, usually by food-gathering supplemented at most with a few cattle. The brahmin tradition of study, which remained in force nearly till the Christian era and theoretically remains obligatory to this day, required each acolyte to serve an apprenticeship of twelve years under a senior teacher settled in some such clearing; to tend his cattle, master the unwritten Vedas by heart, perfect himself in every detail of ritual, and finally emerge as a fully initiated brahmin himself. Neither hunting nor agriculture were practised in these study colonies. The period was early enough for some intermarriage with the Nāga aborigines to be permissible; the pioneer brahmin rarely had any womenfolk with him of his own caste, till later days when the fashion of forming a study grove (*gurukula*) was firmly established. There was no reason for conflict with the Nāgas, who were never fighters (unlike the modern Assam 'Nāgas') or food-producers, hence very thinly scattered through the jungle. The badly fired, low-grade, ochre-washed pottery of Hastināpura I is presumably late Nāga production. The Nāgas came over to agriculture by gradual absorption as the forest was cleared. The *Mahābhārata* shows that at least one Nāga line was friendly to and in some special relation with the Kurus, though not the Pandus. The descendants of such Nāgas would naturally retain their original cults, and be on friendly terms with the first bards who sang of lost Kuru glory. The Nāga genealogies and myths are given high place in the opening canto of the great epic, though almost completely irrelevant to the main war story. In striking contrast, the Yadu hero and demigod Krishna, whose rise to 'all-god' status is clearly discernible through various strata of the epic, had his saga and genealogy relegated to a supplement, the *Harivaṃśa*. In later Indian iconography, the Great Cobra finds employment in many different situations. He is supposed to bear the whole earth upon his head, to keep it from subsidence into the waters. He serves also as bed and canopy for Vishnu, who sleeps upon the waters and whose incarnation Krishna eventually became; the Cobra is also a garland for Śiva, a weapon in the hand of Ganeśa, and an independent deity in his own right with a special day of the year to himself on which the orthodox can do no digging and use no metal. At the same time, he is the Indian peasants' favourite 'guardian of the fields' (*kshetrapāla*, a name also given to Śiva). The Great Epic is decidedly more interesting for the process of reciprocal acculturation which it reveals than for its negligible and very doubtful historical content.

The cultural importance and normal misinterpretation of the *Mahābhārata* make a brief recapitulation essential. The earliest stories in the epic have three distinct sources: Pūru-Kuru war ballads, aboriginal myths, and Yadu sagas. These discordant tales had somehow to be fitted together to suit the combined but still primitive society. The melting-pot was the Delhi-Meerut-Mathurā area, at a time when metals, especially iron, were known but in short supply. Late-Vedic Aryans, Nāga food-gatherers of the forested divide, and Krishna's neo-Vedic cattle-herders could together form a more efficient food-producing society if only they stopped fighting each other. The environment and shortage of metals made it impossible for any one of the three to subdue the others by naked force. So the myths had to coalesce. Recombination of the human elements was helped by the Kaśyapas; the editing of legends was done by another brahmin clan, the Bhrigus. The mutual acculturation was so effective that the *Mahābhārata* continued to be inflated and the *Purānas* rewritten on the same model throughout the medieval period. The process failed only when grouping people together on the basis of joint superstition could no longer help to create a more productive society. This failure was made patent by the relative ease of the Muslim conquest. But by then, 'Live and let live' had long been equated to 'Believe anything the priests say, regardless of logic, material reality, or ordinary common sense'.

CHAPTER FIVE

From Tribe to Society

5.1. *The New Religions*

To hundreds of millions outside the country, India is simply the land of the Buddha. Buddhism, and not any political system or material export, still remains for all time the most important discovery of India for the great majority of Asian people. The art and architecture of Burma, Thailand, Korea, Japan, and China, and hence world art, would be much poorer without Buddhist motifs developed under Indian influence. The Buddhist scriptures constitute by far the greater part of classical Mongol and Tibetan literature. The entire state machinery of Tibet consisted till 1959 of a few Buddhist monasteries and their nominees. The people of Ceylon, Burma, Thailand, and Indo-China not only follow the Buddhist creed (as they understand it), but regard that religion as the prime civilising influence at the dawn of their various histories. The powerful and indispensable role of Buddhist monasteries in the economic development of China, especially of the hinterland during the fifth and sixth centuries A.D., has only recently been realised. Countless pilgrims from many distant countries braved and still suffer the rigours of deserts, high snow-clad mountains, and typhoon-swept ocean to visit Indian sites connected with incidents in the Buddha's life. The westward spread of the religion was even more marked in its day than that to the east. The gigantic 60-metre-high statues of the Buddha carved out of the living rock at Bamiān (Afghanistān) would by themselves be sufficient testimony. Innumerable ruined *stūpas* (relic monuments) in central Asia bear further witness. The religion not only influenced Manichaeanism but must earlier have helped in the formation of Christianity. The scholars who wrote the Dead Sea

96

scrolls, though good Jews, show peculiarities that appear to be of Buddhist origin. Their practice of living in a monastery almost on top of a necropolis would be repulsive to Judaism, though quite agreeable to Buddhists. The 'Teacher of Righteousness' mentioned in the documents of this (probably Essene) Palestinian foundation bears the precise title of the Buddha. It is not, therefore, surprising that the Sermon on the Mount should sound more familiar to Buddhists than to the followers of the Old Testament who first heard it preached. Some of the Christ's miracles such as walking on the water were current much earlier in literature about the life of the Buddha. For that matter, the Christian saint's legend that goes under the title 'Barlaam and Josaphat' is a direct adaptation of the Buddha's life-story. The Barmecides, an important ministerial family under the Abbasid Caliph Harūn al-Rashid of Baghdād (immortalised in the *Arabian Nights*) were once the hereditary abbots (*paramaka*) of the Buddhist monastery of Nao-behār. As new converts to Islam, they came under suspicion of retaining some heretical doctrines from their old religion.

This extraordinary diffusion has two striking but mutually inconsistent features. The dissemination outside India was without force of arms or corresponding growth of Indian political influence. The name of Asoka (Sanskrit, Aśoka) is venerated far beyond his own country because he was the great Buddhist emperor, not for any conquest or other manifestation of power. The Kushānas did rule parts of central Asia and India together; but they also patronised, besides Buddhism, several other Indian cults and gods such as Śiva, whose worship nevertheless did not travel far. Beginning with Min-ti of the Han dynasty, a long line of Chinese emperors went out of their way to invite Buddhist missionaries. Yet, in the very land of its origin, Buddhism vanished but for traces on the north-eastern fringe of India. This complete internal eclipse unaccountably runs contrary to the external success. Even today educated Indians would generally be aghast or indignant if told that Buddhism—which they regard as a passing aberration—was their country's outstanding contribution to world culture. The 1500 years of the full cycle of the rise, spread, and decline of Buddhism saw India change over from semi-pastoral tribal life to the first absolute monarchies and then to feudalism. The varying roles played at different stages by this religion inside the country of its origin must therefore occupy a central place in any serious treatment of Indian civilisation. At the same time we must try to explain the dual and puzzling development of the doctrine within and outside the country.

The sixth century B.C. produced the philosophy of Confucius in China and the sweeping reforms of Zoroaster in Iran. In the middle of the

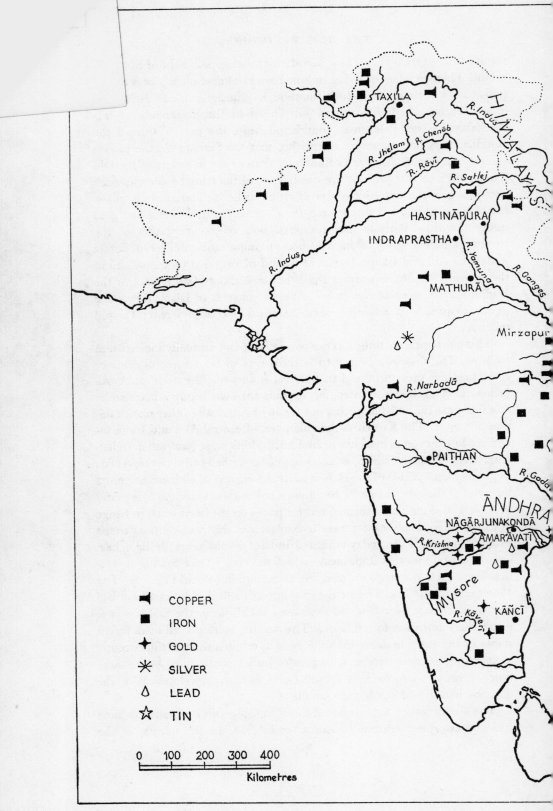

TAXILA

R. Indus
R. Jhelam
R. Chenāb
R. Rāvi
R. Satlej
HASTINĀPURA
INDRAPRASTHA
R. Yamuna
R. Ganges
MATHURĀ
Mirzapur
R. Indus
R. Narbadā
PAITHAN
R. Goda
ĀNDHRA
NĀGĀRJUNAKONDĀ
AMARĀVATĪ
R. Krishna
Mysore
KĀÑCĪ
R. Kāveri
HIMALAYAS

COPPER
IRON
GOLD
SILVER
LEAD
TIN

0   100   200   300   400
Kilometres

Met

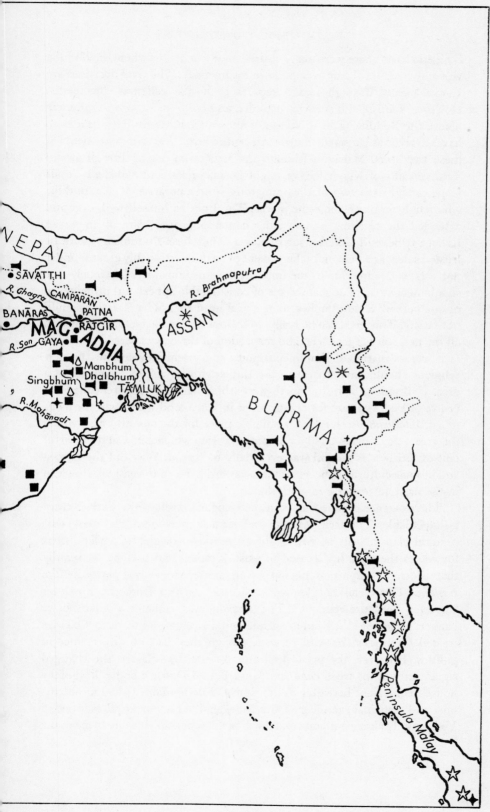

NEPAL

SĀVATTHI

R. Ghagra CAMPĀRAN

BANĀRAS PATNA

MAG·ADHA RĀJGIR

R. Son GAYA

Manbhum
Dhalbhum

Singbhum TĀMLUK

R. Mahānadi

△ R. Brahmaputra

✳ ASSAM

B U R M A

Peninsula Malay

Gangetic basin there were many entirely new teachers of whom the Buddha was only one, not the most popular in his own day. The rival doctrines are known mostly through biased reports in hostile religious documents. However, Jainism still survives in India, and traces its origins to founders before the Buddha. The Ājivikas are known from Mysore inscriptions to have survived as late as the fourteenth century A.D. The main proponents of these two sects, Mahāvira (though the Jain claim a long line of earlier Tirthamkaras of whom Pārśva might be historical) and Makkhali Gosāla respectively, were two of the numerous contemporaries of the Buddha who taught in much the same places. The Buddha himself took over and extended the teaching of two elder contemporaries, Alāra of an Aryan Kālāma tribe, and Uddaka, son of Rāma. Therefore, Buddhism cannot be treated solely as a personal achievement of its unquestionably great founder nor was its decline due to the imperfections of humanity. Obviously, the simultaneous rise of so many sects of considerable appeal and prominence in one narrow region implies some social need that older doctrines could not satisfy. This need can be analysed by looking for the factors common to all the new lines of teachers, and inspection of the new classes of disciples. If it were a matter of simple continuity and gradual evolution, the new religions should have arisen on the Indus with its ruined memories of a great civilisation, or in the north-west which had been and remained the centre of Vedic culture for centuries, or in Kuru-land which was the locus of the *Mahābhārata* story and a suitable place for the morality with which the great epic is overloaded, or at Mathurā from which a new and powerful cult of Krishna as all-god was eventually to spread. Why did the newest and in some cultural respects rather backward lands of the east take the lead in the most advanced forms of religion?

The existence of new classes in the Gangetic basin of the sixth century is undeniable. The free peasants and farmers were one. The neo-Vedic pastoral class of vaiśyas within the tribe was replaced by agriculturists for whom the tribe had ceased to exist. Traders had become so wealthy that the most important person in an eastern town was generally the *śreshthī*. The term, not known earlier, is derived from the word for 'superior', or 'pre-eminent'. The *śreshthī* was actually a financier or banker, sometimes the head of a trade guild. Even absolute, despotic kings treated these *śreshthīs* with respect, though they had no direct voice in politics. However, the prime indicator for the new class is the changed significance of the word *gahapati* (Sanskrit, *grihapati*); literally 'lord of the house', equivalent hereafter to the Roman *paterfamilias*. It had meant the host and principal sacrificer at any considerable but not royal sacrifice in Vedic and Brahmana literature. Now, for the first time, it came to mean the head of a large patriarchal household of any caste who commanded respect primarily because of his wealth, whether gained by trade, manufacture, or farming; but no longer wealth measured simply in cattle. The *gahapati*, as the executive member of the new propertied class, could do what he liked with the riches at his disposal, though obliged to support members of the household and bound by the inheritance laws of his kinship group; but he was no longer bound by tribal regulations. The new class position was obscured for a while by formal ties of caste and kinship, which became progressively lighter. Even the word *gotra* ('cowpen') used earlier to denote the exogamous clan unit would hereafter mean also the *gahapati's* large patriarchal family, though the older meaning of *gotra* was never lost like the older meaning of *grihapati*. Both agriculturists and traders suffered from the constant warfare which was regularly preceded by Vedic *yajña* fire sacrifice. The trader had to be on good terms with people beyond the territory of his tribe and state; but he also needed safe trade routes, free from robbers. A part of this demand could be satisfied only by the growth of a 'universal monarchy', a single state that would end petty warfare and police the entire countryside. But trade always extended beyond political frontiers.

The existence of free, tenant or land-owning peasants (*kassaka, karshaka*), necessarily implied by the existence of *gahapati* and *śreshthi*, is clear from the texts. As explained, large-scale slave labour was not available. Food-gatherers were too few, rarely inclined to perform the hard, regular labour of a farm. They were drawn into food production mostly when their lands were cleared by others; in feudal and modern times, by famine. (This last led to the formation of 'slave' castes like the Hāris, out of aboriginals who had contracted away their freedom for bare but regular subsistence; their labour, known to the last generation, was inefficient and unproductive.) The real peasantry had to derive in the main from more advanced 'Aryan' tribesmen, who had begun to clear land on their own, in small groups not always in touch with most of the tribe. The only incentive they had to produce any surplus came from trade in that surplus. This in turn was possible only if there were no clan obligation to share the surplus food, if cattle were not owned in common, and the plots were not subject to redistribution by tribal councils—in a word, private property in farm animals, in land and its produce. The Panjāb remained conservative in this respect; tribal life continued much as before, with nearly the same type of chieftain-king as in the *Brāhmanas*. Yajurvedic kingship was a powerful deterrent to unlimited agrarian production by individual households, and an insupportable burden for the peasantry. Peace and lower taxes were essential. Cattle and other animals were requisitioned in increasing number for the *yajña* without payment. This is shown by Pāli stories of royal fire-sacrifices. The strain upon regular agriculture was intolerable. Only a few brahmin priests (such as those to whom the sixth-century monarchs like Pasenadi and Bimbisāra gave away whole villages) gained permanently. Thus, it is natural that all the new sects denied flatly the validity of any ritual, especially of Vedic ritual. This included brahmin teachers, as, for example, Pūrana Kassapa and Samjaya, son of Belatthi.

Regular human sacrifices had gone out of brahmin fashion by the time of the *Śatapatha Brāhmana*, in spite of the human victims listed in the Yajurveda. Sporadic human sacrifice did continue, being considered neces-sary to make impregnable such strong points as bastions and city gates and to prevent dams from being swept away by flood waters. The victim had to be buried in the foundations of the new construction in such cases. But these exceptional sacrifices were very rare, frowned upon, and never con-ducted according to Vedic rites. The horse sacrifice was also rather rare. None is, in fact, definitely recorded for the Gangetic basin till a brief and futile revival in the second century. The main Vedic sacrifice was of cattle, natural in a predominantly pastoral society. How completely the sixth-century reform drove this, too, out of fashion is seen by the absolute Hindu tabu upon cattle-killing and beef-eating which is still in force, though now senseless, uneconomic, and cruel to the cattle in a land short of pasturage. A modern orthodox Hindu would place beef-eating on the same level as cannibalism, whereas Vedic brahmins had fattened upon a steady diet of sacrificed beef. The *Śatapatha Brāhmana* gives ritual arguments in a famous passage why the flesh of cow and cart-ox (*anaduh*; nothing is said about the bull) should not be eaten. The whole passage ends in a blunt and now embarrassing statement by the leading brahmin party of Yāj-ñavalkya: 'That may very well be; but as long as (it puts) flesh on (my) body, I shall continue to eat it.'

Two quotations suffice to prove the economic basis of the tabu on beef-eating. Archaic verses ascribed to the Buddha read, "Cattle are our friends, just like parents and other relatives, for cultivation depends upon them. They give food, strength, freshness of complexion and happiness. Knowing this, brahmins of old did not kill cattle" (*Sutta-nipata*, 295–6). There was no question of beef-eating as a sin in the earlier days of the ban. Mao Tse-tung's *Report* of March 1927 on the peasant uprising in Hunan says, "Draught-oxen are a treasure to the peasants. As it is practi-cally a religious tenet that 'Those who slaughter cattle in this life will themselves become cattle in the next', draught oxen must never be killed. Before coming to power, the peasants had no means of stopping the slaughter of cattle except the religious tabu. Since the rise of the Peasant Associations, they have extended their jurisdiction even over cattle and have prohibited their slaughter in the cities. Of the six beef shops in the county town of Hsiangtan, five are now closed and the remaining one sells only the beef of sick or disabled cattle. Cattle slaughter is prohibited throughout the county of Hengshan. A peasant whose cow stumbled and broke a leg had to consult the Peasant Association before he dared kill it . . .". That the Chinese peasant did not use the cow's milk, butter, cheese or curds presumably accounts for the difference between his position and that of the Indian peasant.

When the *Upanishads* were added to supplement the various *Brāhmanas*, no direct acknowledgement was made of any change; but the contents of brahmin books became entirely different. The *yajña* was now cited primarily for some mystical philosophy with generally fantastic interpretation, not for its original blood-and-guts performance. The Upanishadic brahmins, who had once finished their studies near or to the west of the Indus, now went even to eastern kshatriyas like Aśvapati Kaikeya and Pravahana Jaivali to learn the 'inner significance' of the sacrifice. There appeared a new concept, Brahmā, an undefined divine essence whereof the attainment is superior to all other human endeavour. For the rest, the questions dealt with by the Upanishads are just those which the other sixth-century Gangetic philosophers treated: What is the nature of the soul, if there is a soul? What happens to man after death? What is the supreme good for man? No reference was made to Buddhism or any other anti-brahmin religious sect. This has led many to believe that the oldest Upanishads must all precede Buddhism. The mention of a past king 'Ajātaśatru of Kāśi' in the *Upanishad* attached to the *Śatapatha Brāhmana* shows that this cannot always be true, for that king was the Buddha's younger contemporary. The nascent doctrines were 'in the air' of the sixth century.

The exact parallel to the development of a universal monarchy would have been a single exclusive religion with a strict unitary ritual. This was impossible for the society in question without an immense use of force. The limitless Gangetic forest could have sheltered those for whom a separate common ritual was an indispensable common bond, as ritual observances remain even now in India. The new eastern teachers rose above all ritual and broke the strongest tabu by eating cooked food from the hands of another caste however low, or even left-overs of soiled food. What the last means is difficult to explain to anyone who does not know that most Indians would rather go hungry, and many have preferred death by starvation to eating soiled food or that prepared by a person of lower caste. The leaders of the various innovating sects and their monkish followers (not the lay believers) gained their livelihood mostly by alms. This was at base a reversion to food-gathering. Many continued to prefer a life of solitude in the jungle. They killed nothing and obtained what food they required from vegetation. Only salt was acceptable from human hands to these extreme ascetics. Celibacy and abstinence from holding property made the new teachers much more economic than greedy fire priests in an acquisitive society. The Yajurvedic and later brahmins hoped for rich gifts in unlimited quantity and actually claimed to have received them from legendary ancient kings: numberless elephants, cattle, chariots, beautiful slave women, and many pieces of gold. The sharp impression made even upon brahmin practices by the new asceticism was indelible; poverty and penance remained high ideals ever afterwards. The Upanishads, too, tell of a famished brahmin accepting soiled food from a low-caste elephant driver. Another such brahmin spied upon a chant-and-dance for food by dog-totem tribesmen. The *yajña* was ended for the easterners in all but theory; the brahmin of the future would eventually agree to serve all castes as priests and to adapt new worships to old forms in order to gain his livelihood—paying lip service to the Vedas all the while.

5.2. *The Middle Way*

The roots of the main schools of later Indian philosophy can clearly be discerned in the sixth century B.C. Ajita, nicknamed 'with the hair blanket' (*kesakambali*), preached a thoroughgoing materialist doctrine: good deeds and charity gained a man nothing in the end. His body dissolved into the primary elements at death, no matter what he had or had not done. Nothing remained. Good and evil, charity and compassion were all irrelevant to a man's fate. The Lokāyata school from which the brutally practical theories of Magadhan statecraft were to develop seems to have taken a great deal from this Ajita, though the outstanding name in Indian materialism is that of Cārvāka, whose original teachings are lost. Pakudha Kātyāyana added three more to the list of primary indestructible elements (which were normally taken as earth, water, air, and light): namely, happiness, sorrow, and life. These, too, could be neither created nor destroyed. The sword stroke that seemed to end life was a mere passage of metal between molecules of flesh and bone, with no power over man. This could be the origin of the Vaiśeshika school of later times. Pūrana of the Kassapa brahmin *gotra* may have laid the foundations of Sāmkhya doctrine in regarding the soul as distinct from the body, unaffected by anything that happened to the body. His immediate following later merged into that of Makkhali Gosāla, a teacher who believed that the soul had to pass through a vast, immutable cycle of foreordained rebirths, regardless of any action by the particular body to which it was attached in each birth.

The Jain Mahāvira followed the four rules ascribed to his predecessor Pārśva: Taking no life (*ahimsā*), taking no property from others, possessing no property of one's own, and truthfulness. To these he added a fifth, celibacy. Though a kshatriya of high Licchavi tribal birth, Mahāvira reached his ultimate state of knowledge by the severest penance and constant meditation. He abandoned even the three sheet-like togas allowed for a monk by Pārśva, to go stark naked. His followers would not drink water without straining and filtering it, lest some life be destroyed thereby. A careless step might kill some insect. The in-breath must also be filtered through a piece of cloth, not for hygiene but to save any life floating in the air. Castigating one's own flesh by long hours in the hot sun and the rain was not only a Jain fashion but also the practice of many other teachers and sects of the day. Gosāla also went naked, but drank and practised orgiastic sexual rites which doubtless originated in contemporary primitive fertility cults. Even so did later Tantric rites originate, but they were not always put into practice, being more often sublimated through mystical interpretation and symbolic innocuous substitution. It should never be forgotten that there always existed a marginal population to whom sorcery, fertility rites and secret tribal cults seemed essential. People who felt dissatisfied with official 'civilised' religion continued to learn and adopt these secret rites through the ages down to Muslim times and even later, in the belief that they thereby achieved some special powers or at least a short cut to perfection. Gosāla's actions were regarded as obscene self-indulgence in his own day, but the reports are of hostile origin. Tribal medicine-man's rites left other marks upon ascetic life in the form of punishing observances: total abstinence from food and water for incredible periods, control of breath, maintaining excessively contorted bodily postures—all these and many other senseless exercises were supposed to confer extraordinary powers. It was thought that true adepts could become invisible or fly through the air at will. Later *yoga* practices and physical poses developed from this. Yoga within limits is a good system of exercise in a hot climate for people who do not live by muscular exertion and hard physical labour. The most that one can attain by it is some measure of control over normally involuntary functions of the body, and good health; but no supernatural powers.

Buddhism stood between the two extremes: unrestrained individualistic self-indulgence and equally individualistic but preposterous ascetic punishment of the body. Hence its steady rise, and its name 'The Middle Way'.

The core of Buddhism is the Noble (*ārya*) Eightfold Path. The first of the eight steps is proper vision: this world is filled with sorrow generated by uncontrolled desire, greed, cupidity and self-seeking on the part of mankind. The quenching of this desire is the path to peace for all; the eightfold path is the way that leads to this end. So much for the first step, proper vision. The second step is proper aims: not to increase one's wealth and power at the expense of others, not to be lost in the enjoyment of the senses and in luxury; to love others in full measure and to increase the happiness of others—this is proper design. Third step, proper speech: lies, calumny, vituperation, useless chatter, and such misuse of the tongue spoils the organisation of society. Quarrels arise that may lead to violence and killing. Therefore, correct speech must be truthful, conducive to mutual friendship, endearing, and measured. Fourth step, proper action: taking life, theft, adultery and such other actions of the body would lead to great disasters in society. Therefore it is necessary to abstain from killing, stealing, fornication; and to do such positive deeds as will lead to the benefit of other people. Fifth step, proper livelihood: no man should make his living by means that harm society, *e.g.* by the sale of liquor, dealing in animals for butchery, etc. Pure and honest methods alone should be followed. Sixth step, correct mental exercise: not to let evil thoughts enter the mind, to remove evil thoughts already in the mind, to generate good thoughts actively in the mind, and to carry to fulfilment the good thoughts that are already within the mind. This sort of active mental self-discipline is the sixth of the eight steps. Seventh step, correct awareness: to be ever conscious that the body is made of unclean substances, to examine constantly the sensations of pleasure and pain in the body, to examine one's own mind, to meditate upon the evils that come from bonds of the flesh and attachments of the mind; and to meditate upon ways for the removal of these evils. Eighth step, proper meditation: this is a carefully worked out mental training in concentration. Briefly, it is to Buddhism what 'gymnastics' was to the Greek body.

Clearly, this was the most social of religions; the applications of its various steps are carefully developed and expounded in a long series of discourses ascribed to the Buddha. There were regulations specially meant for the monk, such as celibacy, which were not binding upon the lay follower. The Buddhist monastic Order was organised and conducted its meetings precisely on the lines of the tribal *sabhā* assembly. The total number of monks in the Buddhist *samgha* (Order) could not have exceeded 500 during the Teacher's lifetime, nor is there any credible record of their having all gathered together at any one time till after his death. The rules of the Order which form a special *vinaya* ('discipline') section of the

Buddhist Canon are all ascribed to the Buddha himself in order to lend them his authority; but they are obviously of later origin for the most part, though formulated not long after his death. During his lifetime, and even long afterwards, any group of six or more almsmen could, if so minded, frame their own special rules and follow their own separate discipline without interference by the rest of the Order, provided, of course, they respected the main doctrine. The monk was permitted no property beyond a begging-bowl, a water-pot, at most three pieces of plain, unembroidered, patternless cloth (preferably pieced together from rags) for wear; oil-jug, razor, needle and thread, and a staff. The more delicate were allowed plain sandals. Though he might beg his food in a village or town, the one daily meal of left-over scraps (mixed together to minimise any pleasure of taste) had to be eaten before noon. Nor could the almsman stay in a householder's dwelling even for a single night (later altered to permit three nights or less). His residence had to be outside the settlement, in a grove, cave (originally, natural cave), under a tree, or by a corpse-enclosure into which dead bodies were thrown to be eaten by birds and animals, or sometimes cremated. These were just the places where the most gruesome primitive rites were practised, including cannibalism for the attainment of magic powers. The monk was enjoined not to let the terrifying sights move him, but to overcome all such perils by his own firm determination. For the three or four months of the rains the residence had to be in some one place. Otherwise, he must travel on foot (never by chariot, elephant, horse, cart, or pack-animal) to preach to the people. The early monks, like the Buddha himself, were expert food-gatherers, as is evident from their recorded arguments about begging soiled food from other human beings; long trips through the wilderness did not trouble them. Generally they would accompany caravans, but even then pass the night outside the camp. The Buddhist monk was forbidden labour for profit and for agriculture, having to live on alms or by gathering food in the forest without the taking of life; only thus would he be free to concentrate upon his social duties, the obligation to lead all to the proper Way. His own salvation was freedom from the cycle of rebirth, *nirvāna*, a mysterious ideal never fully explained.

The Buddha would refuse to answer questions as to the existence or non-existence of a soul. However, the doctrine of rebirth and transmigration (no matter what part of personality was reborn) seemed natural to contemporary society. The Vedas and Upanishads did not have this. Though it was only one step from the primitive conception of return of the departed individual to an animal totem, the step was of the utmost importance. Primitive reversion to one specific totem was obligatory, independent of the individual's will. Buddhist transmigration depended upon *karma*, the man's action throughout his life. *Karma* as merit would correspond not only to a store of acquired money or harvested grain, but would also come to fruition at the proper time as a seed bore fruit or a loan matured. Every living creature could perform some *karma* which would raise it after death to rebirth in a suitable body; a better body if the *karma* were good, a mean and vile one, say of an insect or animal, if the *karma* were evil. Even the gods were subject to *karma*. Indra himself might fall from his particular heaven after the course of his previous *karma* was fully run; an ordinary man could be reborn in the world of the gods, even as an Indra, to enjoy a life of heavenly pleasure for aeons—but not for ever. The Buddha and the truly enlightened monks were released from the otherwise endless chain of births, death, and rebirth. The eightfold path and the Middle Way, a pure life of no possessions and no worldly attachment, dispassionate and compassionate, devoted to helping mankind discover the right trail through the maze of conflicting personal desires, would achieve ultimate liberation for the best of the *bhikshu* almsmen.

5.3. The Buddha and his Society

The life of the Buddha is well worth a brief sketch, not only to reach the original nucleus buried beneath a mass of later legend but also because of the social picture of his times. The founder was born with the name Gotama, later improved by the devout to Siddhārtha, in the small, undifferentiated kshatriya tribe of the Sakyans (*Sakka*). The Sakyans spoke an Aryan language and claimed to be Aryans. The name in the precise Pāli form Sakka is reported for a conquered tribe in the Elamite version of the inscriptions of the Achaemenid emperor Darius I, late in the sixth century. There may be no direct connection between the two, but the Aryan origin of the Sakyans becomes plausible. There were no brahmins or caste-classes within the tribe, nor have high Vedic observances ever been reported of the Sakyans. In spite of being kshatriyas who wielded arms at need, the Sakyans also worked at agriculture. All Sakyans including the Buddha's father put their hands to the plough. In addition, they had a few trade colonies (*nigama*) outside their own territory. The Sakyan chief was elected by rotation, which led to the later fable of the Buddha being born a prince and living in magnificent palaces amid the most refined pleasures. Actually, the title *rājanya* denoted any kshatriya eligible for election to chieftainship. The Sakyans generally managed all their own affairs, but had not power of life and death. Such power was reserved by their overlord, the Kosalan monarch (at that time Pasenadi: Sanskrit Prasenajit), whose suzerainty was acknowledged by the Sakyans. In this they differed from the more powerful and completely independent Aryan tribes such as the Mallas and Licchavis, fighting oligarchies similar to the Greek republics of the time, over whom no external king had any authority and who also elected their office-holders in rotation. The date of the Buddha's birth would have been a priceless datum and reference point for our chronology. He died at the age of 80. One Indian tradition puts the decease in 543 B.C., but there is an un-explained jump of sixty years in the record, corresponding to one complete sixty-year cycle by which Indians and some other Asiatic people count their years. The year 483 seems to be reasonably consistent with the chronology of later events and is supported by a record of one dot per year after the Buddha's death, placed on an Indian palm-leaf manuscript which was taken to Canton in a known Chinese year.

The tiny Sakyan region, primitive and poorly developed, lay on both sides of what is now the Indo-Nepalese frontier along Basti and Gorakhpur districts. The Koliyan neighbours of the Sakyans had also listened to the Buddha and claimed a share of his ashes after his cremation. Nevertheless, many of them were at the time in a more primitive stage of tribal existence, with the Kol (*Zizyphus jujuba*) tree as a tribal totem; some followed personal rites of the bull totem. The Koliyans as a whole were therefore often counted among the aboriginals with the generic label Nāgas. The Sakyans, fighting with them over the waters of the Rohini river, had naturally no compunction in poisoning that water, against all rules of warfare among Aryans. The Buddha himself was born in a grove of *sāla* (*Shorea robusta*) trees sacred to the mother goddess Lumbini, just after his mother had bathed in the adjoining sacred investiture *pushkara* (artificial lotus pond) of the Sakyans. The *sāla* was the Sakyan totem tree, so that the mother Māyā (who died within a week of Gotama's birth) kept all the observances then in force, in the manner of most Indian women of whatever class and historical period. The goddess is still worshipped at the same spot under much the same name (Rummindei) by people who have forgotten the Buddha altogether.

Young Gotama received the normal Sakyan kshatriya training in the use of weapons, management of the horse and chariot, and tribal custom. He was married to a Sakyan lady Kaccānā and begot a son Rāhula. But the influence of the new philosophies made itself felt in the urge to solve the problems of life, the cause and removal of sorrow from humanity. At the age of 29, just after Rāhula's birth, Gotama left his house and tribe, cut off his hair, assumed the garb of an ascetic, and began his quest of salvation for mankind. Six years or so went in seeking guidance, in the beginning from various teachers and then by direct experiment, without satisfaction. The life of a reasonable almsman was soon abandoned for extreme physical penance, at times in complete isolation from all humanity in the deepest jungle. The final discovery was made near Gayā, on the banks of the Nerañjarā river, seated under a pipal (*Ficus religiosa*) tree that probably had been a humble cult spot and became a great centre of pilgrimage afterwards, with cuttings planted in distant places like Ceylon and perhaps China. The first sermon was preached at Sārnāth (*Isipatana*) near Banāras to former disciples who had left him in disillusionment when he gave up rigid austerities. The remaining forty-five years of his life were spent wandering on foot, except during the obligatory monsoon retreat, to preach his new discovery. Occasionally, he would retire to absolute solitude to think out the answer to some important social problem. Later in his life, a young disciple Ānanda accompanied him to look after his welfare as far as the simple daily routine allowed. Tradition ascribes to this Ānanda the repetition from memory of many of the discourses that the Buddha preached, none of which were written down during the Teacher's lifetime. More of the sermons were delivered at the Kosalan capital city Sāvatthi than in any other place. The Buddha's travels could not have taken him much beyond Kosambī, and probably not as far as Mathurā on the Yamunā river, though he did visit Kuru-land more than once. In the opposite direction, he passed regularly through Rājgir and Gāya and visited the newly cleared region of Dakkhiṇāgiri near Mirzāpūr, just south of the Ganges. Nothing is reliably known of his appearance. There were no contemporary portraits, and, in fact, the Buddha is represented for centuries after his passing away only by a tree, his footprints, or the Wheel of the Law in sculptures such as at Bhārhut. The peripatetic life with its simple and spare diet kept him healthy through a long life, with little recorded illness. Though he spoke jestingly of his aged body, 'held together somehow like an old worn-out cart', he seems to have swum across the Ganges at Patnā in his seventy-ninth year, while less hardy disciples looked for boats and rafts to ferry them over. Death came to him at Kusinārā of the Mallas, on the way from Rājgir to Sāvatthi.

The life was not without its adventures and risks. At Dakkhiṇāgiri ('the southern mountain') and near Mathurā, there were cruel *yaksha* cults where strangers were caught, asked riddles, and sacrificed if the answer was not satisfactory. The Buddha managed to convert some of these *yakshas* (presumably their human representatives) to bloodless sacrifices. King Bimbisāra offered the young and then unknown Buddha command of the Magadhan army, after making certain that the young almsman of distinguished appearance and impressive physique was a trained kshatriya. The King and the Buddha remained good friends after the refusal. A brahmin Māgandiya offered his beautiful daughter in marriage to the Buddha, regardless of caste and vow of celibacy. The refusal made a lifelong enemy of the rejected beauty, who later married a prince and tried for revenge. There were false accusations by rival teachers and manifestations of contempt from those who felt that a healthy man should take to farming or some other productive occupation. The ferocious brigand Amgulimāla, outlawed for killing every wayfarer he caught, was converted after trying in vain to intimidate the Buddha, and joined the Order to end his days in peace as a monk. The richest and most generous merchant of the time, Sudatta (styled Anāthapindika, 'he who feeds the helpless') acquired the grove of Prince Jeta outside Sāvatthi by covering its soil with silver pieces, just to give the Buddha and his followers a place of rest during the monsoon. There were many other men and women of the trader and well-to-do householder (*gahapati*) class who listened with special attention to the duties the Buddha worked out for the ordinary citizen who was content to remain within the power of *karma* and rebirth. A most charming story tells of his preaching to a couple happily married for many years, who asked for nothing more than to be reborn as husband and wife again, in whatever condition. They were told how to achieve this by performing the simpler duties of a righteous family life. The brahmins Sāriputta and Moggallāna, the leading disciples during the Buddha's own lifetime, were actually better known than the Teacher when they left the following of Samjaya to join the Order; the Buddhist *samgha* owes its growth, early philosophy, and organisation to them. But there were other disciples from all walks of life. The first in the traditional line of *samgha* patriarchs was Upāli, a lowly barber (but almost certainly a Sakyan, too) before initiation. The Buddha's Sakyan cousin Devadatta wanted a more austere discipline for the monks, with less social contact; he is accused of having tried to murder his pre-eminent leader, who refused so unsocial a rule. A scavenger, a dog-eater, members of the lowest castes, were highly respected monks, too, initiated by the Buddha himself. There was also a separate Order of Buddhist nuns, with their own organisation. The two greatest kings of the day, no longer tribal chiefs but absolute monarchs, offered respectful patronage. The blacksmith Cunda served the aged Buddha a special dish of mushrooms which later brought on a relapse of an earlier attack of dysentery and led to the Teacher's final illness; but he, too, received as much attention in a special discourse on morality as the richest merchant or most noble princeling.

One story from the archaic Buddhist canonical work, the *Suttanipāta*, is worth detailed report for the information it conveys, both about the spread of Buddhism and about contemporary India. The Kosalan brahmin Bāvari had left the capital (Sāvatthi) to go down the southern trade route (*dakshināpatha*, the modern Deccan). He settled with a few young disciples at the junction of the Mulā and Godāvari rivers, in the territory of the Assakas ('Horse People', the tribe that later developed into the Sātavāhanas). There he lived by food-gathering, taking wild grain and nuts from plants and tubers or roots from the earth. Eventually a good-sized village (*grāma*) came into being in the neighbourhood. With whatever he could gather from the surplus of this village, Bāvari arranged to perform one of the major *yajña* sacrifices in Vedic style. The ceremony was upset by a brahmin who turned up after the gifts had been distributed and cursed Bāvari for not having anything more to give. Then Bāvari sent sixteen of his brahmin acolytes north to question the Buddha, whose fame had reached far down the trade route and who seemed to be the only person who might enable the curse to be foiled. These pupils went first to Paithan, the terminus of the Dakshinā-patha trade route (which lay to the south-east of the hermitage); then presumably with some trade caravan past Aurangābād, to Maheśvar on the Narmadā; Ujjain, Gonaddha (unidentified but in Gond country), Bhilsā, Kosambi, Sāketa (Fyzābād), Sāvatthi. There they joined the eastern section of the northern trade route (*uttarāpatha*) to go to Setavyā, Kapila-vastu (Sakyan headquarters), Kusinārā and Pāvā (both of the Mallas), Bhoganagar, Vesāli (modern Basārh; then chief town of the Licchavis), Rājgir. There they found the Buddha at the Stone Chaitya outside the city. Some of the questions asked were: What covers this world, what keeps it from the light? What can take man out of the cross-currents of life? Who is the fully contented man in the world? What constrains sages, kshatriyas, brahmins and other people to offer sacrifices to the gods? What is the source of the many sorrows of the world? Is the real sage he who has philo-sophic knowledge, or the master of (Vedic) ritual? What is the nature of that salvation which is gained by whoever frees himself from desires and doubt? Such queries are typical of the early Upanishads.

These questions speak for the spirit of the times. The southern trade route from Paithan to Sāvatthi is outlined in detail by our source. Kosala was more important at the time than Magadha and direct transport from Kosambi to Banāras and further east not too popular, whether by land or river. It is clear that there was no agriculture on the Godāvari till the middle of the sixth century, after which village settlement spread rapidly, presumably because iron and knowledge of iron-working as well as the heavy northern plough had then just reached the region. The emergence of the Deccan from prehistory is thus rather accurately dated with reference to the life of the Buddha. This, incidentally, tallies with excavations at Maheśvar on the Narmadā and Nevāsā near the junction of the Godāvari to the Pravarā-Mulā complex; it also explains the 'intrusion' stratum in southern excavations. The territory from Nevāsā to Pravarāsangam remained holy for southern brahmins throughout recorded history. It was here that the Mahārāshtrian saint Jnānśevara took refuge at the end of the thirteenth century A.D. from the persecution of his fellow brahmins at Alandi, to write his metrical translation of and comment on the *Bhagavad-Gitā*. This work gave the Marāthi language its form and provided inspiration for a long line of successors of all castes. But the impetus for the new language and for the agricultural settlement, without which the *Gitā* and its translation would have been unnecessary for the region, both came from the north, effectively in the sixth century B.C.

Buddhist scriptures work out the duties of a householder and peasant regardless of caste, wealth, profession—and with no attention whatever to ritual. They argue against brahmin pretensions and specialised ritual with consummate skill but in the simplest words. Caste might exist as a social distinction; it had no permanence, no inner justification. Nor did ritual, which was irrelevant and unnecessary for the good life. The canonical writings, almost all supposedly from the Buddha's discourses and dialogues, were in everyday language and plain style without mysticism or lengthy speculation. This was a new type of religious literature addressed to the whole of contemporary society, not reserved for a few learned initiates and adepts. Most important of all, the Buddha or some anonymous early disciple ventured to propound new duties for the absolute monarch: the king who merely collected taxes from a land troubled by brigands and anti-social elements was not doing his duty. Banditry and strife could never be suppressed by force and draconic punishment. The root of social evil was poverty and unemployment. This was not to be bribed away by charity and donations, which would only reward and further stimulate evil action. The correct way was to supply seed and food to those who lived by agriculture and cattle-breeding. Those who lived by trade should be furnished with the necessary capital. Servants of the state should be paid properly and regularly so that they would not then find ways to squeeze the *janapadas*. New wealth would thus be generated, the *janapadas* liberated from robbers and cheats. A citizen could bring up his children in comfort and happiness, free from want and fear, in such a productive and contented environment. The best way of spending surplus accumulation, whether in the treasury or from voluntary private donations, would be in public works such as digging wells and water ponds and planting groves along the trade routes.

This is a startlingly modern view of political economy. To have propounded it at a time of Vedic *yajña* to a society that had just begun to conquer the primeval jungle was an intellectual achievement of the highest order. The new philosophy gave man control over himself. What it could not give was limitless scientific and technical control over nature with the benefits to be shared by all mankind according to individual and social need.

When the Buddha passed away by an obscure village, attended only by one disciple, his own Sakyan tribe had been massacred, both his great royal patrons dead in miserable circumstances; his brilliant pupils Sāriputta and Moggallāna had already attained Nirvāna. The doctrine continued to grow nevertheless because it was eminently fitted to the needs of a rapidly evolving society.

5.4. The Dark Hero of the Yadus

The creed which would survive to the twentieth century as the 'true religion' for millions in India was not to be Buddhism but the heterogeneous worship of Krishna, a personal god to whom anyone could pray for succour in distress as one could not to the human teacher Buddha. The two contrast at every step, though a great deal of doctrine later palmed off in Krishna's name was surreptitiously borrowed from Buddhism; as for that matter were some epithets (Bhagavat, Narottama, Purushottama). Where the Buddha was an historical figure, it is difficult to find anything historical about any of the numerous Krishnas whose myths and legends coalesced to form the dark all-god. Later Buddhism was ruined by increasing layers of myth and the progressively divine status accorded the Teacher; Krishna worship was founded entirely upon and gained strength from the cumulative myths of divinity. The serene and limpid presentation in the simplest words and plain logic which characterises early Buddhist discourses is not to be found in the teachings foisted upon Krishna. The *Gītā* with its brilliant Sanskrit and superb inconsistency is a book that allows the reader to justify almost any action while shrugging off the consequences. The many-faceted god is likewise inconsistent, though all things to all men and everything to most women: divine and lovable infant, mischievous shepherd boy; lover of all the milkmaids in the herders' camp, husband of innumerable goddesses, most promiscuously virile of bed-mates; yet devoted to Rādhā alone in mystic union, and an exponent of ascetic renunciation withal; the ultimate manifestation of eternal peace, but the roughest of bullies in killing his own uncle Kamsa, in beheading a guest of honour like Śiśupāla at someone else's fire sacrifice; the very fountain-head of all morality, whose advice at crucial moments of the great battle (in which he played simultaneously the parts of *deus ex machina* and a menial charioteer) nevertheless ran counter to every rule of decency, fair play, or chivalry. The whole Krishna saga is a magnificent example of what a true believer can manage to swallow, a perfect setting of opportunism for the specious

arguments of the *Gitā*. It reflects the relationship between a highly composite society with a relatively primitive level of production and its religion.

The full narrative would go at least to the twelfth century A.D. and the
Vishnuite reform of the great *ācārya* Rāmānuja. We shall take the story
only to the fourth century B.C. for the present. The sole archaeological
datum about Krishna comes from his traditional weapon, the missile discus,
a wheel that could be thrown and was sharp enough to behead an enemy.
This is not Vedic, and went out of fashion long before the Buddha; but a
cave drawing in Mirzāpūr district (the Buddhist Dakkhināgiri, in fact)
shows a charioteer attacking the aborigines (who drew the picture) with
such a discus. The date would therefore be about 800 B.C., roughly the
time when the first settlement at Banāras was founded. The charioteers
would be Aryans exploring the region across the river for iron ore, the rich

FIG. 8. Discus-throwing charioteer in a Mīrzāpūr Cave, *circa* 800 B.C.

haematite with which the cave pictures were drawn. On the other hand,
Krishna in the Rigveda is a demon, enemy of Indra, his name being the
generic designation of hostile dark-skinned pre-Aryans. The basis of the
Krishna legend is that he was a hero and later demi-god of the Yadu tribe,
one of the five main Aryan people (*Pañca-janāh*) in the oldest Veda; but
these Yadus were alternately cursed or blessed by the hymn-singers,
according to current alignment in the constant fighting between Panjāb
tribes. Krishna is also a Sātvata, an Andhaka-Vrishni, and fostered in a
gokula (cattle-herders' commune) to save him from his maternal uncle
Kamsa. The transfer related him, moreover, to the Ābhiras, an historical
and pastoral people early in the Christian era, progenitors of the modern
Ahir caste. The prophecy had been that Kamsa would be killed by a son of
his sister (or in some versions daughter) Devakī, who was imprisoned
accordingly with her husband Vasudeva. The child Krishna-Vāsudeva
(son of Vasudeva) grew up in the *gokula*, saved the cattle from Indra,

115

trampled down and expelled—but did not kill—a poisonous many-headed Nāga, Kāliya, who blocked access to a convenient pool of the Yamunā river near Mathurā. Then Krishna and his even stronger brother Balarāma knocked off Kamsa's bravos in the arena before fulfilling the prophecy. It should always be remembered that, in certain primitive societies, the sister's son is heir and successor to the chief; also, the chief has often to be sacrificed by the successor. Kamsa's death has good support in primitive usage, and shows what the Oedipus legend would have become in matrilocal society.

Krishna's next step beyond his tribe was taken with the mother goddesses. As a child, he had killed one of them, Pūtanā by name (later a goddess of the smallpox, perhaps), who had tried to nurse him with her poisonous milk. She must have survived the killing, as did Ushas after her brush with Indra, for a part of the Mathurā region continued to bear Pūtanā's name. The *gokula* where Krishna was fostered (to save him from Kamsa) boolied or shifted permanently to a grove across the river from Mathurā, the *Vrindāvana*. The name means 'forest of the group goddess'. Krishna is still married every year at a fixed date to this goddess, represented by a holy basil (*tulasī*) plant; the annual repetition of the ceremony indicates that the consort of the goddess's human representative was originally sacrificed—a custom apparently broken by Krishna. The habit of marrying mother goddesses and dallying with nymphs grew uncontrollably upon the vigorous hero, the total number of Krishna's official wives (besides Vrindā and Rādhā) being given as 16,108. Some of them represented older, foreign tribes, as for example Jāmbavati, daughter of a 'bear' clan chief. Rukmini ('the golden') was associated with the Bhojas, also savages at the time. Thousands of these unnamed 'wives' were simply *apsarases*, water nymphs. As a result, Krishna worship could encroach peacefully upon local cults. It continued to spread long after the Yadus had killed each other off to the last man, thirty-six years after the supposed *Mahābhārata* battle. It is known that by the sixth century B.C., Mathurā was occupied by the Śūrasenas; the Yādavas or Jādhavs of medieval times were upstarts given the usual spurious genealogy by brahmins paid to link them to Krishna's Yadus. However, the Śūrasenas, though unrelated to the Yadus, maintained the cult of Krishna which continued to be centred upon Mathurā. The dark god's marriages were a vital step forward in assimilating patriarchal Aryans to some matriarchal pre-Aryans. It must always be remembered that not only would food-gatherers rise to food production, but Aryans could also degenerate into food-gatherers because of the environment; at both stages, fusion between the two sets of people was possible and facilitated by mutual adoption of cults. The divine

1. Village hut, Ambarnāth.

2. Thatched hut-and-stable with stone and mud walls, Cākan.

3. Cattle-dung cakes being dried for use as fuel, Poona. Deforestation, and the acute shortage of firewood, compels this removal of potentially useful fertilizer from the soil-cycle.

4. Caravan buffalo, just after coming up the difficult Nānaghāt Pass for Junnar; the type has not changed for over 2,000 years.

5. Potter's disc, used only by women. Left, ready for use; right, the two halves open to show the boss and socket (now metal-lined) and lubrication.

6. The fast potter's wheel being set in motion with a stick. The wheel, carefully balanced, turns on an inset agate bearing, supported on a sharp-pointed pivot of *khadira* (*acacia catechu*) wood. The support may be moved to any spot; the stick is inserted in a slotted fitting of wood.

9. Potter's disc in use; it is handled only by women. The pots are the base-portions of large water-jars, built up in three stages; the rough nature of the product can be seen. The jars are paddled down and finished by men.

Modern potter at Poona enlarging a pot with a wooden ddle; the stone anvil is inside the pot in his left hand. This ocess finishes the surface and compactifies the clay, which f poor quality in Poona. The pots are porous water jars; the iginal, shown in the foreground, is pushed out to a much gger size, which could not be turned directly with the local pe of clay.

8. Potter's wheel in use for mass-production, Poona. The pots are identical in size, though no template or tool is used; shaping is done entirely by the potter's fingers and only a wet string is used to remove the pot from the unformed clay left on the wheel.

10. Terracotta shrines of Mhasobā, the cattle-god and also the buffalo-demon. The central shrine is modern the others older, modelled after a type of "soul-house" or hut now unknown in the Khandālī region.

11. Indian humped Sacred Bull dedicated to Śiva, Banāras, 1937. The *sandaka* protected by an Asokan edict was of the same kind. These bulls are now a public nuisance and have to be numbered; the brand mark registers the beast.

12. Water-buffalo, now the standard milch-beast of India; not sacred and not tamed till after the Vedic age. The swamps and forests of the Gangetic basin could not have been opened up without this animal; the bulls are used for ploughing wet muddy lands (paddy fields) where ordinary cattle cannot work.

13. The bull that draws the sacred palanquin on the annual pilgrimage to Panddarpur. The beast is of the type on the Indus seals. The embroidered cloth shows a modernized version of the tiger-strangling Gilgameś.

14. Modern plough derived from the Kushāna type, in use near the Ganeśa Lenā Buddhist caves at Junnar.

15. Kushāna plough, *circa* 200 A.D. with vertica handle and curved yoke-pole Detail from the Bodhisattva's First Meditation, Gandhāra relief. *Lahore Museum.*

16. Harrowing and sowing the fields; the seed tubes are handled by the women.

17. Treading out the corn,
here sorghum (*jowar*), a
millet-like grain, Talegaon.
The oxen are muzzled,
against Biblical injunction.

18. Tanners soaking
buffalo-hides in lime pits
for tanning. The tanners
are from a low caste, not
intermarrying with any
other, and are normally
regarded as untouchables.

19. Donkey caravan descending the Nānaghāt Pass, almost exactly as in Sātavāhana days. The pack-saddles are horned and the horn is always turned down-hill to prevent the load from sliding off. The steps are artificial, and zig-zag in an ancient water-course. The packs are loaded with onions and potatoes from Junnar; the vegetables are exchanged against low-grade grain in the Konkan backlands, and the grain brought up the Pass for sale.

20. An outrigger sailing ship of the type carrying trade across the Indian ocean. Borobudur, Java, *circa* 800 A.D.

21. Illustration from an unknown manuscript of about 1600 A.D. showing feudal porterage in Kásmir (?)

22. Orissā famine, 1944.

23. Orāons dancing.

24. Muria boys beating a
pitorna drum made from
hollowed-out blocks of
wood.

25. Tribal employees in
tea garden *mela*. The
plantation is in Assam,
but the labourers were
recruited from Orissā,
Bihār and Madhya
Pradesh. Note the sense
of strain in pose and
expression, as contrasted
with the ease and freedom
of the original tribal
dancers.

26. Nachari women
fishing in a stream,
Assam.

27. Garos fishing from a
dug-out canoe in a
stream, Assam.

28. Bhīl sisters embracing each other. The married sister, in her wrap, is greeted on her arrival for a visit by the young unmarried one, who by custom remains unclothed to the waist. Rājasthān.

29. Miju Mishoni women carrying water in joints of giant bamboo, Assam.

30. Juang women making leaf cups.

31. Archer of the forest, Koli tribal caste, in front of the Buddhist caves, Pale, near Mahad. The bow is of bamboo, the "string" of cane, the arrows short with long blade tips, deadly at short range. This hunter served in the Indian army during World War II, and had seen Rome and other foreign lands; but he has reverted to his original life, with only a cleaner-than-usual loin-cloth to show any special influence of war-service.

32. Juang youth carrying his plough. The only metal part is the short steel tip of the shave.

33. Saora youth collecting palm-toddy, Orissā.

34. Bhīls husking and winnowing wheat, Rājasthān; normal peasant technique.

35. Drawings on the wall of a Bhīl hut, Rājasthān.

36. Warli peasant setting fire to dry leaves on a hill slope for slash and burn shifting cultivation, Mahārāshtra. Much the same method is used by ordinary peasant farmers for preparing seed-beds of rice-paddy.

37. Microliths of the pre-pottery track, not associated with larger tools or with megaliths; these belong to the "thin-Skins" people. Some are surgical instruments, presumably for gelding.

38. Microliths found on early terraces, associated with rock-engravings which characterize the Deccan megaliths. Note the scalloped edges, made by pressure-flaking; the technique is more advanced, though the microliths are thicker and less delicate.

39. Front of a jar with naked female figure, Maheśvar (Nāvdā Tolī excavations), second millennium B.C. The piece undoubtedly depicts a mother-goddess, herself symbolized by the pot, which is the homologue of the womb.

40. Painted potsherd showing dancers with joined hands, Maheśvar (Nāvdā Tolī excavations), second millennium B.C.; such ring-dances are still performed by girls towards the end of the monsoon, as the remnant of a fertility rite.

41. Mohenjo-dāro saddle-quern and muller stone. The lower end would be held between the knees; used for grinding grain. The rotary quern was not known to the Indus culture.

42. Prehistoric megalith still in worship as the shrine of the mother-goddess Bolhāi. The goddess herself is represented by a smooth oval lump of red-coated stone under the arch. The capstone is about seven feet long, and rings like a bell when struck, or even when rubbed with another stone in a ritual still practised. The whole structure was fashioned without metal tools.

43. The so-called "Pippala House", a rectangular stone cairn at Rājgīr. It represents the *pāsanaka cetiya* where the Buddha rested so often and which occurs in the Bāvari story; but it is much older than the Buddha, presumably an Aryan relic. It was a watch-tower and drum tower, with a prehistoric natural cave just behind; probably a cult-spot too.

44. General view of Mohenjo-dāro under excavation, 1925-6.

45. The Great Bath on the citadel mound at Mohenjo-dāro; the prototype of the later *pushkara* lotus pond.

46. (Left) Indus seal showing a boat with sail, oars and rudder or steering oar. 47. (Centre) Indus seal showing a sacrifice. The lower row of gowned figures is seven in number, presumably the original brahmin clan-founders; though the head-dresses may suggest vegetation deities. The three-horned god in a *pipal* (*ficus religiosa*) tree is adored by an eighth priest; the animal behind the officiant is a chimera with goat's horns, fish-head, ram's body and perhaps clawed feet. The object on the low altar might be a foreshortened human head. 48. (Right) Indus seal representing a bull-man, similar to the Sumerian Enkidu, killing a horned tiger.

49. (Left) A rather anaemic Indus hero strangling two tigers; like the Mesopotamian Gilgameś, who is represented killing lions in this fashion. 50. (Centre) Indus seal representing a man-tiger, prototype of the man-lion incarnation of Vishnu (*narasimha*). The first two ideograms are harrow-signs. 51. (Right) Button-seal from Mesopotamia, representing merman and mermaid; though not known on Indus seals, this conception developed as the fish incarnation of Vishnu (*matsya*) in India.

52. (Left) Cylinder seal; two bearded heroes grapple with a lion and a bull. Sumerian; Akad period, late 3rd millennium B.C. 53. (Right) Cylinder seal; naked goddess, perhaps Ishtar, under a winged canopy and mounted on a humped bull. One of the flanking figures is dressed in Egyptian style. Syria, middle of the 2nd millennium B.C. The naked goddess fits some Vedic descriptions of Ushas.

54. Cylinder seal; heroes and lions in combat. Sumerian; early Dynastic period, middle of the 3rd millennium B.C.

55. (Left) Medallion commemorating the expedition of Alexander the Great to the Panjab, and his defeat of Poros in 326 B.C. From Babylon(?)

56. (Right) Sophytes (Saubhūti) an Indian king contemporary with Alexander the Great; the style and legend of his coins is Greek.

57. (Left) Silver coin of Peukelaotis (Pushkarāvati) in the lower Kabul valley. The legend reads: *Pakhalavadi devada Ambi*, "the goddess of Pushkarāvati", the Tyche of the city shown as a lotus-bearing mother goddess.

58. (Right) reverse of the *Ambi* coin of Peukalaotis, bearing a humped bull, presumably sacred, the badge of the city. The legends: Kharosthi *usabhe*, Greek *tauros*, "bull".

59. (Left) Antiochus I. Graeco-Bactrian, *circa* 261-247 or 246 B.C.

60. (Right) Demetrios. Graeco-Bactrian.

61. (Left) Eukratides. Graeco-Bactrian, founder of a new line; great rival to Demetrios, whom he deprived of his kingdom *circa* 175 B.C.

62. (Right) Coin of Menander, King of Sialkot, *circa* 180-160 B.C., found in 1940 circulating in a Poona open-air market as equivalent of a half-rupee.

63. (Left) Silver punch-marked coin, of northern weight standard; probably late Mauryan or early Sunga.

64. (Right) Coin of Rajuvula, Indo-Scythic Mahākshatrapa mentioned on a lion capital at Mathurā. His coins, circulated in the Mathurā district, imitate those of the Greek prince Strato I Soter.

65. (Left) Silver portrait coin of Nahapāna, Śaka Kshatrapa of Mahārāshtra, whose capital was at or near Nāsik. Dates uncertain, but he is recorded in inscriptions of 119-124 A.D.

66. (Right) Sātavāhana Kumāra, silver. The Sātavāhanas re-conquered the Western Deccan *circa* 126 A.D. and their princes continued to re-strike Nahapāna's coins; the prince on this example is unidentified.

67. (Left) Cashtana, Saka Kshatrapa and Mahākshatrapa of Malwa, whose capital was at Ujjain, *circa* 124—*circa* 150 A.D. It is significant that the reverse of most of his coins shows a *caitya* symbol; this may derive from the coins of the Andhra dynasty, which feature the *caitya* prominently, often in association with a tree and railing. The *caitya* also appears on some coins of Taxila and north-west India. It became the standard reverse symbol of the coins of Cashtana's successors.

68. (Above Right) Silver coin of Damajadaśri I, Saka Kshatrapa of Malwa, *circa* 150-*circa* 178 A.D.

69. (Left) Jīvadāman, son of Damajadaśri, Saka Mahākshatrapa *circa* 178-198-A.D.

70. (Right) Rudrasimha I, brother of Damajadaśri, Saka Kshatrapa 180-196 or 197 A.D. His fully dated coins are evidence of his contention for power with Jīvadāman.

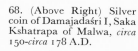

71. (Left) Kanishka I. Kushāna, *circa* 120-*circa* 144-50 A.D.

72. (Right) Huvishka. Kushāna, *circa* 150-162 A.D.

73. (Left) The only known coin (silver) of the Vrishni tribe, from East Panjāb, who claimed Krishna of the Yadus as their ancestor, real or imaginary. The coin bears a pillar with capital composed of an elephant and a lion. From Hoshiarpur, Panjāb, 3rd century A.D.

74. (Right) Gold coin of Candragupta I with his queen, the Licchavi princess Kumāradevī. Gupta, *circa* 320-*circa* 330 A.D.

75. (Left) Samudragupta with lyre. Gupta, *circa* 330-*circa* 380 A.D.

76. (Right) Candragupta II. Gold coin bearing an archer. Gupta, *circa* 380-*circa* 415 A.D.

77. (Left) Gold coin showing Kumāragupta I on horseback hunting the rhinoceros; the coin commemorates his reputed feat of cutting off the tip of the horn while sparing the life of the beast. Gupta, *circa* 415-*circa* 445 A.D.

78. (Right) Silver coin of Sāmantasena, showing a feudal cavalier with pennon.

79. Bull capital from an Asokan pillar, polished sandstone. From Rāmpurvā, 3rd century B.C.

80. Section of stūpa railing, red sandstone. From Bhārhut, Central India; Sunga, 2nd century B.C.

81. Anāthapindika, the richest śresthin of Sāvatthi, purchases the grove of Prince Jeta for the Buddha, as a refuge outside the city. Anāthapindika's servants cover the ground with punchmarked coins, thus taking literally a word said in jest by Jeta, who was unwilling to part with the land. In the centre, Prince Jeta makes the gift-libation to the Buddha, who is represented only by the tree with railing. Sandstone relief from Bhārhut, 2nd century B.C.

82. The Nāga Rāja Erāpātra, attended by *nāgas* and *nāginis*, paying devotion before a *siris* (acacia) tree. In the time of Kasyapa Buddha, Erāpātra was condemned to lose the power of assuming human form until the next Buddha should appear in the world. When he heard of Sakyamuni's enlightenment, he came in serpent form to the new Buddha; on approaching the six *siris* trees where the Buddha was seated, he instantly regained the power of appearing in human form. Bhārhut, 2nd century B.C.

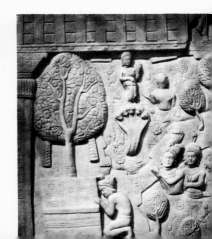

83. North gate of the Great Stūpa, Sāñcī. Early 1st century A.D.

85. The Buddha subdues the raging elephant
Nālāgiri. The narrative is continuous, showing
at left, Nālāgiri trampling down people in the
streets of Rājgīr; at right, Nālāgiri calmed by a
quiet word of gentle reproof by the Buddha.
Relief medallion from Amarāvatī, 2nd century
A.D.   84. (Right) Māyā, the mother of the
Buddha, seated on a lotus, lustrated by two
elephants. This subject was later interpreted
as *gajalakṣmī*, the goddess Lakṣmī, consort of
Vishnu-Nārāyana. From the East gate of the
Great Stūpa, Sāñcī.

86. Interior of the Caitya cave, Kārle. The vault beams are of wood, formerly painted, and are purely decorative in function. The radiocarbon dating for the wood was found to be 280 B.C. *plus or minus 150 years*, much earlier than suspected.

87. A capital from one of the pillars in the Caitya cave, Karle. Note the loving couples, rather strange decoration for an assembly of celibate monks who had renounced the world to found a refuge in the wilderness.

89. Mithuna couple, Kārle.

88. (Left) Kārle, the capital of the right 13th pillar, away from the nave and in almost total darkness. The woman is mounted on a horse, but the man is on a sphinx. The pillar was dedicated by a Greek *yavana* from Dhenukākata named Dhamadhaya, which is Buddhist-Indian in form. The pillars were not all finished at one time, but over many centuries as special donations became available; this pillar may be of any period till the 1st century A.D., possibly a little later. The front facade has no relation to the Caitya hall or the rest of the monastery, but depicts the interior courtyard of a five-storied palatial house.

92. Cell of a Buddhist cave monastery, Sirval, 1st century A.D.(?). The doorway shows sockets for a solidly framed wooden door and lock-hole through which a chain was inserted; there are also arrangements for a grilled window.

90. Demons of Māra's army. Note the Graeco-Roman panoply of the two soldiers in the lowest row; the scales of the cuirass at the left are turned the wrong way, showing that such armour was not in common use by Indian soldiers, and not generally known to the artists. Gandhāra, 2nd-4th centuries A.D.

91. Centaurs on the capital of a small engaged column in the Indrasabhā cave, Bhāja; perhaps 1st century B.C.

94. The Elevation of the Begging Bowl, relief medallion from the great Stūpa at Amarāvatī, 2nd century A.D. The stūpa was demolished in the 19th century, and much of the marble was burnt to provide lime.

95. Hunting mythical animals; fragment of a frieze from Amarāvatī, now in the British Museum.

93. (Left) Frieze of figures on the facade of Chaitya cave no. 1, Kondane, note the 6-foot bow of the *kṣatriya* dallying with two ladies at once. 2nd century B.C.

96. Durgā slaying the buffalo demon Mahishāsura, Māmallapuram, early 7th century A.D.

97. Ellora, the Kailāsa cave; rock-cut temple carved out in the second half of the 8th century by Rāshtrakūta king Krishna I (Akālavarsha). Repairs and stucco reliefs on the exterior were made as late as the 1780's by Ahalyābāī Holkar of Indore. On top of the hill, not visible in the photograph, is the site of a late stone age settlement.

98. Seated Buddha. Sandstone; from Sarnāth, 5th century A.D.

marriages reflected human unions. The resultant social combination was more productive, with a better mastery of the environment.

There was one further early exploit of Krishna which accelerated his rise: he protected the cattle of the *gokula* against Indra. The fight seems to have been three-cornered, for Indra saved most of the Nāgas whom Krishna and the junior Pāndava branch of the Kurus crushed whenever possible. Krishna is really foreign to the *Mahābhārata*, a late intruder in the epic. The legend says that he joined the Pandus in burning down the Khāndava forest to clear the land. The ambiguous position of the Yadus in the *Rigveda* and Krishna's dark skin may be another step in the recombination of Aryan with aborigine, just as the irreconcilable Nāga stories are a clear step in that direction. Both types of stories would not be acceptable in one epic unless the audiences contained elements that derived from both types of people. The conflict with Indra had a remarkable consequence. Late in the fourth century, invading Greeks found that the worship of an Indian demigod whom they equated immediately with their own Herakles was the main cult of the Panjāb plains, while 'Dionysos' continued to be worshipped in the hills. This Herakles was unmistakably the Indian Krishna. The Greek hero was traditionally a matchless athlete burnt black by the sun, who had killed the Hydra (a many-headed snake like Kāliya) and violated or wedded many nymphs. In addition, the manner of Krishna's death was more familiar to Greek myth than to the Indian. The Yadu demigod died of an arrow shot into the heel by the wild hunter Jaras, really his half-brother. Indians still cannot understand how such a wound could be fatal. The stories of Achilles and so many other Greeks of mythological antiquity show that the peculiar death must have been due to a ritual killing connected with a poisoned weapon often wielded by the brother (or tanist) of the sacrificed hero. The other Indian god whom the Greeks recognised as conquering Dionysos can only be Vedic Indra, whose hard-drinking and hard-fighting character rages berserk through the *Rigveda*. The immense significance of this Greek report has been missed. It shows that although the Yadus were extinct, the cult of Krishna had already driven that of Indra out of the best-cultivated portion of the Panjāb. Moreover, this occurred even though Indra-Dionysos (in the Greek record) had first brought knowledge of iron and metals, use of oxen for agriculture, and the art of house-building to India after his 'conquest'.

The historical steps, chronological order, and precise details of this displacement of Indra by Krishna are unfortunately lost; but the reason for the change is obvious. The pastoral life was yielding to the agrarian. Vedic sacrifice and constant fighting may have suited the former, but would have become a costly, intolerable nuisance for the latter. Krishna was a protector of cattle, never invoked at a fire-sacrifice where animals were offered up, as Indra, Varuna, and other vedic deities were regularly invoked. Whatever sacrifices the Yadus might have made to an ancestral founder-god, there was no reason for their continuance by other tribes. On the other hand, the pastoral tribes who were changing over to agriculture would certainly prefer Krishna to Indra; so would the pre-Aryans who had begun to learn from and intermarry with the herdsmen, but still worshipped some one of the innumerable local goddesses conveniently made into wives for Krishna. The pure agriculturists—developing rather slowly in the Panjāb —were placated by Krishna's Titan brother Balarāma, also called Sam-karshana, 'the ploughman', with the plough as his special attribute weapon where the sharp missile wheel discus (*cakra*) was Krishna's. Not only was this brother the logical god of ploughmen, but the aboriginal Nāgas, too, were adopted through him; Balarāma was often taken to be the incarnation of the great primeval Cobra who is supposed to raise this earth upon his head above the waters of the vasty deep. (Buddhist legends, too, could not dispense with human, divine, or cobra Nāgas. The Buddha converted tribal Nāgas, tamed the poisonous reptiles, was protected against the elements by the divine Nāgas like Mucilinda, and had himself been an ambivalent 'good Nāga' in some previous birth. Prominent Buddhist monasteries like Nālandā and Samkasya derived their origin from Nāga cult spots; sometimes the original Nāga appeared on special days in the guise of a benign snake, to receive food offerings from the monks.) One question remains: Why should strange tribes begin to worship a god not their own? The answer seems to be some alliance between the Yadus and the other tribes, combined with a westward scattering of the tribesmen from Mathurā, supposedly in flight to escape an invasion from Magadha, which lay to the east.

Fundamental differences had already begun to show between people who thought of themselves as Aryans all. Brahmins and kshatriyas went from the Gangetic region to the north-western end (Taxila and beyond) of the *uttarāpatha* trade route for higher education: the *yajña*, brahmin *mantra* incantations, proper Aryan manners, medicine, and correct Sanskrit. For, the easterners had begun to use a simpler *lingua franca* on their trade tracks, with an Aryan base but without the formidable complications of Sanskrit grammar and Vedic tone accent. Their lisping pronunciation, poor syntax, rustic accent, and often downright barbarous vocabulary must have seemed unspeakably comic pidgin in the west. Still, these provincials were accepted as good pupils in Taxila and neighbouring lands without too close an inquiry into caste and lineage, as is attested both by Upanishadic and Buddhist texts. The frontier upper class were white-skinned. They believed that a dark man 'seen seated in the market-place like a heap of black beans' could not possibly be mistaken for a brahmin. At the same time, eastern brahmins could go through a curious rigmarole described in the *Brihadāranyaka Upanishad* to beget a dark-skinned but brainy son. There was no colour bar once caste obstacles were known to be absent. The beauty of a lady of any skin colour (as of any hair colour in Europe) was appreciated. On the other hand, caste observances were so slack on the frontier that easterners began to look upon Madra, Gandhāra and Kamboja people as loose-lived and barbarous. The far north-west had only two real castes: Ārya, which denoted 'free'; and Dāsa, which meant 'slave'. Any member of one could change over to the other without the least fuss. That is, these distant, colder regions where food-gathering was quite difficult and commodity production indispensable had developed slavery comparable in some ways to the classical Greco-Roman; while the east at the same time had no slavery but maintained progressively rigid caste distinctions for the various occupations. The brahmins east of Kuru-land might have admitted intermarriage to some extent with Nāgas, or at least condoned it; but they were scandalised where a man of Peshāwar or Balkh did brahmin's work though his brother was a ploughman, another in the same family a warrior, or barber (very low in the caste professions). Such brothers might even exchange their several tasks at will, without shame. The women of the frontier were quite unrestrained in their behaviour, with neither the shyness before strangers nor modesty in the presence of elder males of the family which Indians of good breeding expect even now from their womenfolk. Both sexes ate meat and drank strong liquor; there would be mixed public dancing in a state of undress. Such a way of life was positively obscene to eastern brahmin eyes. The custom of bride price (instead of its opposite, the dowry) which prevailed in the north-west seemed degrading to easterners; so did the marriage by bride capture that Krishna's people had practised in the *Mahābhārata* and the historical Ābhiras continued to use. Both types of marriage were ultimately forbidden by brahmin scriptures as un-Aryan. Nevertheless, the beauty, loving nature, and utter fidelity of the Madra and Bāhlika women remained proverbial. A warrior's widow in those regions would even immolate herself with her husband's corpse. This horrifying custom of *sati* was then completely unknown in the east and would so remain till early feudal times, say the sixth century A.D. Just what the westerners thought of their snobbishly exclusive and yet rather countrified eastern acolytes is not in the surviving record; but it is known that the more enterprising low-caste youths from the east could travel west, acquire the brahmin's bag of tricks, and ultimately pass themselves off (where their origin was not known) as brahmins. The little attention paid by their learned frontier teachers to caste limits upon occupation—really a primitive class differentiation—made this quite easy.

The *uttarāpatha* traffic ran as strongly in the opposite direction. The first to become the Buddha's lay followers, just eight weeks after the Teacher had obtained perfect insight, were two caravaneers from Peuke-laotis or Balkh, passing Bodh Gayā on their way from Orissā to Rājgir. The names of the brothers, given as Tapussa and Bhalluka, imply association with the metal trade: lead or tin, and copper, respectively. Kapphina, a kshatriya from Kaśmir with characteristic, thin, high nose, was one of the earliest Buddhist monks in the east. The Pāli verses that stand in his name smack rather of Hellenic paganism than ascetic doctrine. A 'king' of Taxila, Pukkusa by name, who had exchanged gifts at long distance with Bimbi-sāra, died in his old age on his first and last trip to Magadha, a week after meeting the Buddha whom he had come to see; the story goes that he was gored to death by a cow.

The bond that held so heterogeneous a society together, that made it a society rather than a set of tribes, was not so much common ritual and common language as a whole aggregate of common needs satisfied by reci-procal exchange. The eastern philosophies were disseminated precisely by the intercourse that went on along the *uttarāpatha* and the *dakshināpatha* trade routes. Commodity production bound the far-flung Aryans and their mixed offshoots firmly together, though Vedic language and ritual were falling apart because of differences in environment, while new gods as well as new theories of religion had begun to move the minds of men.

5.5. Kosala and Magadha

The new moral philosophies of the sixth century B.C. that formulated and preached a doctrine beyond the tribe had their political counterpart. There was a parallel move towards a universal government for all society. The basis was identical both in religious and secular movements: the new needs of *gahapati*, trader, and farmer. Whereas the founders of the great monastic orders had considered tribal patterns of organisation quite suitable and perfectly natural for their own *samghas*, especially the Jain and the Buddhist, the theoreticians of state policy could think of only one way to break tribal exclusiveness—a dictatorial absolute monarchy. Ancient Greeks would have recognised this as transition from the Homeric *basileus* to the Peisitratid *tyrannos*. A cold, inexorable, grimly calculating, logically formulated and carefully reasoned political theory lay behind the prolonged struggle for absolute power. There was never the least pretence of morality or specious excuse of doing good to others. The theorists of this new polity were as important and as capable thinkers in their own way as the contemporary religious leaders. Their names survive only in one book, a compendium by the greatest and the last of the line, the *Arthaśāstra* of Kautalya, which will be considered in the next chapter. The roster is quite impressive: Bharadvāja, Kātyāyana, Parāśara, Ushanas, and Brihaspati bear good brahmin names; some of them represent an entire traditional school each, as with the older religious sects of the time. A 'son of Bāhudanti', Kiñjalka, Kaunapadanta, Piśuna, Viśālāksha, Vātavyādhi, and Dirgha-Cārāyana were presumably kshatriyas; the main school of importance in the kshatriya line bore the name of Āmbhi. The list given here is by no means complete. The full teaching has survived for none, though the views of each are cited and discussed in the *Arthaśāstra* where relevant, very much in the analytical manner of a jurist reviewing former enunciations of legal principles. The historical context is never given and is not otherwise known except for 'Long' Cārāyana. This obscurity is natural. Where the teachers of religion had to convince the multitude and win over people in all walks of life by open and widely disseminated preaching, advice on state policy could be effective only if kept secret, reserved for the chosen few. The great religious almsmen-teachers of the sixth century were far above the all-too-common parasitic beggars and thick-headed cult leaders of later India, because the former participated vigorously in the formation of a totally new type of society. This is precisely the difference between the tale of war, intrigue, assassination and broken faith that unfolds itself in the sixth century and similar actions in later absolute tyrannies where the throne had no constitutional check. The sixth-century monarchies were the first, an innovation to suit the formation of a completely new social stage; the medieval 'oriental despotisms' were changes at the top without effect upon the social basis, which had long been crystallised.

There had traditionally been sixteen principal *janapadas* (territories) in the seventh century B.C., perhaps even a century earlier. Of these sixteen only four retained any importance in the final struggle for power that was fought out at the end of the sixth and beginning of the fifth centuries. Two were powerful tribal oligarchies acknowledging no absolute ruler, namely the Licchavi or Vajji ('pastoral nomads', which shows that they settled down rather late) and the Mallas. These two tribes conducted their affairs by tribal assembly and constantly practised military exercises. They had tribal constitutions renowned for justice and equity; but both were developing patrician groups over subordinate agricultural people (not all of whom were members of the tribe) while the oligarchs were beginning to be further divided among themselves by private property. The Licchavi chief town and meeting-place was Vesāli, modern Basārh; the Mallas had several branches of which two were about the small headquarters towns of Pāvā and Kusinārā. Each tribe could put a formidable army into the field at need. They formed a redoubtable aggressive confederacy at the beginning of the fifth century which had either to conquer other territory or to lose its own independence, but could not be ignored. For these two groups blocked the portion of the *uttarāpatha* trade route that ran southwards from the Nepal frontier through Camparan district down to the Ganges and then across the river to the ores that produced iron and copper for everyone. To their north-west lay Kosala; to the south and south-east Magadha, both absolute monarchies. Kosala and Magadha had been tribes (like the rest of the sixteen *janapadas*), as shown by the regular use of the plural, 'the Kosalas', 'the Magadhas', to designate the countries. However, nothing is ever recorded of a Kosalan or a Magadhan tribe in any of the Buddhist or Jain records, nor of tribal councils and meetings. The word Magadhan earlier meant 'bard', later 'trader', which shows the development of two special guilds from the original tribe; otherwise the brahmin scriptures refer to the Magadhan as a mixed caste. The word *janapada*, literally 'foothold of a tribe', is later used for 'country', 'state', or even 'district'; which shows fairly well how the course of development ran in the Gangetic basin.

These Aryan and Aryanised tribes were comparable to Greek tribal states of the sixth century B.C., with one crucial difference. Argives, Boeotians, Lacedaemonians, etc., seem by then to have developed private holdings in their restricted and relatively less fertile lands. Indian tribal lands, always ample in extent and generally under shifting cultivation, remained territory rather than property. A holding was formally subject to reassignment by tribal assembly, even when cultivated by the same family for a long time. In contrast, the very existence of the absolute monarchies depended upon regular taxes from permanently fixed private holdings in steadily cultivated plots.

Of the two great monarchies, Kosala was the older and at the beginning of the sixth century definitely the more powerful. The sixth-century Kosalan capital lay at Sāvatthi, though the older chief city had been to its south at Sāketa, the traditional Ayodhyā ('impregnable') city from which the mythical epic hero Rāma had set out into voluntary exile through what was then unbroken wilderness. This supposed route of exile later developed or was extended into the southern trade route, the *dakshināpatha* that gave its name to the modern Deccan. The Bāvari narrative shows that Sāvatthi lay at the junction of the two major routes for sixth-century trade. In addition, Kosala also commanded the Ganges, having annexed Kāsi (Banāras) after a long series of battles. The conquest should lie in the seventh century, for nothing is ever heard of the Kāsi tribe. Only some legends of the good 'King Brahmadatta of Kāsi' show that the place, whereof the early first-millennium date is now confirmed by archaeology, had some traditional importance. The name of the kingdom was thereafter hyphenated to 'Kāsi-Kosalā', so important was Banāras as a river port. The cotton, silk (tussore), and other manufactures of Banāras were already famous; its well-known orange-brown dye *kāshāya* gave the first colour for Buddhist robes and retains its popularity even now under much the same name as the famous Banāras *katthai*. Already, the most daring navigators could reach the sea from Kāsi, sometimes trading even beyond the delta and doubtless relying on salt for their earliest and steadiest item of profitable trade.

Magadha appeared to be rather badly placed on the trade route, beyond the river and towards the end of the track where the route disappeared into trackless forest. But this kingdom, destined to grow into India's first 'universal monarchy' and empire, controlled something much more important than a caravan track, namely the supply of metals. The capital Rājgir (Rājagriha, 'King's House') was the solitary old-Aryan settlement south of the river, for a very good reason. The hills near Rājgir have the northernmost Dhārwār outcrop, a geological formation in which iron is rather handily available. Flakes of iron oxide occur therein as considerable encrustations which can be scraped off the rock with hardly any mining, reduced by charcoal fire, and then hammered out at white heat into tools or utensils. Rājgir has the added convenience of an easily defended perimeter of hills, fortified quite early with cyclopean outer walls twenty-five miles in length, enclosing the inner walled city. This was Rājgir proper, of about one square mile, with a third intermediate circumvallation. The enclosed area has an excellent water supply from springs both hot and cold, and could hold out indefinitely against a hostile environment, in view of the excellent grazing between the walls. To the south-east lies Gayā, an early Magadhan colony. Beyond Gayā came the primeval forest through which hardy explorers passed to locate copper and iron ores in the hills to the south-east, the richest such deposits in India. The ore was mined and reduced on the spot, the metal brough back to be traded in the central Gangetic basin. The reason is that the hill-land of the ores is not so profitable to cultivate as the riparian alluvium. This, then, was Magadha's great source of power, for that state used the metal systematically to clear land and to bring it under the plough.

The sixteen were by no means all the *janapadas* and peoples to be taken into account. The virgin forest which covered the greater portion of the land was infested with a thin population of food-gathering savages who still used stone axes (*pāsāna-muggara*), and would be increasingly dangerous to trade caravans as time went on. Even on the two main trade routes, this primeval forest separated the *janapadas* by long distances through which the convoys had to pass with care, generally under heavy escort. A minor tribe like the Sakyan is known to us only because it produced a great man. Others like 'the Būlis of Allakappa' were important enough at the time to claim and receive a share of the Buddha's ashes, but are not known beyond the solitary reference. Mithilā was the name of a city and a *janapada*, but the tribe was extinct; its last king, Sumitra of the direct Ikshvāku line, died about the time of the Buddha's birth. Whether Mithilā had annexed Videha before being taken over by Kosala, or was attached to Videha after the Kosalan conquest of both, neither people had any independent existence towards the middle of the sixth century. Magadha had absorbed the Angās, which lay to the east on both sides of the river. The capital Campā (Bhāgalpūr), become an inconsiderable village, was donated to a brahmin sacrificial priest by King Bimbisāra of Magadha.

More important than ordinary tribesmen were the traders, generally called *sathavāha* (caravaneers) or Vaidehikas. The latter name means 'men of the Videha tribe'. Though all traders no longer belonged to any one tribe or *janapada* and the Videha tribe had vanished, the nomenclature shows the origin of the profession as with a particular tribal guild. The groups of merchant-caravaneers extended in a long chain from Taxila to the very end of Magadha. The bolder went beyond any known *janapada* limits, especially on the Deccan route. The trade was no longer of the primitive type confined to 'trade friends', unless perhaps with some of the forest savages who might still retain the institution. Regular coinage had come into use before the end of the seventh century, to judge by the coins found. The eastern standard of weight for silver coins was the *kārshāpana* of 3.5 grams weight in Magadha, while the solitary Kosalan hoard known is of 3/4-*kārshāpana* standard. The weight goes back to the Indus valley culture, which had, in fact, produced accurately cut stone weights of just this magnitude. Taxilan currency belonged to a foreign weight standard just above 11 grams, which would approximate to the Indian rupee in historic times. The *kārshāpana* was of 32 units weight, whereas the frontier coin, shaped like a bent bar, was 100. Originally the coins were issued as silver blanks by the traders themselves, and the weights checked regularly by their guilds during the period of circulation. The checking was shown by tiny marks punched on one side, which guaranteed weight and purity to all who knew the code of guild marks. These punch marks extended beyond the *uttarāpatha* into Afghanistān and Irān; sometimes they are found even on a few Achaemenid darics, presumably such as had circulated in Gandhāra. Some of the punch marks themselves derived from Indus characters, probably from the descendants of the Panis whom we have named and noted in passing. The other side of the silver piece was originally blank at the time of issue. By the sixth century the kings had stepped in to put their own issuing marks on the coins, on the side that had once remained blank. This was a regular system of four marks for Kosala and five for Magadha and the rest. Because of the marks, we can distinguish between dynasties and say approximately how many kings there were in each, but giving the individual king's name is still not simple, and generally remains a matter of conjecture. Violent changes of dynasty are revealed by counterstruck coins; the new king restruck coins of the displaced ruler found in the treasury with his own marks before issuing them again for circulation.

The weights are as accurately adjusted as for modern machine-minted coins, with very low tolerance. This type of coinage, even the very existence of regular coinage so carefully weighed, implies highly developed commodity production. We read about whole villages (especially near Banāras) settled by basket-makers, potters, smiths, weavers, and the like. These artisans, though kinship groups, generally formed guilds (*śreni*) naturally with a tribe-like organisation inherited from their own past. This process is still visible in semi-tribal areas, e.g. Assam. The guild as a unit often had considerable wealth at its disposal which was not the private property of any member, but might be disbursed at need by the headman or guild council either to any member of the guild or to some external individual or organisation. This happens to be the present-day custom in the poorer Indian professional castes, the prototypes of which are clearly to be traced back to this period or earlier; the late-Vedic craftsman had normally been a member, presumably of the vaiśya caste, of the *grāma* on the move. Not all the production of the artisans was consumed in the nearest town, for cities in the seventh or sixth centuries were still very small. A good deal, like cloth and metal articles, travelled over very long distances. Of natural products, salt could not be as handily mined in Bihār as in the Panjāb salt range, hence needed exploration (even down to the sea) and long hauls. Bamboo was special forest produce that had become an indispensable commodity for baskets, construction work, and the like. Sandalwood rubbed into wet paste was one of many coolants and cleansers in great demand for the bath (a necessity rather than a luxury in the hot climate), especially as soap had not yet been invented. All these materials and trade articles were carted by caravans of 500 or more ox-wagons at a time. The carts had spoked wheels and rawhide tyres, which would suffice for the soft soil of the *uttarāpatha*.

The *dakshināpatha* country was hilly, with difficult passes, broken and stony ground, and without broad, clear tracks comparable to the northern; there, pack trains of animals and on occasion porters with head-loads had to be employed. To exchange for the commodities, there had to be a considerable local surplus of grain, hides and so on, which could best be guaranteed by private property (in land, cattle, etc.) and the use of organised labour, generally the labour of śūdras, whether hired workers or the occasional slaves. In wild country the trading had to be through the tribal chief, who could gather the surplus for the trader; either such chiefs or the groups that had advanced from a 'trade friends' position would eventually become independent of the rest of the tribe because of the new property thus acquired, so that the progressive dissolution of the more accessible tribes was to follow. The horse was a valuable article of trade, being now mounted for riding; it had reached the Deccan before the sixth century. The elephant was much more valuable, but reserved for royal and army use and not a common trade object. The society of the day was still very far from being the caste-ridden, helpless, apathetic village-covered aggregate into which it would evolve within a dozen centuries, with a corresponding worn-out landscape. Nevertheless, the fruits of aggression were already considerable enough to be tempting. Furthermore, some authority backed by irresistible force was increasingly necessary to ensure an unhindered flow and exchange of commodities, which naturally involved regulation by law of intercourse between groups.

Let us digress a little to consider the theoretical position. The essential tool for the new state which was becoming necessary had to be a powerful, well-trained and properly organised professional standing army, whose recruitment and action would not be fettered by tribal prerogative, tribal law, or tribal loyalties, but which would serve society beyond the tribe—a society that exclusive tribal life does not recognise. Such an army could not be a tribal levy called up at need by the chief for a seasonal campaign. It had to be carefully disciplined, constantly drilled, regularly paid, well equipped at state expense, and suitably lodged in strategic garrison. All that was impossible without regular taxes to which tribal oligarchs normally would not submit. Neither the Licchavis nor the Mallas ever managed to create such a free standing army whose soldiers lived entirely on their pay. Only an absolute monarch unhampered by law could break through the barriers between various coherent groups which would not always regard themselves as adherent members of a wider society based solely upon property rights. This course was suggested by Machiavelli in a different context; his book *Il Principe* was advice to the prince to ride roughshod over wrangling Italian cities and unite them into a nation. But there Machiavelli stopped. Neither he nor his favoured candidate Cesare Borgia nor any other Italian saw the need to change the productive basis of late feudal Italy—even though the Renaissance had already passed into the Baroque. Magadhan theoreticians proposed a relentless conduct which might have caused any Borgia to blench; but their openly declared principal aim was to change the face of the land. The main task of their king and source of profit for the state was to clear the heavy jungle, to bring all wasteland under the plough, aided by a state monopoly of mining and metals. This sort of kingship had to burst all barriers of tribal privilege, property-sharing, and exclusiveness; later despotisms merely ruled over a passive substratum already in the fully developed agrarian stage. To round out the discussion, modern analogies of a kind may be shown. In certain east European countries, China, newly liberated portions of Africa, and the Arab world, some leaders assert that dictatorship is necessary to bring the country to a new stage, whether socialist or bourgeois-democratic. Latin-

FIG. 9. Silver punch-marks on the coins of Pasenadi, emperor of Kosala, contemporary of the Buddha. The marks themselves have to be restored from comparison of many different specimens, for they overlap and are often incomplete. Note that the Kosalan system was of four marks, and the weight 3/4 *kārshāpana* standard.

American republics, until the latest Cuban revolution, generally followed the other type of dictatorship which never changed the class position but at best regulated the greed of the ruling class—as did the better Roman emperors.

The sixth-century kings of Magadha and Kosala met most of the requirements. Both were of low birth, without tribe or tribal assembly to restrain them. The Magadhan Bimbisāra's lineage is not given in Pāli records, but the Sanskrit Purānas ascribe him to the Śiśunāga line. Certainly, the royal house and dynasty ended as Śiśunāgas about ten generations later. The termination *nāga* for the name would be impossible in Vedic usage; here, it should indicate aboriginal blood, or at least aboriginal cults. The brahmin records speak of the dynasty with contempt as the lowest of kshatriyas, *kshatra-bandhu*, which means at any rate that they paid scant attention to Vedic customs, except an occasional *yajña* for victory. Indeed, the most prominent pre-Buddhist shrine at Rājgir (Maniār Math) was dedicated to some Nāga cults and maintained its character through the centuries till the place was deserted. Bimbisāra of Magadha had the special epithet *Seniya*, 'with an army'. This indicates that he was the earliest king to have a regular standing army unconnected with any tribe. The Kosalan Pasenadi claimed descent from King Ikshvāku of Vedic fame; but the claim was not admitted in his own time and place. When he asked for a Sakyan girl in marriage, the demand embarrassed the Sakyans, though he held powers of life and death over them and they, too, claimed descent from the same King Ikshvāku. Ultimately, they cheated the monarch by sending the lovely Vāsabha-khattiyā, daughter of Mahānāma Sakya by a slave woman Nāgamundā. The mother's name again shows aboriginal birth. The deceit was later exposed, but the son of this union, Vidūdabha, remained heir-apparent. Pasenadi's chief queen Mallikā was daughter of a flower gardener, hence technically of low caste; but even the eastern caste system was not very rigid at the time, except for some brahmins.

Pasenadi went a step beyond Bimbisāra in creating a new office of commander-in-chief, *senāpati*, for his son and heir, who is always referred to as Vidūdabha-senāpati. No *senāpati* ('Lord of the army') is known before him. The king had, like the earlier tribal chiefs, personally to lead and manage the army. However, the Malla Bandhula had virtually held supreme command over the Kosalan army and was treacherously murdered at Pasenadi's orders under suspicion of wanting to usurp royal power. This was an error of judgement, especially as Bandhula's nephew Digha-Kārāyana was allowed to retain the senior ministerial office. This minister is undoubtedly the master of statecraft referred to as Dirgha ('long') Cārāyana in Sanskrit. (Not only is such change of pronunciation attested in other cases, *e.g.* Asoka's queen Kāluvāki for Cāruvāci, but the Kashmirian Kshemendra actually gives the name as Cārāyana in his Buddhist narrative poem *Avadānakalpalatā*.) For the time being, however, neither Kosala nor Magadha provoked a war. Both kings were of relatively unaggressive temperament; both patronised the new religious philosophers with pleasure. They are reported as being close friends and admirers of the Buddha, but also as generous supporters of all major sects of the time, including a few Vedic brahmins. There was even a marriage alliance, for Pasenadi's sister was Bimbisāra's chief queen and some accounts make his daughter wife to Bimbisāra's son. However, both armies were in constant action against forest savages and perhaps small Aryan tribes; both kings performed costly *yajñas* for victory in battle. That they gave away entire villages in priestly fee has been mentioned. Vivid descriptions remain of the misery and dismay of the peasantry when innumerable beasts were requisitioned—without payment, of course—for the royal fire sacrifices. Thus, the leading kings were not yet entirely free of the Vedic malpractices which no longer suited the new class society.

The first step towards the inevitable conflict was taken by Ajātaśatru, son of Bimbisāra. This prince, undoubtedly with some unreported theoretician of statecraft behind him, imprisoned his own father and eventually had the aged and good-natured Bimbisāra starved to death in the dungeon. Even so the Buddhists, though shuddering at the parricide, admit that Ajātaśatru was a just and able ruler; we have noted that he appears as a philosopher-king in a major Upanishad. Pasenadi's reaction was to rescind the gift of a village in the Kāsi *janapada* which had formed part of his sister's dowry. This was too valuable to be surrendered, a bridgehead for Magadha across the river from which both the Ganges and a branch trade route could be blockaded. The Magadhan hold upon the *janapada* was retained in a series of battles, all won by Ajātaśatru. The Kosalan side was not slow in countermoves. The chief minister, Dīgha-Kārāyana, handed

FIG. 10. Silver punch-marked coins of Magadhan type, probably of Ajātaśatru, *circa* 480 B.C. The system is of five marks, and the weight when new was about fifty-four grains of silver, the full *kārshâpana* based on a weight system going back to the Indus valley, but not known outside India.

over the royal insignia in his keeping to Vidūdabha, who already controlled the army and was promptly installed as king. The aged Pasenadi, deserted by all except one servant woman, fled for refuge to his nephew. The gates of Rājgir were closed for the night when the royal fugitive arrived; before they opened the next morning, Pasenadi had died of exhaustion outside the walls of the Magadhan capital. Ajātaśatru gave a sumptuous funeral to his uncle's corpse and had a claim thereafter to the throne of Kosala.

The claim could not be pressed for the moment. Not only Vidūdabha but powerful free tribes like the Mallas and Licchavis had to be crushed. Such tribes were relatively the more dangerous to any monarch's progress, both as survivals of democracy and as formidable military obstacles. Vidūdabha moved along parallel lines by a massacre of the Sakyans, ostensibly to avenge the insult of his ancestry, but actually as part of a general move to end tribal freedom on the *uttarāpatha*. The Licchavis had by this time extended their control to the Ganges from the north and levied tolls from all trade on the great river. The traders complained bitterly of the double imposts collected by these tribesmen and by the Magadhan king, who also claimed full control over the stream. So a fortified stockade was set up on the Ganges at Pātaliputra (Patnā) by the tri-junction with the Gandak and the Son (which flowed into the Ganges at this point till the fifteenth century A.D.). The Buddha traversed the still incomplete project on his final journey. The brilliant future he is supposed to have prophesied for the place began a hundred years later, when Patnā became the capital of Magadha, Rājgir being no longer conveniently situated for changed administrative needs. The Licchavis countered Ajātaśatru's manoeuvre by a working agreement with the Mallas. The Licchavi tribe and the confederacy were broken up from within by a technique carefully described in the great book of Magadhan statecraft. A brahmin minister of Ajātaśatru went over to the Licchavis in simulated disgrace (like Zopyrus, minister of Darius I to the Babylonians). Though the Licchavis and Mallas had no brahmins within the tribe and followed no known Vedic practices, the guest's status, prestige, and supposed knowledge of the Magadhan king's intentions made him welcome. He utilised this trust to set one oligarch against another, to encourage each Licchavi to claim more than his allotted share; and to make the tribe neglect tribal meetings, collective army drill, and the tribe's judicial assembly. Such 'boring from within' would not have been possible unless inner decay of the tribe had advanced far, under the influence of wealth collected as tribute and taxes, but retained as private property of the oligarchs. That internal disruption had preceded Ajātaśatru's emissary is proved by the rise of an outstanding religious teacher like Mahāvira among the Licchavis; and by the Mallas Bandhula and Cārāyana taking service outside the tribe. Life even among the best of the free tribes no longer offered full satisfaction to the ablest of the tribesmen. Eventually the rot progressed so far that the Licchavis would not meet regularly for the tribal council and tribal affairs. Then the secret agent sent word to Ajātaśatru, who marched in suddenly to easy victory over his disorganised opponents. No details are known of the final defeat of the Mallas, but their ruin soon afterwards is not to be doubted. It was so thorough that the word Malla came to mean only 'wrestler' or pancratiast, from the original tribe's fondness for exercise. A western Malla tribe, whether related to the Gangetic Mallas or not, was slaughtered about 150 years later on the middle Indus by Alexander's army. Some Licchavis, however, did survive Ajātaśatru's campaign, so that the war was not to wipe out the tribesmen but to extinguish the sort of tribal life they led. The cunning Magadhan brahmin minister is referred to only by his nickname Vassakāra, 'he who subdues', derived from this spectacular intrigue. He was undoubtedly one of the great past masters of statecraft whose opinions and policies must have been cited in the *Arthaśāstra* under his unknown official name.

The Kosalan question was settled by an unexpected bit of luck for Magadha. Vidūdabha had been so careless as to pitch his army camp in the dry, sandy bed of the Rāpti river. A sudden cloudburst upstream swept away the whole Kosalan encampment and was regarded as retribution for the massacre of the Sakyans. There remained neither king nor armed force thereafter to contest Ajātaśatru's claim to the vacant throne of Kosala.

It must not be imagined from all these episodes that the extant sources present a connected historical narrative. The pieces have first to be sorted out from the many different stories and legends and then fitted into some plausible sequence. No description of the countryside, no account of any battle or campaign survives. We do not even know how far Ajātaśatru extended his rule; it is certain that his successors had a great deal left to do. There is passing mention that the Pradyota king of Avanti was about to invade Magadha, for which reason Ajātaśatru's high ministers Vassakāra and Sunidha refortified the capital Rājgir. The Avanti kingdom was rich and powerful, one of the sixteen 'great *janapadas*', in fact, with the capital Ujjain on the southern trade route. It fell eventually to Magadha, but how and to what particular Magadhan king is not known. The Vatsa (Vamsa) kingdom of Kosambi on the Yamunā was also in the list of sixteen. Their king, Udayana, is known for his standing quarrel with Ujjain and famous as hero of a charming cycle of romance which involves his enchanting queen, Vāsavadattā. But all this does not say how long the kingdom lasted, or when Magadha took it over at last. The Kurus, Śūrasenas, Matsyas (perhaps descended from the Rigvedic tribe of the Ten Kings battle), were all tribal states in the list of sixteen; they did not last beyond the fourth century, though the Śūrasenas of Mathurā were known by repute to the Greeks.

At a date which cannot be later than 470 B.C. and not more than sixty years earlier (which is wonderful accuracy for ancient Indian chronology!), Magadha had become the major dominant though not yet paramount power in the Gangetic basin. An absolute monarchy, with complete control over the richest deposits of ore and over the north-eastern ends of the two main trade routes, it was still faced with a massive task: that of pushing back the great forest and bringing more land under regular cultivation with the plough. There was no significant military rival left, but numerous small tribes remained unsubdued. The process of aggression could not be stopped till the 'whole earth'—which to Indians meant only the whole country—from the snowy mountains of the north to 'the four oceans', was brought under one rule. This fulfilment of the 'manifest destiny' took another two centuries. Then came a totally new problem: how long could the state continue ruthlessly to violate all law and ethics while its citizens had begun to live by an exceptionally decent moral code? The economic reality underlying this formal contradiction was a conflict of interest between state and trader, private enterprise and production under the government's direct supervision. The older problem of transition to an agricultural society had then been so completely solved that people forgot it had ever existed in history.

CHAPTER SIX

State and Religion in Greater Magadha

6.1. Completion of the Magadhan Conquest

THE fifth and fourth centuries B.C. are known to Indian archaeologists as the high age of NBP, the northern black polished ware. This describes an excellent grade of pottery first made as trade ceramics (presumably for wine and oils) about the sixth century; it went out of fashion a century or two before the beginning of the Christian era. No literature, records, or clearly dated inscriptions of these two centuries survive, but a firm historical date is supplied for the first time by Alexander's invasion of the Panjāb in 327 B.C. The raid, which left no lasting effects upon Indian life, culture, or history, also provides an indispensable frame of reference through reports of the Indian scene as it appeared to the Greeks. It has always to be remembered that India was an exotic, even a fantastic land to Greek observers, as to most foreigners. There were extraordinary and incredible beasts like the elephant which could nevertheless be tamed. Wool grew on trees (cotton). Indian reeds were gigantic (bamboos), and the country produced a white crystal that tasted sweeter than honey—sugar. Rivers of fabulous size (even when compared to the Nile), swift current, unexplored length, and unplumbable depths impressed those who lived by what Indians would call rivulets. The land miraculously yielded two or three bumper crops a year with minimum toil, where Greeks broke their backs to reap one harvest out of stony hillsides. It was baffling to see the Indians manage so well with no chattel slavery, an institution without which the noblest Greek philosophers such as Plato could not even imagine a viable city-state. The ultimate contrast with the chicanery and endless litigation of Greek civic life was the remarkable Indian ability to honour in full an agreement concluded by mere word of mouth, in the absence of any written, signed, and witnessed contract; says Arrian, 'But indeed, no Indian is ever known to lie'! All this has to be allowed for in the interpretation of the record, particularly when a philosopher like Diodorus Siculus, looking for examples from which to construct an ideal society, misinterprets the words of a Greek traveller. Normally sceptical Greeks could believe almost anything of India.

The region to the west of the Indus had been the twentieth satrapy of the Persian Empire since its conquest by Darius I about 518 B.C. It seems to have been the most profitable of Achaemenid provinces. According to Herodotos, the annual tribute in gold dust was 360 talents, say close to nine tons—an astounding treasure washed out of river sands on the upper Indus and placer-mined on the highlands of Tibet or Kaśmir. The wool and superb woollen cloth of the satrapy and its adjoining regions were famous even in India. Some local contingents fought in Xerxes's army, so that the Greeks knew of India long before Alexander. The principal trade city of the province was Pushkarāvati, modern Chārsaddā, Peukelaotis to the Greeks. The name means 'with the artificial lotus-pond', the *pushkara* which we have traced to the Indus culture. The one known coin of this city, of Indo-Greek times and fabric, preserves ancient memory by showing a magnificent Indian humped bull on one side, while the mother goddess Ambi of Pushkarāvati appears on the obverse bearing a lotus in her hand. To the east of the Indus, but apparently a section of the same tribal *janapada* of Gandhāra, lay the great cultural and trade centre of Taxila (Takshaśilā). Hoards of punch-marked coins excavated at Taxila show that Magadhan coinage was by far the most used currency even on the northwest frontier in Alexander's time. These coins reached their finest quality and greatest numbers with the successors of Ajātaśatru; whence it follows (studying the hoards) that Magadha had begun to dominate the whole *uttarāpatha* trade, say from the end of the fifth century B.C.

Alexander had to complete his own conquest of the Achaemenid empire to its last frontier, the Indus river. A succession of easy victories in Persia and the obvious wealth of the fabulous country beyond the river would whet the all-consuming ambition of one who had at his command an unequalled military apparatus backed by the entire hoarded wealth of the Persian treasury. Chārsaddā was reduced after a thirty-day siege; the defences against siege works have been verified by archaeologists who dug up encircling trenches. The first results after crossing the Indus unopposed were very encouraging. Āmbhi, king of Taxila, surrendered without a blow, paying tribute with the remark that there was enough for both, why quarrel? Taxilan culture and wealth were not yet reflected in housing or civic construction; the city was almost as miserable a collection of hovels as Alexander's Macedonian capital Pella must have been at the time. The real difficulties began immediately afterwards, though the army had rested, found a perfect supply base, and the Taxilans fought on the Greek side against their own powerful Indian neighbours. The free tribal cities had to be reduced one by one, each fight being bitterly contested in spite of overwhelming Greek superiority in armament. The Indians still used chariots in warfare, helpless against the 21-foot-long lances (*sarissa*) of the Macedonian cavalry. The war chariot became obsolete in the field, except at times to show a high officer's rank, after Alexander had passed through the frontier region. The invading soldiers wore bronze armour; a relative shortage of metal led Indians to fight with no other protection than a shield and leather cuirass with, perhaps, a metal helmet. Indian elephants could break through any infantry mass, if properly handled. The qualification was essential, for a wounded elephant in panic would trample down men on his own side as easily as on the enemy's; the charging elephant had to be protected by a good screen of cavalry, archers and foot till he could close in. The one clear Indian superiority was with the bow, a fathom-long weapon whose irresistible shot would drive an arrow through shield and breastplate to kill the Greek hoplite. Alexander's most serious wound was from such an arrow which, shot from close quarters, penetrated his armour to lodge deep in a rib, proving very painful and nearly fatal. The Indian tribes would not unite against the invader, but fighting was their normal pastime. They were helped by kshatriyas who had by this time begun to serve cities not their own, for pay. Ultimately, Alexander broke his promise of immunity to fall suddenly upon these professional contingents as they were marching away with the honours of war after a capitulation, slaughtering them to the last man—a breach of faith never condoned by his biographers.

The next river of the Indus system, the modern Jhelum (Greek, Hydaspes) bounded the ancient territory of the Pūrus who had occupied these regions from Vedic times. The king, known by the tribal name as Poros to the invaders, put into the field the biggest single army to oppose the Greeks in their Indian venture. Alexander crossed the river by a feint and the Pūru aristocracy who raced in their chariots to intercept the invader were wiped out in one sharp cavalry action. The main and desperate battle against King Poros lasted the entire day, to end with the slaughter of the Pūrus and the dignified surrender of the gigantic Indian chief, severely wounded and hopelessly overmatched on the battlefield. The

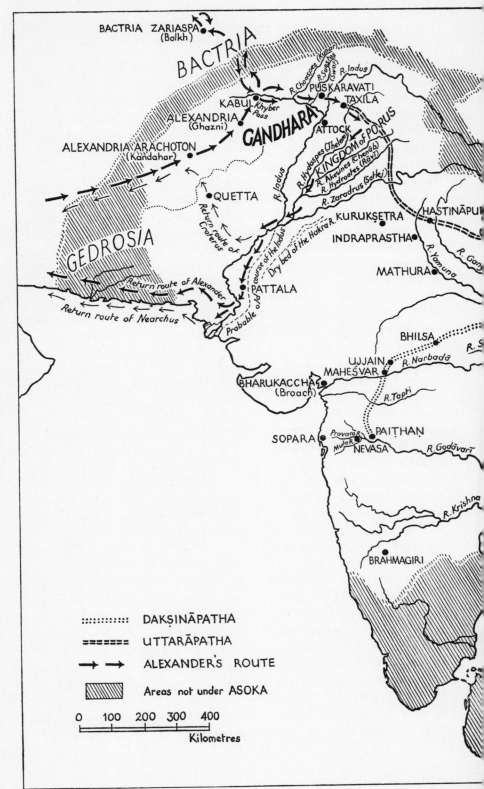

BACTRIA ZARIASPA
(Balkh)

BACTRIA

R.Choaspes (Kunar)
R.Soastos (Swat)
R.Indus

KABUL Khyber
Pass
PUSKARAVATI
ALEXANDRIA
(Ghazni)
GANDHARA
TAXILA

ALEXANDRIA ARACHOTON
(Kandahar)

ATTOCK

KINGDOM OF PORUS
R.Hydaspes (Jhelam)
R.Akesines (Chenab)
R.Hydraotes (Ravi)
R.Zaradrus (Satlej)

R.Indus

QUETTA

Return route of Craterus

Dry bed of the Hakra
R.KURUKŞETRA
HASTINAPU
INDRAPRASTHA
R.Yamuna
R.Gang

MATHURA

GEDROSIA

Old course of the Indus

Return route of Alexander

PATTALA

BHILSA
R.S

UJJAIN R.Narbadā
MAHEŚVAR

Return route of Nearchus

Probable old course of the Hakra

BHARUKACCHA
(Broach)

R.Tapti

SOPARA
Pravara R.
Mula R.
PAIṬHAN
NEVASA
R.Godāvarī

R.Krishna

BRAHMAGIRI

:::::::::: DAKṢINĀPATHA

======= UTTARĀPATHA

→—→ ALEXANDER'S ROUTE

Areas not under ASOKA

0 100 200 300 400
Kilometres

The Mauryan er

SAVATTHI
KOSALA ŚĀKYAS
KAPILAVASTU
KUSĪNĀRĀ MALLAS
AYODHYA LICCHAVIS
BANĀRAS VESĀLI
R. Ganges
KOSAM PATNA CHAMPA
GĀYA RĀJGĪR
MAGADHA
R. Brahmaputra

TĀMLUK

KALINGA

Alexander's raid.

effects of the engagement are best described in the words of Plutarch:

'But this fight took the edge off the Macedonians' courage, and stayed their further progress in India. For, having found it hard enough to defeat an enemy who brought but twenty thousand foot and two thousand horse into the field, they thought they had reason to oppose Alexander's design of leading them to pass the Ganges, too, which they had been told was thirty-two furlongs broad and a hundred fathoms deep, and the banks on the further side covered with multitudes of enemies. For they were told the king of the Gangaridans and Praesians (*prācya*, 'easterners') expected them there with 80,000 horse, 200,000 foot, 8,000 armed chariots, and 6,000 fighting elephants. Nor was this a mere vain report, spread to discourage them. For Sandrokottos (Candragupta Maurya), who not long afterwards reigned in those parts, made a present of 500 elephants all at once to Seleukos (Alexander's general who took over the eastern part of his conquests after the leader's death) and with an army of 600,000 men subdued all India.'

The depth of the Ganges is exaggerated, but the width when swollen in the monsoon flood has to be measured in miles. As the Yamunā and the Ganges were at that time the main arteries of heavy transport for the whole eastern basin controlled by a single expanding and vigorous empire, the rivers would have been much better defended than any in a Panjāb divided by tribal rivalries. The battle with Poros was the last bitter lesson for an intelligent general, however ambitious, whose mutinous soldiers had had their fill of fighting. Alexander created a new satrapy on the Indian side of the Indus under Poros. A flotilla was built of Himālayan pine rafted down the Indus and the Greek army departed by the ancient trade route of the forgotten Indus culture. All along the combined march, tribal armies had to be fought and tribal citadels reduced with considerable slaughter. The disgusted conqueror took his exhausted forces along the deadly coast of Irān to Babylon, losing a good half of them in the desert. At Babylon, hard drinking and malaria put an end to one of the most spectacular military careers in history; but Alexander had already joined the immortals of legend and romance in his brief, meteoric lifetime.

The invasion, or rather raid, for it was too ephemeral to be called anything else, passed completely unnoticed in Indian tradition, though a certain school of foreign historians still presents it as the greatest single event in ancient Indian history. There was an immediate, unexpected by-product of the utmost importance: it hastened the Mauryan conquest of the whole country. The Magadhan army was spared the difficult task of reducing the west Panjāb, tribe by indomitable tribe, with a pitched battle over each trifling *janapada*. This complex obstacle had mostly been smashed by the Macedonian attack and by the Greek practice of taking as many slaves as possible in war, for sale or for drudge labour of the army. The cattle of west Panjāb were booty and food for the invaders; their loss made tribal and pastoral life difficult after the raid. Within five years or so of Alexander's withdrawal Poros was brushed out of his new satrapy into oblivion; the Rigvedic Pūru tribe finally disappeared from history. Candragupta Maurya took the whole of the Panjāb with Taxila; the rest of Gandhāra deep into Afghanistān was wrested from Seleukos Nikator by about 305 B.C. after some more fighting. A marriage alliance is reported between Seleukos and the victorious Mauryan, which accounts for the 500 elephants presented according to Plutarch. Seleukos was free to wage war against his former fellow generals who had partitioned Alexander's conquests among themselves; but he had thereafter to leave India severely alone. The Greek reports about India which have been cited here from time to time derive mostly from the ambassador of Seleukos to the court at Pātaliputra (Patnā). A few fragments of the account by this envoy Megasthenes survive as quotations in other works; the original is completely lost. It is said that a daughter of Seleukos was bestowed as bride upon Bindusāra, the son of Candragupta. This is not improbable, though two objections have been raised, namely Greek marriage rules and Indian caste. The Macedonians were decidedly rude border-Greeks who did not follow the usual Greek laws of city-states like Athens; Alexander had set the example by marrying two Persian princesses. Caste rules meant little to Magadhan kings and less to the Mauryans who were, though Aryanised, of aboriginal or mixed descent. The name Maurya (Pāli: Moriya) indicates the peacock totem and could not be Vedic-Aryan. Asoka's first queen was the daughter of a merchant near Sāñcī or Bhilsā. (The vaiśya Pushyagupta who administered Girnār for a while was Asoka's *rāshtriya*, which should be translated 'brother-in-law' and not 'Collector of *rāshtra* taxes' as has been done elsewhere.) It is just possible that Asoka had a Macedonian or Perso-Greek stepmother; but unlikely that his mother was a *yavana* woman.

The armies of Candragupta and later of his son Bindusāra overran the whole country as far as the terrain allowed. Only the Coorg and Wynaad jungles at the end of the Mysore plateau seem to have stopped them. The peninsula was still mostly undeveloped, in spite of the *dakshināpatha* trade. The prehistoric megaliths at Brahmagiri in Mysore continued to be erected and even increased in size after the Mauryan occupation, which must mean that the local tribes were not immediately converted to the innovation of an agrarian life by the availability of iron. The *topi-kal* hat-dolmens of Kerala are a bit later than the Mysore megaliths, so that the Mauryans had nothing worth conquering in the extreme south. The peninsula had been circum-navigated long before this; the ports of Sopārā (perhaps the Ophir of the Bible) and Broach (Bharukaccha; Greek, Barygaza) with their precious overseas trade were under Magadhan control. This incidentally made Patnā into an international port. Copper mining developed extensively to the south-east of Bihār; the metal was traded through the copper port of Tamluk. There was surely trade by sea with Burma and the islands of Indonesia, to an unknown extent. The silks of China which came (like the furs of Balkh) by the overland route appeared in Magadhan trade, as did the Mediterranean coral exported through Alexandria which was in great popular demand. The silver of Assam had already been tapped, because western imports of the metal no longer sufficed to meet the greatly increased demand for currency. On the other hand, Bengal was cleared and cultivated only in a few patches accessible by river. Orissā (Kalinga) when taken by Candragupta's grandson Asoka about 270 B.C., after a devastating cam-paign, had just become worth the conquest, without having developed into a kingdom.

It was a decidedly mixed empire, over subjects ranging from Stone Age savages to people who had heard and understood the original discourses of Aristotle. At least two subsidiary capitals, Taxila and Ujjain, generally in charge of princes of the ruling house as viceroys, were created for adminis-trative purposes. Asoka, as viceroy under his father Bindusāra, is reported to have quelled a popular revolt at Taxila. That region had produced the great Sanskrit grammarian Pānini, one of the outstanding names in the study of linguistics, but was soon to lose its traditional pre-eminence as a centre of culture. The most ambitious Taxilan intellectuals would naturally move to the capital, Patnā. Trade also suffered for a time, though in this matter the really glorious period of Taxila lay in the future, under the Kushānas. The *dakshināpatha* gave the greatest opportunities for profit; gold and iron were to be had in plenty, though silver and copper were in short supply. Here, the traders and monks who had long preceded the armies had begun to stimulate the first great development of barter and agriculture on virgin land. The great *caitya* cave at Kārle has woodwork dated by radiocarbon to 280 B.C., while the first cells of the monastery, now collapsed, must have been carved out a hundred years earlier. This monks' retreat was accompanied by a settlement of Buddhist Greek traders, in a nearby village then called Dhenukākata. One of Asoka's Buddhist mis-sionaries was a Greek named Dhammarakhita from beyond Afghanistān. That these were not isolated cases is shown by a whole series of sphinxes carved in various Buddhist cave monasteries, the most instructive being at Kārle on a pillar dedicated by a Dhenukākata Greek and obviously copied from a statuette or picture that must have come from Alexandria. Continuity was preserved by a later Greek invader of the early second century B.C., Menander. Though born at Alexandria, he encouraged Buddhist preachers and styled himself *dhammaka* as well as *dikaios* on his coins; both the Pāli and the Greek word mean 'just'. He is immortalised by a late Pāli book: 'The Questions of King Menander' (*Milindapañho*), which is a fairly intelligent dialogue about Buddhist doctrine. The Indian form of his name, Milinda, was borne by a second-century A.D. physician of Dhenukākata, who also dedicated a pillar at Kārle; the name is still given to an occasional Indian boy. This should help clarify the question of interaction between Greek and Indian cultures.

The conquest to the logical boundaries of the whole country and broad cultural penetration were completed by the beginning of the third century B.C. We have now to examine more closely the harsh political theories which were systematically put into practice to achieve this end.

6.2. Magadhan Statecraft

Kings of the Gangetic basin may have listened with sympathy and appreciation to preachers of all the new sixth-century religions. This did not prevent a prince like Ajātaśatru from killing his own father. Similarly, the benign advice to the *cakravartin* to rule by creating full employment, to provide cattle and seed for the farmer and capital to the merchant, was very far from the actual practice of the growing Magadhan state of the fifth and fourth centuries B.C. In what follows, it will be necessary to analyse the textbook upon which this royal policy was based. It has been said by A. B. Keith of this work: 'It would indeed be melancholy if this were the best that India could show as against the *Republic* of Plato or the *Politics* of Aristotle, or even the common sense and worldly wisdom of the author of the tract on the constitution of Athens formerly ascribed to Xenophon.' This is a bit of pretentious irrelevance. Aristotle's royal pupil Alexander did not put the learned Stagirite master's political ideas into action. Athenian democracy failed after a singularly brief span, for all the supposed practical wisdom of its constitution, precisely because of Plato's closest friends. These were the aristocrats like Nikias, Alkibiades, Kritias and others who appear so often as disciples and admirers of Sokrates in the *Dialogues*, but who did less than nothing to bring the Sokratic ideal *Republic* into existence. In contrast, the Indian state we have described grew without a setback from small and primitive beginnings to its intended final size. The Greeks make excellent reading; the Indian treatise worked infinitely better in practice for its own time and place.

The main source of information about state policy and management is the *Arthaśāstra*, a book in Sanskrit rediscovered in 1905 after centuries of total eclipse. The author Cānakya or Kautalya was a brahmin minister of Candragupta Maurya, at the end of the fourth century B.C. Tradition puts his education also at Taxila. He became famous in later legend and romance as the irascible master of intrigue who set Candragupta firmly upon the throne of Magadha. The Sanskrit play *Mudrārākshasa* by Viśākhadatta, written late in the fourth century A.D., gives quite obviously fictitious and improbable details of the involved plotting whereby the best ministers of a murdered Nanda king were won over to support the new rule of an extraordinarily spineless character, the Candragupta Maurya of the play. The state portrayed in Cānakya's book is so different from anything known at any other period that the authenticity of the *Arthaśāstra* was doubted. Though these doubts have since been removed by long discussion, two points must be specially noted. The author does not describe the administration of the Mauryan empire, but discusses theories and principles of the state: 'This book, composed after colleting the various works on statecraft by ancient masters, has been written for the purpose of gaining and maintaining (sovereignty over) the whole earth.' Secondly, the treatise we now possess has lost between a fifth and a quarter of the original. No one section is missing; small pieces have dropped out of every portion of the text in recopying. The nature of the state and army had changed to such an extent in later days that a great deal of the administrative and military practice given was no longer applicable. Many technical terms were not even understood. The sections on army organisation and tactics have suffered most. The immense Magadhan standing army with regular cash payment to retainers, soldiers, and officers vanished after the second century B.C. Tactical units of later times were entirely different, too.

The title *Arthaśāstra* means 'The science of material gain'—for a very special type of state, not for the individual. The end was always crystal clear. Means used to attain it needed no justification. There is not the least pretence at morality or altruism. The only difficulties ever discussed, no matter how gruesome or treacherous the methods, are practical, with due consideration of cost and possible after-effects. The citizen, on the other hand, was subject to a most rigid set of laws, better administered than at any other period of ancient Indian history. This double standard gave the formal excuse for the eventual obsolescence of the *Arthaśāstra*, though leading men of letters continued to read it for its clear-cut arguments and rugged prose till the twelfth century A.D. The work remains unique in all Indian literature because of its complete freedom from cant and absence of specious reasoning. The real cause of its ultimate neglect was the formation of a totally different society (brought into existence by the very success of Magadhan statecraft) to which those methods no longer applied.

Every state rests upon some class-base. The tribal state of the *Brāhmanas* with its overdeveloped *yajña* ritual found its main prop in kshatriya kinship groups which supported their king in keeping down vaiśyas and śūdras and in fighting against other tribes. Later feudal states in medieval India were based upon a powerful landowning class that collected taxes, supplied cavalry and officers for the army, and was held together by a strong chain of direct personal loyalties that bound retainer to baron, vassal to lord, noble to king. At the time the *Arthaśāstra* principles were formulated, the Aryan pastoral tribes had still to be destroyed, though gradually falling apart under the internal pressure of private holdings in land. The overwhelming primeval forest was yet to be cleared; the land it covered was naturally without private owners. The Kautalyan state appears so fantastic today because it was the main land-clearing agency, by far the greatest landowner, the principal owner of heavy industry, and even the greatest producer of commodities. The ruling class was, if not virtually created by and for the state, at least greatly augmented as part of the administration: the higher and lower bureaucracies, the enormous standing army of half a million men (by 300 B.C.) with its officers of all castes and diverse origins; as important as either, a second but hidden army of spies and secret agents—these were the main supports of the new state. It is clear from the *Arthaśāstra* itself that the two sections of the bureaucracy were numerous; Greek accounts tell us that they had become castes, inevitable in a caste society. These two official castes did not survive the Magadhan empire. However, the Kāyastha caste was similarly formed a few centuries later from heterogeneous elements who worked for the state as recorders and scribes.

Espionage and the constant use of agents-provocateurs is recommended on a massive and universal scale by the *Arthaśāstra*. The sole purpose of every action was the safety and profit of the state. Abstract questions of ethics are never raised or discussed in the whole book. Murder, poison, false accusations, subversion were to be used at need by the king's secret agents, methodically and without a qualm. At the same time, the normal mechanism of law and order continued to function for the common man with the utmost vigilance and severity. Such a state could have had no firm basis except its own administration—and even that had to be kept under the most careful observation by spies. After detailing all precautions against corrupt state servants, Cānakya admits ruefully that it is as difficult to detect an official's dipping into state revenues as it is to discover how much water is drunk by the swimming fish. The *Arthaśāstra* state was not characteristic of a society in which some new class had already come into possession of real power before taking over the state mechanism.

This seems to be the place to note an important difference between the Indian and the Chinese course of development. The chief minister of the first Chinese emperor, Chin Hsi Hwang-ti (221 B.C.), was a merchant. The merchant class was later reduced in status, but continued to exercise some real power through those of its members who entered the Chinese civil service, with its regular system of examinations. The Indian *gahapati*-farmer-trader class which called the new Gangetic state into existence was not represented in the ministerial councils, though the early *śreshthis* received the consideration due to their wealth, not granted to their feudal descendants.

The supreme head, symbol, and expression of the state was the king. Kingship required exceptional qualities at the time. Every minute of the day and night was apportioned into suitable periods for the ruler's various administrative duties: hearing of public reports and confidential reports; consultations with the ministerial council, treasury, and army heads. The intervals for rest, sleep, meals, entertainment, or pleasures of the harem were severely restricted by schedule and time-table. Far from 'wallowing in oriental luxury', the *Arthaśāstra* monarch was the hardest-worked person in his realm. Not every king could stand the pace, particularly as the most detailed precautions had to be taken at all times against poison and the assassin's knife. The resulting palace revolutions and changes of dynasty are attested by sudden changes in punch-marked coinage. The line of Ajātaśatru was displaced in a couple of generations by some popular uprising. The new king, Susunāga (Skt. Śiśunāga), restamped existing coins besides issuing new ones of his own. His successors ushered in the great period of punch-marked coins. Magadhan trade and currency dominated the whole of the *uttarāpatha* hereafter, to judge from Taxilan hoards. A later peaceful change, with the same 'wheel of sovereignty' (*cakra*) on coins, brought in a junior but related line, the Nandas or Nandins; their prosperity remained a byword ever after. By this time, about a hundred years after the death of the Buddha, the capital had finally shifted to Patnā, which became (and remained for a century or two) the greatest city in the world. A capable upstart whose most likely name is given as Mahāpadma Nanda then usurped the throne without violence. The murder of Mahā-padma's last son brought the crown to Candragupta Maurya.

Strife for the throne is treated as a minor occupational hazard of kingship by Cānakya. No regard for morality or filial piety is ever in question. He quotes a predecessor's axiom: 'Princes, like crabs, are father-eaters.' The various opinions of previous teachers are considered dispassionately:

methods of training a prince, testing him for untimely ambition, spying out his secret vices and hopes, and restraining him when necessary. The very next chapter advises the ostracised (*aparuddha*) heir-apparent how to circumvent his father's precautions against a short cut to the throne. Neither names nor specific historical examples are given. The context, however, makes it clear that the *aparuddha* prince was no longer merely ostracized, as he had been in the older days of small tribal states. The growth of absolute royal power and of the territories of the new monarchies meant that the person was now restrained in some way by being relegated *ad insulam* as under Roman law, or perhaps even *deportatus ad insulam* with complete loss of all civil rights.

None of the dynastic changes had the slightest effect upon the steady expansion of Magadha. No civil wars interrupted state policy, external or internal; nor does the *Arthaśāstra* ever contemplate such interruption by whatever happened in the palace. The state was too well put together for that. The eleventh book (probably shortened in transmission) of the *Arthaśāstra* is devoted to the methods of systematically breaking up free, powerful, armed tribes of food-producers that had not yet degenerated into absolute kingdoms. The main technique was to soften them up for disintegration from within, to convert the tribesmen into members of a class society based upon individual private property. So, the leaders and the most active tribal elements were to be corrupted by cash bribes, ample supplies of the strongest wines, or by encouraging personal greed. Dissension would be sown by spies, secret agents, brahmins and astrologers, women apparently of good lineage, dancers, actors, singers, and harlots. Senior members of the tribe should be encouraged not to eat at the tribal common table (*ekapātram*) or intermarry with the lesser who in turn were to be egged on to insist upon meals in common and intermarriage. Recognised status within the tribe was to be upset by every sort of internal provocation. Royal agents could needle the younger people, who were allotted a minor share of tribal lands and revenues by custom, to question the apportionment. Murder of tribesmen by ambush or poison (for which the blame would be put upon known rivals within the tribe) and rumours that chiefs had been bribed by the enemy would also help lead to open clashes. Then the king of the *Arthaśāstra* state would intervene directly with armed force. The tribe was to be fragmented, the tribesmen deported to be settled upon distant lands in units of five to ten households, well away from each other so that they should not be able to master tactical manoeuvres in the field. The actual tribes named are as of two kinds: those like the Kamboja and Surāshtra kshatriyas who practised arms as well as husbandry (agriculture and trade) and those who lived solely as (fighting) kshatriya oligarchs (not condescending to lesser occupations) such as the Licchavi, Vriji, Malla, Madra, Kukura, Kuru, Pañcāla and others. The Licchavis or Vajjis had been already extinguished as a tribe by Ajātaśatru, but not exterminated. A few inscriptions in Nepal show that the name survived for nearly a thousand years. The Gupta king Candragupta I of the fourth century A.D. could boast of no better title to nobility than his marriage with the Licchavi 'princess' Kumāradevī. A bitter line in the brahmin *Purānas* laments that the Magadhan emperor Mahāpadma Nanda exterminated all kshatriyas, none worthy of the name kshatriya being left thereafter. This can refer only to the Kurus, Pañcālas, and neo-Vedic tribes of east Panjāb, of whom nothing more was ever heard except in legend and poetry. The rest of the work was mostly done by Alexander. The Madra and Kamboja tribes would not come into direct contact with the Magadhan state till the time of Cānakya himself, but he must have seen them at close range as a frontier brahmin of Taxila. So the book gives an

FIG. 11. Silver punch-marked coins of Mahāpadma Nanda, the last great Magadhan king before the Mauryans. He is credited with the final destruction of the free 'Aryan' tribes, presumably including the Kurus, *circa* 350 B.C.

abstract of long-established principles brought up to date, based upon the actual methods employed—as by Ajātaśatru's brahmin minister Vassakāra against the ancient Licchavis. Though the overwhelming and irresistible Mauryan army could simply flatten out opposition on the field of battle, earlier Magadhan kings had found that circumspection would cost less in men and money. For the rest, nomadic herding tribesmen not in permanent occupation of land, neither engaged in agriculture nor sufficiently well armed to be a military danger, continued to exist. Megasthenes states that these pastoralists were one of the seven major classes of the Indian population in the third century B.C. Some of the *Arthaśāstra* methods, including strong drink and poison, were used in the U.S.A. against the 'Redskins' for much the same reasons as in ancient Magadha.

6.3. Administration of the Land

The *Arthaśāstra* must appear strange and unreal to those who visualise the Indian countryside in its later form. The unit of administration was the *janapada*, which might now be translated district. The original meaning 'seat of a tribe' no longer applied. Tribal settlers had often merged into a far wider peasantry. The districts did not touch each other, but were separated by considerable forests inhabited solely by food-gathering *āṭavika* savages. The forest between villages of the same *janapada* would supply fuel, timber, hay, game, edible produce, and grazing, but was normally clear of dangerous humans. The frontiers of each *janapada* were heavily guarded against attack, whether a raid by the savages or foreign invasion. Movements and intentions of the savages would be spied out by special agents, usually disguised as hermits; if too powerful but nevertheless ripe for change to food production, the forest tribes could be subverted by the methods of the last section. These disjointed *janapada* internal frontiers of the kingdom were as important as the boundaries with other kingdoms till the third century B.C. Trade caravans between *janapadas* had to pay customs duties at the points of entry and of exit. Every individual crossing the *janapada* frontier had to produce a duly stamped official pass, to be obtained only for good reasons by paying a heavy fee. The high ministers and boards of local officials belonged to the *janapada* they administered. Occasionally, a top governor might seem to be a stranger like the Persian Tushāspha under Candragupta Maurya, but a long line of rapidly Indianised foreigners later held the same post at Girnār, presumably because there was a powerful settlement of Iranians in that area.

The administration was duplicated, *janapada* by *janapada*. The highest officials held the rank of minister to the king; the officials just below them sat in boards (*bahumukhyāḥ*; noted by the Greeks). The men destined for top appointments were carefully chosen and examined for intelligence, honesty, courage, loyalty, and weakness in the way of money, women, vices, or ambition, through temptations held out by secret provocateurs. The special qualities and defects of each were docketed. Every official was spied upon for the whole of his career. Spies disguised as men of substance, penitents, or ordinary citizens ascertained public opinion, even helped mould it at need. This was a substitute for the public opinion poll and newspaper editorial campaigns of some modern countries. The lower bureaucracy extended to the registrar of every village or of each block of streets in town. Every such 'guardian' (*gopa*) had to keep a full record of births, deaths, movements of any person into or out of his registry. Strangers and guests, stray travellers, traders, any sudden access of wealth or suspicious behaviour on the part of any person had at once to be reported and closely watched. There were spies in every traders' caravan. The king was omniscient; nothing was allowed to escape the notice of royal agents. Any news item of interest or importance was conveyed immediately to headquarters by messenger or carrier pigeon and orders passed to the proper official by the same methods.

The *janapada* lands fell into two distinct categories: those paying *rāshtra* taxes; and the *sītā* lands settled as well as farmed directly under crown supervision. The former had developed out of earlier Aryan tribal settlements. They normally had their own small headquarters city to which surrounding farmlands supplied the necessary produce. The administration here was allowed to run along traditional lines provided no practice endangered the power of the emperor. Among these *rāshtra* units were the 'free cities' reported by the Greeks, understanding the words in the sense of Aristotle's 'free states' where oligarchs ruled by sanction of the people. Some, under Mauryan hegemony, issued their own coins with a mint-mark of the central treasury; the wheel-symbol of sovereignty that appeared on royal coins was replaced by tiny human figures, or by a shield and arrows. The *rāshtra* taxes were also based on former tradition, though now

FIG. 12. Silver 'Tribal' coins, struck by people who had not an immediate king—though under the ultimate suzerainty (in this case) of the second Mauryan emperor Bindusāra (who defeated Seleukos Nikator). Such coinage tallies with the existence of Indian 'free cities' mentioned by Megasthenes.

.gathered by a special minister of the king. Some villages paid a single commutation tax, individual shares being settled by the residents among themselves. The main assessment was the sixth portion of the harvest. A tax 'for army rations' represented the tribal contributions that had formerly supported local levies; the *bali* evolved out of traditional gifts to the king at the tribal *yajña*; some taxes had emerged out of presents to the chief at the birth of a son, convocation of a general assembly, etc. The chief and the (volunteer but practised) tribal army had often disappeared; nevertheless the new state regularly collected every one of the old taxes. The state also levied a tax on orchards and a nominal tax as compensation for supposed damage to crops by herds; a cess was charged for water-works (dams, canals reservoirs) constructed at state expense. Some of these taxes are confirmed by the inscriptions: Asoka freed Lummini village of the *bali* and reduced the sixth to an eighth of the harvest ('because the Buddha was born here'). The personal gifts, etc., reappeared or continued as baronial prerogatives in feudal times.

The situation was entirely different in *sitā* lands. These soon formed so great a proportion of the cultivated area that Greek visitors (who must have gone to Patna along the Ganges and not by the gradually deserted *uttarā-patha* land route) believed all land belonged to the Indian king. The *Arthaśāstra* king vigorously promoted the direct settlement of wastelands, whether former clearing that had reverted to jungle or virgin soil cleared for the first time. The settlers might be immigrants from outside the *janapada* given special inducements to settle, or śūdra families deported forcibly from the king's own domains, whether overcrowded town slums or overpopulated villages. We know that some were taken and resettled under compulsion from newly conquered lands, for the precise verb (*apavah*) is used by Asoka to describe the results of his Kalinga campaign. However, these villagers were not slaves, not even serfs, but free settlers—with restrictions on such freedom of action as might cause fiscal losses. The new villages were to be three miles or so apart, with the precise boundaries between villages carefully demarcated, whether all the land was cleared or not. The settlement unit was a village of between 100 and 500 śūdra peasant (*karshaka*) families each, so grouped that villages could protect each other. There were administrative headquarters, presumably with garrisons, for groups of every 10, 200, 400, and 800 villages. It might be that Śiśu-pālgarh was established as a town of the last kind; the details have yet to be checked by comparison against the *Arthaśāstra*, but the archaeological date is the third century B.C.

The land in each crown village was assigned only for life to the holder. It would not be reassigned if he were the first to clear it and would go to his heirs if properly cultivated. The holding could not be transferred by the assignee without special permission; any failure to cultivate might result in reassignment of the field to someone else. The *sitā* taxes might be remitted when the clearing and settlement was new, or in times of distress. Otherwise, they were much heavier than in the *rāshtra*, the least being a fifth of the harvest, while up to one-third would be charged for lands irrigated by the state. Timber, forest produce, fish, game, and elephants were reserved for the state. The elephant forests were not cleared; anyone convicted of killing an elephant would be put to death. The elephant was indispensable to the army, not only in battle but for heavy transport, building bridges, and heavy auxiliary duties; in addition, there was the prestige value. Officials, veterinaries and doctors, state messengers and the like could be allotted a holding of *sitā* land for the duration of service; but they had no ownership rights and could not even mortgage the plot. Land under culti-vation for a long time was to be directly farmed, if it fell vacant, by the minister of crown lands (for the particular *janapada*) with hired labour and

149

penal slaves who were thus allowed to work out their sentences or their fines. There was no large-scale slave labour as such; penal slaves, however, could be sold for the prescribed term. Unfarmed lands could also be assigned on half-shares, generally to those who had nothing to supply but their bodily labour. The seed would be deducted and the womenfolk of the assignees subject to work at milling the grain taken by the state as its portion. Apparently the representative of the state arranged even for tools and oxen in such cases. This half-share-cropping, incidentally, persisted in Bihār through feudal times and was recognised by the British as the land-lord's prerogative wherever sanctioned by custom. The survival has again led to the view that there was no change in India. That there were no feudal intermediaries in Mauryan times or earlier between the state and the farmer is then overlooked. About the only concession made in *sitā* lands was to soldiers or ex-soldiers, who would be granted easier terms if they could not take up land even on a fifth-share payment to the state; such people continued to be favoured under feudalism and eventually became a special class which supplied recruits to the army.

The king looked after orphans, the aged, infirm, widows, and pregnant women who had no one else to fend for them. This type of protection was nearer to the care of the master for his cattle than of a father for his children. No form of assemblage whatever—except for a kinship group (*sajāta*) if it existed, or for the necessary public works (dykes, drainage channels, etc.)—was to be permitted in the *sitā* village. Whoever did not supply labour or bullocks at the proper time for the obligatory communal labour was fined. Otherwise no workers' associations or trade guilds, none of the new religious preachers and proselytisers were permitted entry into the crown village; at most an individual non-preaching hermit might pass through. (This is why *sitā* villages receive no mention in Buddhist or Jain tales. The Buddha and Mahāvira lived in a period of *rāshtra* or tribal land-holding, while their followers were barred from crown lands during just those two intervening centuries before Asoka when the system of direct exploitation by the state reached its vigorous peak.) No *sitā* villager was allowed to become a monk (*parivrājaka*) without first making provision for his dependents and distributing all his property. A woman was not to be converted at all to the penitent's life. No peasant could leave a tax-paying village to settle in a tax-free village whether of the *rāshtra* type or one of the (very few) special groves in wastelands granted without taxes to brahmins for their study and maintenance. No bards, dancers, clowns, ballad-singers, jongleurs, or other entertainers of any sort could enter any crown village. Indeed, no village building suitable for public meetings, plays, or games could be built at all. Says Cānakya: 'From the helplessness of the villages

and the exclusive preoccupation of men with their fields stems the growth
of revenue for the royal treasury, of the supply of forced labour (*vishti*),
grain, oil, and other liquid produce.' Greek observers of the fourth century
noted with amazement that these peasants (*georgoi*) would continue to
plough their fields in stolid indifference to two armies fighting a pitched
battle within sight. No wonder, because the laws of war gave the totally
disarmed śūdra farmer personal immunity, and whoever won could make
no difference to his way of life. This again has been taken as a feature of the
changeless East. Actually, the idiocy of village life was deliberately fostered
by early state policy. Not only did the apathetic village survive the form of
state that created it but it destroyed that state and left an ineradicable mark
upon the country.

The state was not the sole land-clearing agency. Any group could move
out into the jungle on their own, usually organised as a guild (*śreni*) for
land clearance with temporary or permanent occupation. Their taxes would
be on the respective scale if they were in recognised *rāshtra* or *sitā* areas.
Otherwise, they would be—for the time being—beyond the constantly
expanding frontiers of any *janapada*, hence beyond the king's jurisdiction.
This meant holding out against the forest savages (*atavika*) by force of arms
or direct negotiations. Both were possible, for the *śreni* normally indulged
in trade and often in manufacture, too. Also, they would send contingents
on hire for military service during a campaign. To what extent they were a
stimulus to the development of the *ātavikas* is a matter for conjecture; but
it was an *Arthaśāstra* practice to hire the *ātavikas*, too, as scouts and army
auxiliaries, which needs must influence their future advance to civilisation.

The *Arthaśāstra* gives all the tricks of the trade for aggression against
neighbouring kings: international alliances, war, poison, the fomenting of
rebellion, internal subversion. Treaties, admitted to have been once sacred
even when made by word of mouth, were to be broken at convenience and
for no other reason. But the fruit of aggression was not direct tribute, which
history shows to have been the normal motive elsewhere in antiquity. If the
defeated king were reasonable (he would not survive otherwise), he could
retain his old throne with all his former revenues and officials left intact.
The sole right insisted upon by the conqueror was over wasteland, where
clearing, settlement, and mining would be conducted on behalf of the
winner. If possible, this right was to be gained without war, by simple
agreement with the neighbouring king. Magadha of the fifth and fourth
centuries B.C. was the one state where political economy was clearly understood as a science. The others ate up their own subjects for taxes—something the *Arthaśāstra* king avoided by building up crown income directly.
The Greeks remarked that Indians, meaning those of the Panjāb, knew

little of metallurgy and technology, and were ignorant even of the water-wheel for irrigation. Foreign comment (which has not survived) upon Magadha of the day could not have contained any such reproach. Mining and every form of irrigation had developed to a remarkably high level in the *Arthaśāstra* state—precisely because the *sitā* lands directly under the crown were exploited to the utmost fiscal advantage.

The traditional main tax after the Mauryans, though the exact period of the change is not known, was 'the king's sixth' of the harvest. The distinction between *rāshtra* and *sitā* lands rapidly disappeared. The former word came to mean 'country' or 'nation'. The state continued to get its revenues on the *rāshtra* scale, whether directly from the peasant owner or a new class of intermediaries, the landlords. In the latter case the tenant farmer would pay on the *sitā* or even the half-share scale, the difference between this payment and the sixth portion to the state being the proprietor's share. The system had its roots in Mauryan times, but the later state mechanism had as its basis the new class of intermediate landowners, not uniform in structure but with rights clearly recognised in practice and with special obligations to support a state which had then become their state, though outwardly the same absolute monarchy.

6.4. *The State and Commodity Production*

The *Arthaśāstra* state differed in one other remarkable particular from any other known to antiquity, whether in India or elsewhere: it engaged in commodity production on a large scale. The main income of the state, as we have seen, was from *sitā* lands, which paid a fourth or more of the produce into the state's warehouse; the *rāshtra* taxes, though lower, were also mainly gathered in kind. The grain had to be husked and perhaps milled to flour before it became usable; someone had to press the oilseeds for the edible oil, to card the cotton and spin it into yarn, to grade and process the wool and prepare blankets, to saw and trim down the timber into planks and beams; and so on. The superintendent of crown storehouses had all this done under state supervision, mostly by local labour (both men and women) seasonally engaged when agricultural operations were slack; they were paid a small monthly wage in addition to their food. The full range of operations is described in the *Arthaśāstra*, with the normal loss of every kind of material given at each stage of processing, with the average output of efficient labour, the final weight or measurement of the finished product and so on step by step; we might be reading a factory production manual rather than a book on statecraft. With the system of recording, it would have been difficult to cheat. The inefficient state official was fined in proportion to the loss of revenue caused by his negligence, with rewards for the keener officials who showed income above the estimate by finding new sources not in the budget or by new economies and more efficient methods of processing. In addition, the state storehouses were very important in budgeting and each of them had a rain-gauge whose records helped classify the land for revenue estimates.

The final product was sold. A great deal went to other branches of the state service, such as the army; but it was transferred by sale with full accounting. The state paid its soldiers very well, but as much of the pay was to be gathered back as possible during a campaign by salaried state agents disguised as merchants selling their goods in army camps at double prices and returning the difference to the treasury. Every state servant was paid in cash; the scale of salaries, given in fullest detail, makes impressive reading. The highest pay was 48,000 *panas* per year each for the king's chief priest, high councillor, chief queen, queen mother, crown prince, and commander-in-chief. The lowest was 60 per year for the menial and drudge labour needed on such a large scale in camp and on state works; this was called *vishti*, and there was an element of press-gang compulsion in it, but it was paid for, whereas the same word under feudalism meant the forced unpaid corvée labour which peasants and artisans had to give in lieu of or in addition to taxes as required by the king or the local baron, ostensibly for the public good. A good deal of this labour was for porterage in bad country, roadmaking, digging irrigation canals or fortification ditches and piling up dykes. The scale of 60 pieces of silver shows the minimum then needed to keep body and soul together for a year under conditions of hard physical labour, with perhaps something left over for dependants. (This amounts to 17.5 grams of silver per month, almost exactly what was paid to the lowest Indian labour by the British East India Company in the early eighteenth century.) Carpenters and craftsmen were paid by the state at 120 *panas*. The heavy-armed soldier of the line after being trained in full got 500, which was the scale also for scribes and accountants in state service (generals, senior superintendents, etc., naturally got much more). The expert miner and the engineer received 1,000 a year. So did the best quality of spy who could disguise himself in many ways; also the spy who normally lived unsuspected as a householder, merchant, or man of religion. Whereas these spies were expected actually to follow the normal pastimes of the classes whose disguise they adopted, there were no extra allowances; hence 1,000 *panas* per annum may be taken as the decent minimum for a Magadhan *grihapati's* normal standard and style of living. The lower spies: assassins, bravos, poisoners, the beggar-woman-spy (who had unhindered access to all women's apartments from the palace to normal household), got

153

500, which was also the scale for the registrar who reported on the village or villages in his charge. Royal messengers were paid on a fixed scale, in proportion to the distance travelled, with double rates for the long-distance couriers. There were regular pensions for those disabled in state service, and for the helpless dependants of servants and officials who died during their term. For long service, special bonuses were given in the form of allowances of rice or food-grain, presents of cloth and the like. Never was anything given away which would permanently curtail state revenues; when short of ready cash, the king might add any gift articles from his storehouses that he liked, but not give away land or whole villages. This is a strange injunction from a brahmin minister like Cānakya, seeing the villages given away to *yajña* priests by Bimbisāra and Pasenadi; the latter also granted an occasional village to a prince or army colonel. The *Arthaśāstra* expressly warns against such hereditary gifts, which later became the norm under feudalism. The most that any Magadhan state servant might expect was a plot of *sitā* land assigned on much the same terms as to anyone else, unless the candidate had been disabled or super-annuated in state service, in which case the rates might be reduced; but the land had to be worked and taxes paid regularly.

It follows that the Magadhan state functioned on a powerful cash economy. Some misunderstanding has been caused by the word *pana* or *kārshāpana*, which came later to mean a copper coin. The *Arthaśāstra* *pana* was of silver, as seen from the directions given in the book itself, and from numerous archaeological finds of the period. The age shows plenty of hoards of silver coins of the 3.5 gram standard, but none of gold and very few of copper. The demand upon currency must have been enormous, when we recall the size of Candragupta's army, even taking a goodly part of the camp to consist of menials, *vishti* drudge labourers, and attendants. It must be emphasised that the state controlled all mining in its domains. This is shown by the excellent salary for the miner who directed everything from the prospecting to the refinery. The state monopoly is reflected in Cānakya's dictum: 'The treasury is based upon mining, the army upon the treasury; he who has army and treasury may conquer the whole wide earth.' The Greeks would have understood this basic position of heavy industry very well, though the Indians of the Panjāb did not, nor did Indian politicians in general till perhaps the present day. There are careful though brief directions in the *Arthaśāstra* for reducing and smelting ores, with distinction between various grades. Nowhere is it implied that the state would make the tools and utensils and ornaments in use; a great deal of the metal was sold by the state to the trader, to artisans' guilds, goldsmiths, and individual manufacturers. Even silver coins could be made by a private person provided the pieces were taken to the mint, where the alloy and weight would be checked and the proper punch-marks stamped on if the pieces were up to standard; after which the coin would be legal tender. Counterfeiting involved drastic punishment. It is known that cloth, pots, baskets, etc., were mostly made and traded privately. What were the relations between the private commodity producer and the state?

The trader and merchant could purchase whatever was available from the state, or from any other source. Every peasant was free to sell his surplus, if any, to any purchaser or to barter it against any article of use. The royal storehouses in each *janapada* had to keep a permanent stock not only of grain and foodstuffs but of rope, timber, tools and the like against emergencies. Famine, fires, flood, or an unusually lean year due to epidemic or the like would find public relief given from these stores. An inscribed copper plate found near Sāvatthi and a similar though damaged limestone slab from Bogra prove not only that the storehouses actually existed but that such instructions for storage and relief were given. Except for this reserve stock, anything else could be sold. The merchant's troubles began after the purchase. There was the rigid rule: 'No trade goods to be sold (by the private merchant) in their place of origin.' This implies that the purchased material had to be processed in some way, and generally to be transported to a distant place. The trader had to add value by manufacture, or by transport; the latter was most important in keeping the circulation of goods and money at a satisfactory level. There were periodic checks on all weights and measures (with a licence fee) with the inspection of all wares and stocks. The caravaneer had to pass from *janapada* to *janapada* through forests infested with savages against whom the caravan might protect itself by carrying arms. As soon as the frontier of the next *janapada* was reached, the arms would have to be deposited in the state armoury, unless there were special reasons for which a permit might be issued against the proper fee. No private individual was allowed to go armed within the *janapada* limits without such a permit; even regular soldiers not on active guard duty could not bring their arms into a city. The caravans had to pay tolls and customs duties upon entering and leaving the *janapada*. Smuggling and false declarations of value were not only dangerous but very difficult, because at least one merchant in the caravan would be a spy in the well-paid secret service, and would know of every transaction of the caravan. Often the information would be sent ahead so that the captain of frontier guards could tell the merchants exactly what goods their caravan had brought, without waiting for the formal customs declaration. The goods imported had to be sold at an appointed public market-place at prices that allowed a good profit but no more. Unsold goods might even be put up by the local officials for sale at prices they believed to be fair, based upon their very accurate information; the merchant—unlike his modern counterpart —could not withhold any essential goods in the hope of a better bargain somewhere else, or for under-cover sales at higher prices.

Perhaps the most serious of the restrictions on the manufacturing trader was the limit to his supply of skilled labour. The artisan was free and generally organised in powerful guilds. No śūdra living as a free man could be sold into servitude; the Greeks could not recognise any form of slavery in India, just as the Indians thought that there was only the distinction of Ārya and Dāsa castes on the frontier and in Greek lands. Penal slaves have been mentioned before, and there was a whole purchased class of house slaves, entertainers, and the like. But none of them could be asked to perform any degrading or filthy service; any such compulsion resulted in immediate freedom, as did any attempt at rape, or cruelty. Children of slave and free were free, not subject to sale. Any property held by the slave could not be taken by the master; the labour of any slave would count at its statutory value towards purchasing his or her freedom. The paid workers were protected by a very fair contract law, which bound them as well as those who had contracted for their services. Add to that the endless forest where anyone who had the nerve could find refuge. There it was always possible to live by food-gathering and for people on good terms with the savages to clear a patch for cultivation, untroubled by state or taxes till the *janapada* expanded to that limit. Though the merchant's interests were amply protected in those cases where they did not conflict with those of the crown, the general attitude of the law was that the trader was a natural rogue who would become a public enemy unless carefully watched, controlled, and penalised from time to time. No view more strikingly different from the Buddhist attitude can be imagined.

The cash appraisal of everything is reflected in the table of fines; the list occupies nine and a half columns in the index to a standard translation of the *Arthaśāstra*, and covers many transgressions that would otherwise have been treated as sins or bad manners. Even the brahmin priest was legally bound, just like any other contracting party, by his agreement to perform a ritual. The ascetic who had not the wherewithal to pay a fine for a minor transgression was assessed in terms of prayers for the king. Prostitution was neither a crime nor a sin, but a state enterprise under its own minister; the regulations for public women are as complete as for merchandise or services of less peculiar quality. When they had earned a certain amount, they could retire and become respectable, for the profession was not so dishonoured as it became later; but the debt to the state must be paid. The superannuated courtesan could in turn become a superintending

Madam herself in state service. Wines, too, had a separate ministry that looked after the liquor from manufacture to sale. All gambling houses were also run by the state under a particular superintendent. The penetration of a cash economy into every corner of civic life can hardly be better shown than by these features. Only it must be remembered that by far the greater number of people lived in the deaf *sitā* villages, where every precaution was taken to keep them hard at work on the soil. The prostitute, wine shop and gambling-house were amenities for the cities and towns, not for the country-side in general. When we say that the Magadhan state and its society reduced everything to its money equivalent, the statement applies primarily to urban life, to the caravan trader, and the state official; not to the lowly peasant deported for settlement on crown land.

6.5. Asoka and the Culmination of the Magadhan Empire

Asoka (Sanskrit: Aśoka, 'sorrowless'), son of Bindusāra and grandson of Candragupta Maurya, assumed the imperial throne about 270 B.C. His own edicts form the oldest Indian inscriptions hitherto deciphered. The few scattered details of his life preserved in semi-legendary form are hardly worth collecting as a narrative. Asoka is supposed to have killed his half-brothers to mount the throne, and to have ruled with despotic rigour for the first eight years of a reign that extended over not less than thirty-six years. The site of a legendary 'hell on earth' specially made by him for torturing prisoners was shown to visitors near Patnā centuries afterwards. The earthly 'hell' refers simply to the normal rigours of Magadhan jails, where torture was added to hard labour when a convict whose guilt was not in doubt proved recalcitrant or specially obdurate; the use of torture disappeared under early feudalism, to reappear in later feudal times. The various accounts show some confusion between two Asokas due to the existence of a Magadhan king of the fifth century B.C. whose personal punch-mark on coins was practically the same as that of the great Asoka two hundred years later. Both sets of coins circulated at the time of the second Asoka and afterwards, so that the Śiśunāga king would naturally be called Kālāsoka, 'the ancient Asoka'. The Mauryan Asoka styled himself Piyadasi ('of pleasing mien'), Beloved-of-the-gods; the latter designation (*devānampiya*) was a title for kings in general, but nothing is implied about kingship by divine right, for the word was used also to mean 'simpleton' or 'half-wit'. The authorship of the edicts was settled by the discovery of other inscriptions of the same style at Maski (Mysore state) and Gujarra equating Piyadasi to Asoka explicitly by name. In Buddhist records (Sanskrit, Pali, and Chinese) the name has become immortal though legendary because of the emperor's conversion to Buddhism and liberal donations to the Order. The coins of the great emperor were not identified till recently, for they bear no name or legend, only symbols like all punch-marked coins.

FIG. 13. Śiśunāga coins (silver), of which the upper belongs to a king known later as Kālāsoka (*circa* 420 B.C.) for the fifth mark is almost the same as that of the Mauryan king Asoka. All earlier coins circulated in later realms, though sometimes reissued with marks of the new king stamped on them, if the succession had been by conquest. The lower of these two coins, with the bull (*nandin*) as the king's personal mark, is the most frequent type among pre-Mauryan coins, and betokens a long reign of immense prosperity. The mark probably led to the legend of the prosperous 'Nanda' king or dynasty.

FIG. 14. Coins of the first three Mauryan emperors: Candragupta, Bindusāra, Asoka. Only one coinage of each king is shown here, but Asoka had several dozen different types issued, because of many mints at work during his long and peaceful reign. However, the Mauryan silver coins after Candragupta show a sudden increase in the copper content, with less accurate minted weights—primitive inflation and stress upon currency in circulation.

Asoka himself speaks of a revulsion after the blighting Kalinga (Orissā) campaign, eight years from the time of his coronation. A hundred thousand men were killed in the fighting, many times that number died from the concomitants of war; 150,000 were deported—the verb *apavah* used is identical with that of the *Arthasāstra* for deportation in forcible settlement of crown lands. The victory was the last act of major warfare for the Mauryans. The people of Kalinga—what was left of them—came thereafter under Asoka's special protection as if they were his children. It was about this time that Asoka began to listen to Magadhan religious teachers and became a Buddhist himself. This conversion, compared so often to that of the Roman emperor Constantine to Christianity in A.D. 325, did not create an organised church associated with the state, nor did it put an end to the other Indian religions in the same way that state Christianity wiped out paganism in the Roman empire. On the contrary, Asoka and his successors made generous donations to brahmins as well as to the Jains and Ājivikas. The great emperor made a point of visiting aged people in his domains who deserved respect, interviewed brahmins and ascetics of all sorts during his constant tours of inspection, and helped the worthy of whatever denomination by money or other gifts. The fundamental change was not religious so much as in the attitude shown for the first time by an Indian monarch towards his subjects: 'Whatever exertion I make, I strive only to discharge the debt that I owe to all living creatures.' This was a startlingly new and inspiring ideal of kingship, completely strange to earlier Magadhan state-craft, where the king symbolised the state's absolute power. The *Artha-sāstra* king owed nothing to anyone; his sole business was to rule for the profit of the state, with efficiency as the one ultimate criterion. With Asoka, the social philosophy expressed in the sixth-century Magadhan religions had at last penetrated the state mechanism.

Asoka has accordingly been charged with publishing his edicts solely to promote or preach Buddhism. This view cannot be justified, seeing the support publicly given to all other dispensations, including the brahmins whose pretensions Buddhism deflated and the two major parallel sects of the Jains and Ājivikas which were execrated by all Buddhists with theological intensity. It is true, however, that the emperor regarded himself as a Buddhist. He is credited with building countless *stūpas* over the Buddha's ashes, with other monuments at sacred places. This is confirmed to a great extent by archaeology. His pillar and rock edicts were placed at important crossroads on major contemporary trade routes or near the new centres of administration. Even those which mark the sites of events specially impor-tant in the life of the Buddha were mostly on the older *uttarāpatha*, a trade route which the vastly increased spread of Gangetic settlement would bring into progressive neglect. A special edict on schisms is addressed to the Buddhist Order; this gives the monks no special privileges, only some excellent advice on their study and behaviour. Apparently, the Order was becoming a bit slack from the effects of rapid growth and high patronage.

The third Buddhist Council, traditionally held during Asoka's reign, seems to be historical, as also his sending out missionaries to all neighbouring countries: Ceylon, Central Asia, and probably China. The Pāli Buddhist canon in its oldest extant form was supposedly compiled just after the death of the Buddha, but is most likely to have been given its present content in or about Asoka's time. It survives in Ceylon, Burma, and Thailand.

The edicts go much deeper than personal liking for Buddhism, for they indicate a totally changed basic policy on the part of the state. The first main indication is in public works (even apart from the *stūpas*) that brought no return to the state; Asoka's magnificent new palace at Pātaliputra and similar buildings would be for comfort and ostentation, such as any king might have built. The *Arthaśāstra* palace was more for use and personal safety, with woodwork where Asoka used a considerable amount of stone with a characteristic mirror-like finish. The style, polish, and the beautiful Asokan bell-capital which thereafter came into wide use for Indian pillars, are supposedly derived from Achaemenid construction. The *Apadana* palace of Darius I is presumed to have furnished the model and even the workmen for Asoka. As it was built over 2,000 miles away before 500 B.C. and had been burned down in 330 B.C. during Alexander's revelries, the statement is not to be taken literally. Asokan art, with which I include the great though slightly later gateways at Sāñcī, shows direct translation into stone of a well-developed woodwork tradition. Reliefs at Kārle, Kondāne, and other cave monasteries show that the many-storied houses were mostly of wood; even the characteristic 'Buddhist arch' was originally in woodwork. The late Mauryan audience hall, once mistaken for Asoka's great palace, whose ruins were excavated in the Kumrahar suburb of Patnā, had flooring, ceiling, roof, substructure, and even drains of heavy timber; its beautifully polished stone pillars rested securely upon heavy logs sunk vertically into the soil with a mat of clay. Timber was plentiful in a region now painfully denuded of trees, for roads built of corduroy or trimmed logs ran for miles through Bihār even in the seventh century A.D. The fortifications of Patnā at its greatest were of timber, covered with earth.

Indian art and architecture, not the least valuable part of Indian culture, may be said to begin from Asoka in spite of Indus valley construction. The ruins of the Asokan palace at Patnā were still impressive to Chinese pilgrims in A.D. 400, seemingly the work of genii and supernatural agencies. Asoka spent a great deal on much more important public works that would give no profit to the state. Hospitals were founded all over the empire for men and beasts, with free medical attendance at state expense. Shady groves, wells with steps leading down to the water, fruit orchards and resting-places were systematically laid out on all major trade routes at distances of one *yojana* (from five to nine miles, the original word denoting the distance at which cart-oxen could safely be driven between inspanning and out-spanning on long treks). These new constructions, which must have been an absolute godsend for the traders, especially because of the doctors and veterinaries available at many of the stations, were located not only in Asoka's domains but also beyond his frontiers. This agrees precisely with the duties of the benevolent *cakravartin* emperor which are mentioned in the Buddhist discourse cited in a previous chapter. Such works were not visualised by the *Arthasāstra*, unless some cash return could be obtained for the money; though even that grim book emphasises the need to help the aged, maimed, and orphans.

This does not mean that King Asoka neglected administrative business for charitable works and pious deeds. He notes in so many words that regular reports had gone out of the royal routine for some time—naturally, seeing Candragupta's extensive campaigns, the continuous mopping-up operations of Bindusāra, and the spread of empire over the whole sub-continent. Asoka says: 'I shall receive and consider official reports at all times; even at dinner-table, in the inner apartments (harem), in bed, the toilet, on parade inspection, in the royal park, or anywhere else shall the reports about the condition of the people be brought to me.' The neglected royal schedule of the *Arthasāstra* was now being restored with a special effort to make up for lost time. There were, however, serious changes in the Canakyan administration. (Canakya's retirement is placed by unsupported tradition early in the reign of Bindusāra.) The king himself would now make a complete tour of inspection throughout his domains every five years. Such a tour must have taken up a good part of the five years, which implies constant travelling except in the rains. All previous royal journeys of the sort had been for personal pleasure such as hunting, or on military campaigns. Every high administrative official was likewise ordered to make a similar quinquennial tour through the entire territory under his own jurisdiction. In addition, there was created a new class of plenipotentiary supervisors with control over officials and special funds. The title was *Dharma-mahāmātra*, which can be translated 'minister of morality', and would later be 'senior regulator of charity and religious affairs'. The correct translation at the Asokan stage is 'High Commissioner of Equity'. Equity is the principle beyond formal codified law and common law upon which both law and justice are supposedly based. This corresponds exactly to the early meaning of *Dhamma* and justifies Menander's Greek translation *dikaios* for *dhammaka*. Part of the new high commissioners' duties was to examine the complaints of all law-abiding groups and sects, to see that they were treated fairly; but also to ascertain the tenets and principles of all such groups and

161

sects. This the emperor himself accomplished during his own inspection. Primitive group-law and primitive group-religion cannot be separated. The people in the *Arthaśāstra janapadas* were certainly primitive, especially the villagers. Ritual was considered (then as now) the essential prelude for every agricultural operation from the first ploughing to the final winnowing, while many observances were often inherited from food-gathering society. The problem was to adjust these parochial and sometimes conflicting beliefs to a larger society in food production. This was also the aim of Buddhism, which, however, condemned the fire sacrifice and all ritual killing, where the *Arthaśāstra* ignored the *yajña* and used witchcraft to clear the *janapada* of a plague, whether of serpents, mice, or epidemic.

Asoka did not forbid all killing; only a special list of animals and birds were protected, for reasons unknown, perhaps totemistic. The ox, cow, and bull are not protected, except the *sandaka* bull, set free (even to this day) to graze where he would and useful for stud purposes, though regarded as sacred; beef was still sold openly in the market and at crossroads, like any other meat. The emperor set the example of vegetarianism in his own palace, cutting down the royal household's consumption of meat almost to vanishing-point. The *yajña* was forbidden by decree, as were certain forms of the saturnalia (*samāja*) which led to heavy drinking and public orgies, with crime or deplorable excesses. Even here, the emperor admits that some types of *samāja* are necessary and not evil. It has been noted that one form survives to this day, the *holi* spring festival, whose most obscene features have been mitigated by law and public opinion. It was completely prohibited to burn down forests for driving the game to slaughter or to clear the land. This was not some Buddhist vagary, but absolutely necessary to protect settlements and to conserve natural resources. Even the brahminical *Mahābhārata* in a late addition puts the same injunction in the mouth of the dying Bhishma, who characterises burning down forests as a major sin. The glorious Pāndava heroes of that very epic had cleared the site of Delhi in this way with the god Krishna to help them; so the advice seems quite incongruous in the context. The real meaning is that the ancient Vedic Aryan way of life had passed beyond recovery; society had made the final transition to agrarian food production, so that the rougher customs of the pastoral age would no longer suit. The commissioners of equity were ordered specially to look after the welfare of prisoners. Many convicts, then being kept in fetters after the sentence had expired, were to be released. Others in jail had helpless dependants whom the new commissioners were charged with helping out; prisoners sentenced to death were allowed three days of grace to settle their affairs, but there was no question of abolishing capital punishment.

The Asokan edicts clearly provide the first constitutional checks against the crown, the first Bill of Rights for the citizen. This is made clear by the special instruction to officials that the edicts were to be read out and carefully explained to large public gatherings at least three times a year. The question to be considered briefly is: Why was this extraordinary change necessary?

The Asokan reform is a good example of the ultimate change of quality with change of quantity. The number of householders, peasants, artisans, and the size of the *janapadas* had increased to such an extent that the *rajjuka* assessor of land revenue had begun to exercise full control over several hundred thousand human beings, like the Collector of a district in British times. *Janapada* frontiers were no longer widely separated, nor were the trade routes just a few narrow tracks through dense forest. The forest savages, now relatively few, were becoming a nuisance only, but no real danger. Asoka sent *dhamma* emissaries to them, as to the countries beyond his frontiers. The forest land, increasingly penetrated by daring individuals, also began to sprout many cleared tracts under cultivation, difficult to classify as either *rāshtra* or *sitā*. The overpowering Magadhan army was superfluous and much too costly to maintain on its former scale; indeed, Asoka says that, after his 'rule by equity', the army was used only for parades and public spectacles.

The country fell into three major sections with totally different structure: the Panjāb and the western portion of the empire, open to invasion, needed an alert army with one or more separate local commands. The local commander would naturally be tempted to set up as a king on his own account, or would be driven out by Greeks, Sakas, and other Central Asians. Both these developments took place about fifty years after Asoka. The second region, the Gangetic heartland, needed no army as long as the Panjāb had no hostile occupation. It was still very rich and prosperous. However, the state monopoly of metal was gradually being lost. Copper mines in Bihār had begun to reach water-level; there were no pumps. Iron was needed in quantities much too large to be supplied from Magadha. New sources of iron had been located and developed in the Deccan (as shown by the Bāvari story) to some extent long before the Magadhan invasion, by northern private enterprise. Indian steel had supplied the best swords, even to the Achaemenid court, a hundred years or more before Alexander. The insatiable demand for this product of high metallurgy could only be met by tapping small pockets of the very finest ores, which are scattered down through Āndhra and Mysore, in jungles where the Magadhan state would find it very costly to establish its heavy-handed bureaucratic jurisdiction over the prospectors. This third region, the peninsula, could not be settled in the same fashion as Magadhan *sitā* lands, for the best soil was concentrated in scattered patches, and of a totally different kind to that in Magadha. The future development of this third portion of the Magadhan empire would mean a new growth of local population, local languages, and local kingdoms. At the time of Asoka, there was no other dynastic kingdom whatsoever, only wild and semi-wild tribes, throughout the whole of India not under his rule. The only kings he names are Greeks beyond his western frontier; none is mentioned even for Kalinga, which was to have its own conquering monarch Khāravela within a hundred years. Finally, deforestation meant increasing floods and diminishing returns even in Magadha, where the best lands would be the first cleared and the rest would be difficult to irrigate. One bad season, whether due to flood, epidemic, or poor rains, would entail complete loss of revenue from an increasingly large area, with correspondingly added strain upon the treasury for relief measures. This, like every other problem of the highly centralised administration, was made difficult by slow transport and vast distances.

Asokan currency shows that this is no imaginary reconstruction. The Mauryan punch-marked *kārshāpana* after Candragupta has the same weight as its predecessor, but much more copper, cruder fabric, and such a large variation in weight that the manufacture must have been hasty. This evidence of stress and unsatisfied currency demand is accompanied by debasement (inflation) plus the vanishing of the reverse marks which denoted the ancient trade guilds. The new trader was accordingly less easy to control, while the Deccan actually managed with less coinage, lighter silver coins, and even lead and pewter tokens, which indicates a tremendously increased volume of trade and heavy profits for traders who would barter with tribesmen. The first debasement of currency is attributed to Cānakya himself, who traditionally struck off eight times the number of coins out of the same amount of silver; but the *Arthasāstra* prescribes other measures when the treasury was in difficulties. Special levies were to be made by the financially embarrassed king—just once, not oftener—on the people's capital, stored goods, grain, etc.; the ubiquitous state agents in disguise would come forward with 'voluntary' contributions to whip up public enthusiasm. New cults would be 'discovered', whether *nāgas* or apparitions or the like; the credulous thus duped by secret agents would make contributions that went surreptitiously into the treasury. This sounds a strange method for a brahmin minister like Kautalya to suggest, but many brahmins till the third century could look upon primitive, non-Vedic superstition with contempt. The grammarian Patañjali says in passing that the Mauryans did invent such cults for the sake of money. Finally, instead of the national debt and state loans, the *Arthaśāstra* recommended special measures against merchants. Spies in the proper guise would get a rich trader drunk, rob him, falsely accuse him of crime, or even murder him; the merchant's confiscated goods and money would go to the state treasury. That these deadly methods put a strain upon human character beyond the margin of safety, no matter how carefully the secret agents were chosen, is clear.

Asoka's public works returned a great deal of money into circulation. His tours and those of his officials helped to ease the strain on transport, the local surplus being eaten up wherever it existed. The new attitude towards subjects and new works on the trade routes established a firm class basis for the state, which had till then been managed by the bureaucracy for the bureaucracy. The state developed a new function after Asoka, the reconciliation of classes. This had never been visualised by the *Arthaśāstra*, and indeed the classes of society grew within the pores as it were of the Magadhan state policy of extensive land clearing, land settlement, and severely regulated trade. The special tool for this conciliatory action was precisely the universal *dhamma* in a new sense. King and citizen found common meeting-ground in freshly developed religion. This may not seem today to have been the best solution, but it was immediately effective. It can even be said that the Indian national character received the stamp of *dhamma* from the time of Asoka. The word soon came to mean something else than 'equity', namely religion—and by no means the sort of religion Asoka himself professed. The most prominent future Indian cultural developments thereafter would always bear the misleading outer cover of some *dharma*. It is altogether fitting that the present Indian national symbol is derived from what remains of the Asokan lion-capital at Sārnāth.

CHAPTER SEVEN

Towards Feudalism

7.1. The New Priesthood

THE Asokan reform completed the mutation of the older Aryan tribal priesthood, the brahmin caste. The pastoral life of the Panjāb tribes with their constant *yajña* sacrifices had been the firm basis of the older brahminism. This was wrecked beyond any chance of revival, first by Alexander's devastating raid and then by the immediately following Magadhan conquest. Magadhan agriculture, philosophy and the non-killing (*ahimsā*) sects like the Buddhists, Jaina, and Ājivikas had prevented any real expansion of Vedic ritual into the Gangetic basin, beyond a few sacrifices by the more simple-minded of the sixth-century kings. The *Arthaśāstra* lays no stress whatever on the *yajña*, though its writer was a brahmin. The cult of Krishna has already been pointed out as a symptom of the decline of the Vedic ritual even in the Panjāb. An important class was thus freed for the first time from tribal bonds and traditional Vedic ritual duties. The brahmins were the one group in ancient Indian society with obligatory formal education and with an intellectual tradition. Twelve celibate years in the service of some preceptor (*guru*) in an isolated brahminical grove were considered necessary for the acolyte to master Veda, grammar, and ritual. The sacred books had to be memorised without error of a single syllable or of as much as a tone-accent; yet the Vedas were not committed to writing. This learning by rote and method of training resembled that of the Druids in Caesar's Gaul, but on a higher level of mental achievement. The respect showed by Asoka and his successors to the leading brahmins of the day was due to the important new mission that the caste had already begun to fulfil in education, culture, maintenance of a class structure in society, unification and absorption of originally irreconcilable groups, and in the general spread of an agrarian society. These items must be considered in detail.

Though the Vedic idiom remained immutable in theory, Sanskrit as a living language had begun to show marked regional variation. The task of fixing the language was achieved by a long line of brahmin grammarians of whom the greatest, Pānini, obliterated the memory of his predecessors. Pānini's *Ashtādhyāyi* is perhaps the first scientific treatise on grammar in any language. The most important among his successors was Patañjali (first half of the second century B.C.), whose masterly comment on Pānini's highly condensed rules develops the principles of the Sanskrit language with sharp logic and absolute clarity. Grammar (*vyākarana*) became thereafter the most satisfying of Sanskrit studies. Patañjali's limpid and beautiful exposition still remains about the finest specimen of Sanskrit prose. The emphasis upon memorising all basic formulations (*sūtras*) of any science whatever promoted simple versification, but stultified the development of prose. The structure of Sanskrit shows no essential change through the centuries after Patañjali. Nevertheless, vocabulary and idiom were enriched from time to time by small loans from the steadily developing regional vernaculars of the common people, which followed their own course, but with important influence of Sanskrit. These provincial languages were pidgins formed by the various regional common markets. The Magadhan *lingua franca* could not serve the whole country for long, granted the diversity of people who grew rapidly in numbers because of food production and advanced sufficiently in other techniques of production to participate in the flourishing trade. This is seen by a look at Assam, where almost every little valley has its own tribal group with its special language or major dialect. Such must have been the general situation in India when the Asokan edicts were inscribed.

Sanskrit rapidly became a special upper-class idiom understood by educated men. Formal instruction in this language remained in the hands of the brahmins. The first considerable Sanskrit inscription occurs at Girnār about A.D. 150. The Śaka king, Rudradāman, boasts therein of his rebuilding a dam first constructed under Candragupta Maurya; but he boasts also of his own command of Sanskrit. This means that rich and powerful foreigners could naturalise themselves through Sanskrit as Indians of the nobility—though the simpler Prakrit was generally used for inscriptions till the fourth century A.D. The most highly Sanskritised epigraphs in the Buddhist caves at Nasik come from Śaka donors of foreign descent, while the indigenous Sātavāhana rulers still kept to the simpler Prakrit. The most prolific of Sanskrit authors, King Bhoja of Dhārā (*c.* A.D. 1000–1055), who wrote on science, astronomy, architecture, poetics, and composed verses as well as dramas, seems to have been the son of an aboriginal (Nāga) princess with the Sanskrit name Śaśiprabhā. At least, his father Sindhurāja's courtship and winning of the princess furnishes the theme of the *Navasahāsānkacaritam* of the poet Padmagupta-Parimala. The vaiśyas, though strictly speaking Aryans, soon dropped out of Sanskrit studies, whereas kshatriyas of Indian and foreign ancestry continued to enrich the literature. After the fourth century the language was often used for court documents, too. The clerical Kāyastha caste was helped out in this by model norms for letters, decrees, notices, judicial decisions, and the like; some of these still exist (*Lekhaprakāśa, Lekhapaddhati*).

Sanskrit, with such curious verb-forms as the benedictive, always retained the stamp of a priests' language; it lacks even the simple future tense for everyday use. The brahmin continued to be tied to ritual, though not exclusively the Vedic type. In this, his only rivals were the primitive medicine-men, each of whom was restricted to his own tribal group. Many even of these tribal priests were absorbed with their superstitious lore into brahminism; sometimes, the brahmin would take over and supplement with his own ritual the priestly tasks for a guild caste or even a tribe caste, always excluding or softening the worst features of the primitive rites. Buddhist, Jain, and other monks had abandoned all ritual and could not officiate as the brahmins could and did at the sacraments of birth, death, marriage, pregnancy, and initiation. Only the brahmin could bless the crops at sowing, propitiate evil stars and placate angry gods, determine (and prognosticate by) the calendar. The Vedic *yajña* rites remained supreme only in theory, but were progressively neglected in practice. Occasionally, some king might perform, say, the horse sacrifice (*aśvamedha*); but this was much too rare to be a reliable source of income even for the king's own high priests. The new ritual could become paying only if it served the householder (*grihapati*) class of agrarian and trading society. This service was done by the brahmins regardless of caste, but always for a suitable fee and on condition that due respect was offered to brahmin institutions in general. It would seem that *gahapati* had developed the connotation of landed peasant proprietor or rich vaiśya settler in the third century B.C. The head of a large house and household received the specific designation *mahaśāla*, whether he was a *gahapati* or not.

The brahmins gradually penetrated whatever tribes and guild castes remained; a process that continues to this day. This meant the worship of new gods, including the Krishna who had driven Indra worship out of the Panjāb plains before Alexander's invasion. But the exclusive nature of tribal ritual and tribal cults was modified, the tribal deities being equated

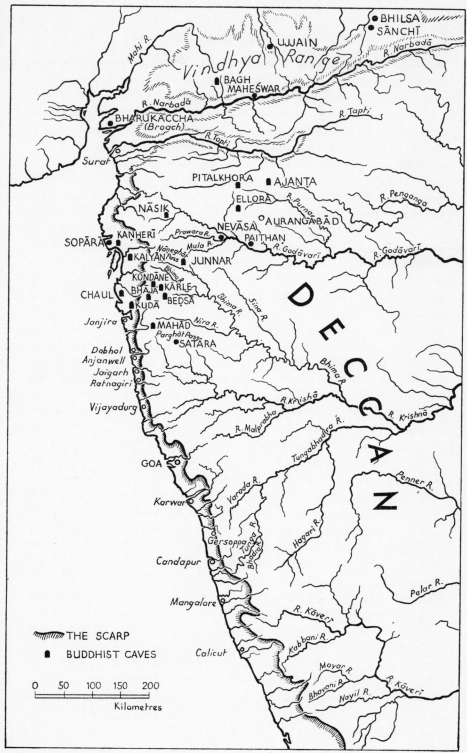

The **Deccan Scarp** showing passes from the West Coast estuaries to the river systems of the Deccan and early Buddhist cave monasteries.

to standard brahmin gods, or new brahmin scriptures written for making unassimilable gods respectable. With these new deities or fresh identifications came new ritual as well, and special dates of the lunar calendar for particular observances. New places of pilgrimage were also introduced with suitable myths to make them respectable, though they could only have been savage, pre-brahmin cult spots. The *Mahābhārata, Rāmāyana*, and especially the *Purānas* are full of such material. The mechanism of the assimilation is particularly interesting. Not only Krishna, but the Buddha himself and some totemic deities including the primeval Fish, Tortoise, and Boar were made into incarnations of Vishnu-Nārāyana. The monkey-faced Hanumān, so popular with the cultivators as to be a peculiar god of the peasantry with an independent cult of his own, becomes the faithful companion-servant of Rāma, another incarnation of Vishnu. Vishnu-Nārāyana uses the great earth-bearing Cobra as his canopied bed to sleep upon the waters; at the same time, the same cobra is Śiva's garland and a weapon of Ganeśa. The elephant-headed Ganeśa is son to Śiva, or rather of Śiva's wife. Śiva himself is lord of the goblins and demons, of whom many like the cacodemon Vetāla are again independent and highly primitive gods, still in popular, village worship. Śiva's bull Nandi was worshipped in the south Indian neolithic age without any human or divine master to ride him; he appears independently on innumerable seals of the Indus culture. This conglomeration goes on for ever, while all the tales put together form a senseless, inconsistent, chaotic mass. The importance of the process, however, should not be underestimated. The worship of these newly absorbed primitive deities was part of the mechanism of acculturation, a clear give-and-take. First, the former worshippers, say of the Cobra, could adore him while bowing to Śiva, but the followers of Śiva simultaneously paid respect to the Cobra in their own ritual services; many would then observe the Cobra's special cult-day every year, when the earth may not be dug up and food is put out for the snakes. Matriarchal elements had been won over by identifying the mother goddess with the 'wife' of some male god, *e.g.* Durgā-Pārvati (who might herself bear many local names such as Tukāi or Kālubāi) was wife to Śiva, Lakshmi for Vishnu. The complex divine household carried on the process of syncretism; Skanda and Ganeśa became sons of Śiva. In the feudal period the pantheon was arranged in a sort of imperial court. The marriages of the gods imply human marriage as a recognised institution, and would be impossible without social fusion of their formerly separate and even inimical devotees. The new *jāti* castes received a status roughly consonant with their economic position in the conjoint society. They would retain the endogamy and the commensality of former tribal existence, unchanged. Their position was guaranteed by the respect their gods now received from society as a whole, while they became an integral part of that society by worshipping other gods along with their own transformed deities. The arrangement resembled the Greek amphictyony except for the inequality of group status with group exclusiveness.

This process of mutual acculturation accompanied the introduction of a class structure where none had existed before. The later brahmin scriptures (*smriti*) are as emphatic as Cānakya, that kingship is essential for the preservation of the social order. The monarch had to use force and the 'Law of the Big Stick' (*danda-nīti*) 'to keep the Big Fish from swallowing up the Little', though tribal society had never felt the need. Several southern kings of tribal origin boast of having had the 'Golden Womb' (*hiranya-garbha*) ceremony performed. This is carefully described in some *Purānas*. A large vessel of gold was prepared into which the chieftain would be inserted doubled up, like the foetus in a womb. The brahmin ritual for pregnancy and childbirth was then chanted by the hired priests. The man emerged from the 'womb of gold' as if reborn, having also acquired a new caste, or even a caste for the first time; this was not the caste of the rest of the tribe when they were absorbed into society, but one of the classical four castes, usually kshatriya, with the *gotra* of the brahmin priest. Some of the 'reborn' medieval kings might claim the brahmin and kshatriya caste at once, like the Sātavāhana Gotamiputra. The brahmin priests received the golden vessel as part of their fee, which made everyone happy. Most of the later kings, even some Buddhists, insist that they support the four-caste class system (*cāturvarnya*), though some of them claimed descent from Nāgas, or from the semi-Nāga Aśvatthāman of the *Mahābhārata*, or some monkey king of the *Rāmāyana*. All this amounted to keeping down a newly created set of vaiśyas and śūdras by brahmin precept and kshatriya arms. The chief, with the backing of a few nobles freed from tribal law, would become ruler over his former tribe while the ordinary tribesmen merged into a new peasantry. Sometimes the brahmin went further than discovering some respectable genealogy for the chief in the epics or Purānas, and beyond writing such ancestries into the record. That is, the brahmin would even marry into the tribe, which would normally create new tribal brahmins. Occasionally, as in central India of about the sixth century, the mixed descendants might rule the tribe. King Lokanātha of Bengal boasts a bit later of such mixed descent from a brahmin father and a tribal clan chief-tainess (*gotra-devi*). The first Indo-Chinese kingdom was similarly founded by a brahmin adventurer named Kaundinya, whose superior prowess with the bow cowed local tribesmen and enabled him to wed the local 'Nāga' chieftainess Somā. Aboriginal matriarchy made such unions quite simple.

Sometimes a regular balance was struck, as in Malabār, where the Nair caste originates from mothers of the local matriarchal population by fathers of patriarchal Nambūdiri brahmin caste. Both groups still retain their separate institutions.

Disruption of the tribal people and their merger into general agrarian society would not have been possible merely by winning over the chief and a few leading members. The way people satisfied their daily needs had also to be changed for the caste-class structure to work. The tribe as a whole turned into a new peasant *jāti* caste-group, generally ranked as śūdras, with as many as possible of the previous institutions (including endogamy) brought over. The brahmins here acted as pioneers in undeveloped localities; they first brought plough agriculture to replace slash-and-burn cultivation, or food-gathering. New crops, knowledge of distant markets, organisation of village settlements and trade also came with them. As a result, kings or kings-to-be invited brahmins, generally from the distant Gangetic basin, to settle in unopened localities. Almost all extant copper plates (which have been discovered all over the country by the ton) are charters which—from the fourth century onwards—record land-grants to brahmins unconnected with any temple. In addition, every village would set apart a plot or two of land plus a fixed though small share of village harvests for the cults and priests, brahmin or not. Brahmins, however, claimed and generally received exemption from all taxes; they even claimed a specially low rate of interest on loans, and other privileges, not always granted.

The brahmin often preserved tribal or local peasant *jāti* customs and primitive lore in some special if modified form, as the priest who had taken them over. This transformed the *dhamma* Asoka found associated with all Indians. Naturally, sanction from holy writ (forged if necessary) would be claimed by the particular brahmin, who had become the repository of tribal usage and tradition, for the laws he had in some way to justify. The general medieval rule is that each *jāti* caste, guild, clan, family, and locality had its own legal customs which must be consulted before the king's judges could give a decision. Even now, the lowest Indian groups adjust their internal differences by argument before the caste *sabhā* (council). Appeal to some higher law comes only with the development of individual property rights, or when members of different groups are involved in litigation. The rigid *Arthaśāstra* judicature which overrode all other usage disappeared soon after the Mauryans.

This procedure enabled Indian society to be formed out of many diverse and even discordant elements, with the minimum use of violence. But the very manner in which the development took place inhibited growth of commodity production and hence of culture, beyond a certain level. The emphasis upon superstition meant an incredible proliferation of senseless ritual. The administrative manuals compiled from the scriptures by two medieval brahmin ministers of state make a strange contrast with the *Arthaśāstra*. These two works are the *Kritya-kalpa-taru* of Bhatta Lakshmidhara (*c.* A.D. 1175), and the *Catur-varga-cintāmani* of Hemādri (*c.* A.D. 1275). The former was a high minister of King Govindacandra Gāhadavāla of Kanauj, and the latter chief minister of the Yādava King Rāmacandra of Devagiri (Daulatābad) in the Deccan. Both compendia are crammed with ritual rules for every occasion and date. Pilgrimages, expiations for every kind of transgression real or imaginary, observances for the dead and purifications take up most of the twelve fat volumes that each work would cover if published in its entirety. All that is obvious from them is that the ruling class had to suffer some quite meaningless disabilities in order to be able to impose rule by superstition upon the lower orders. Of administration as such there is virtually nothing; justice reduces to the rule above that each group should be allowed its own unrecorded laws. The ordeal by fire, hot iron, poison, etc., was admitted when the judge could not decide on the strength of the evidence presented, though not as torture to extract a confession. It is significant that each of the two kingdoms was irretrievably ruined by comparatively small Muslim invading armies within twenty-five years after the corresponding book had been prepared. Hemādri, with all his respect for the *smritis* and his legendary reputation as administrator, is accused in Mānbhāv literature of having taken bribes from Ala'-ud-din Khalji to disrupt the defensive preparations of his own kingdom.

The brahmin never troubled to record and publish the caste laws he defended. The basis for a broad, general common law on the principles of equality or like the Roman *ius gentium* was lost; crime and sin stand hopelessly confused, while juristic principles are drowned in an amazing mass of religious fable which offers ridiculous justification for any stupid observance. The various guild and city records that existed through the Middle Ages were never thought worthy of study and analysis. Indian culture lost the contributions that these numerous groups (tribal, clan, *jāti* caste, guild, and perhaps civic) could have made. The civilising and socialising work of the Buddha and of Asoka was never continued. The tightening of caste bonds and of caste exclusiveness threw away the possibility of finding some common denominator of justice and equity for all men regardless of class, profession, caste, and creed. As a concomitant, almost all Indian history is also obliterated. The fifth-century B.C. tribes (Licchavi, Mallas, and the Aryans in the Panjāb) defended their liberties as stubbornly as any Greek city-state and far more vigorously than Athens against Macedon. Only, no brahmin Aristotle ever studied their constitutions. Their *sabhā* councils saw eloquence (as we know from tradition) comparable to the Athenian in public meetings, but no historian tells us how and what free institutions were destroyed along with the free people. The actual difference between Greek and Indian antiquity was less than appears from comparison of the superb literary quality of the Greek classics with the endless insipid drivel of medieval Sanskrit Purānas. Megasthenes recognised 'free cities' in India, a term with clear historical meaning for the Greeks even when they had been subjugated by Macedon. Aristotle specially notes the common table at Sparta, Crete, and many other Greek cities as an important democratic institution. This is precisely the Yajurvedic *sagdhi* and *sapiti*, eating and drinking in common for which the eighth-century Aryan prayed. It is also the decaying institution *ekapātram* which the eleventh book of the *Artha-śāstra* would use to subvert the freedom of the great Indian oligarchies. It now remains only as a caste tabu on strange food. Greek and Roman religion required fishing about in the reeking entrails of freshly slaughtered beasts before every important action, for centuries after such customs had gone out of Indian fashion; Themistokles sacrificed human victims on the eve of Salamis. Thus, brahmin indifference to past and present reality not only erased Indian history but a great deal of real Indian culture as well. The loss may be estimated by imagining the works of Aristotle, Herodotos, Thukydides and their contemporaries as replaced by priestly ritual re-written for the medieval *Patrologia Latina* of Migne, supplemented by excerpts from the *Gesta Romanorum*.

The 'logic' advanced by the brahmins took good care to avoid all reality. The end result is seen in the philosophy of the great Śamkara (*c.* A.D. 800), who threw out the proposition that 'A thing is either A or not-A', and viewed the universe as divided into metaphysical categories upon several planes. The highest plane was, of course, of speculation about and unity with eternal principles. Material reality did not exist. The philosopher was thus excused if he joined the common herd on the plane of ritual obser-vances. Lip service to Vedic *yajña* blood sacrifices accompanied the *ahimsā* (non-killing) that the brahmin had necessarily to preach after Buddhism. At the same time as obligatory vegetarianism, the *smriti* scriptures also contain a table of various types of meat that was to be fed to brahmin guests at a feast for the souls of departed ancestors. This ability to swallow logical contradictions wholesale also left its stamp upon the Indian national character, noticed by modern observers as by the Arabs and Greeks before them.

The absence of logic, contempt for mundane reality, the inability to work at manual and menial tasks, emphasis upon learning basic formulas by rote with the secret meaning to be expounded by a high *guru*, and respect for tradition (no matter how silly) backed by fictitious ancient authority had a devastating effect upon Indian science. The old Indian system of medicine (*āyurveda*) collected many useful cures, sometimes learned from jungle-dwellers. Even the highly practical Arabs who knew Galen and Aristotle translated an Indian medical work on diagnosis from the Sanskrit for their own use. But many masters of Āyurveda today prescribe a plant *ananta* for certain types of spasms, without being agreed as to just which herb it actually is; no less than fourteen species, from a lowly grass to a full-grown tree, are known in various localities by that Sanskrit name, and all seem to be so prescribed. Similarly, the brahmins had a long list of holy places for pilgrimage all over the country and beyond its frontiers as far away as Baku and Egypt. Many of them remain unidentifiable, as no record of travel and accurate location was ever given. For historical descriptions of ancient Indian scenes and people, sometimes even for the identification of ruins, we have to rely upon Greek geographers, Arab merchant travellers, and Chinese pilgrims. Not one Indian source exists of comparable value.

The dismal tale of rapid growth and long degeneration summarised here covers some fifteen centuries after Asoka. At the end the village brahmin, far from studying the Vedas over twelve years at some distant place, often failed to reach simple literacy. The parasitic caste privileges were never willingly surrendered; a brahmin would at times fast to death rather than pay taxes. An occasional forged copper-plate charter shows that the high-souled brahmin *elite* had come a long way from the day when astonished foreigners like Arrian could say, 'But indeed, no Indian is ever known to lie.' The apparent failure of brahminism, however, was in fact the complete victory of the helpless, apathetic, virtually self-supporting and self-contained, disarmed village which Cānakya had preferred as the productive basis of state power and of the king's treasury. The unlimited growth of superstition showed, as has been remarked, the necessity for the ruling class to subject itself to formal disabilities and restrictions in order to make religion effective in control of society. The advance of culture needs exchange of ideas, growing intercourse, both of which depend in the final analysis upon the intensity of exchange of things: commodity production. Indian production increased with the population, but it was not commodity production. The village mostly managed to subsist upon its own produce. What little was exchanged had first to pass into the hands of feudal lord or tax-collector, often the same person, as ground rent, tribute, and taxes. This curious isolation of village society accounts for the fantastic proliferation of medieval Indian systems of religion and religious philosophy, which failed—but for trifling exceptions in greater Malaysia—to attract the same following outside India that was accorded to Buddhism.

7.2. The Evolution of Buddhism

Just after A.D. 630 the Chinese pilgrim Hsiuan-tsang arrived at the monastic university of Nālandā to perfect himself in the study of Sanskrit and of Indian Buddhism. He had come a long way through desert and over icy mountains, past towering *stūpas* and opulent monasteries from Khotān to Gandhāra, and through the Panjāb, to the homeland of Buddhism within sight of Rājgir. As a distinguished foreign scholar, he was welcomed by the senior Master of the Law, Śilabhadra. The Chinese biographer reports of Hsiuan-tsang's reception:

'He was lodged on the fourth story of Buddhabhadra's house, in the courtyard of king Bālāditya's college. After having been entertained for seven days, he was assigned quarters in a guest house to the north of the house of Dharmapāla Bodhisattva and his daily perquisites were increased. Every day he was provided with 120 *tāmbūla* leaf-bunches, 20 areca nuts, 20 nutmegs, one ounce of camphor, and one *shang* measure of *mahāśāla* rice. This rice had grains larger than the black bean, and when it was cooked it had a fragrance which no other kind of rice posssesed. It was produced only in Magadha and was not found elsewhere. As it was offered only to kings and well-learned monks of great virtue, it was called *mahā-śāla* rice. He was also supplied with three *tou* of oil every month, and as regards butter and milk he took as much as he needed every day. He was attended by one servant and one brahmin and was exempted from ordinary monastic duties, and when he went out he had an elephant to ride on. Of a total number of 10,000 host and guest monks of the Nālandā university, only ten persons including Hsiuantsang enjoyed such privileges. Wherever he travelled he was always treated with respect like this.'

As for Nālandā itself:

'Six kings built as many monasteries one after the other, and an enclosure was made with bricks to make all the buildings into one great monastery with one entrance for them all. There were many courtyards, and they were divided into eight departments. Precious terraces spread like stars and jade pavilions were spired like peaks. The temple arose into the mists and the shrine halls stood high above the clouds. . . . Streams of blue water wound through the parks; green lotus flowers sparkled among the blossoms of sandal trees, and a mango grove spread outside the enclosure. The monks' dwellings in all the courtyards had four storeys. The beams were painted with all the colours of the rainbow and were carved with animal designs, while the pillars were red and green. The columns and thresholds were decorated with exquisite carvings. The plinths were made of polished stone and the rafters adorned with paintings. . . . In India there were thousands of monasteries, but none surpassed this one in magnificence and sublimity. Always present were 10,000 monks, including hosts and guests, who studied both the Mahāyāna teachings and the doctrines of the 18 Hīnayāna schools as well as worldly books such as the Vedas and other classics. They also studied grammar, medicine, and mathematics. . . . The king gave them the revenues of more than 100 villages to support them, and each of the villages had 200 families who daily offered several hundred *tan* of rice, butter, and milk. Thus the students could have the four requisites (clothing, food, shelter, and medicine) sufficient for their needs without going to beg for them. It was because of this support that they had achieved so much in their learning.'

The ruins at Nālandā show that this description was by no means exaggerated, though the archaeologists have so far failed to provide us with accurate details of the successive development of even one monastery. There existed seven-storey buildings in those days, while the Mahābodhi temple at Buddha Gayā had already reached its present height of 160 feet. Of the monks' activities, Hsiuan-tsang himself has this to add:

'The Vinaya (*Liu*), discourses (*Lun*), sutras (*King*) are equally Buddhist books. He who can entirely explain one class of these books is exempted from the control of *karmadāna*. If he can explain two classes, he receives in addition the assignment of an upper seat or room; he who can explain three classes has allotted to him different servants to attend and obey him; he who can explain four classes has 'pure men' (*upāsaka*) lay-followers allotted to him as attendants; he who can explain five classes of canonical books is allowed an attending escort. . . . If one of the assembly distinguishes himself (in disputation) by refined language, subtle investigation, deep penetration, and severe logic, then he is mounted on an elephant covered with precious ornaments and conducted (in procession) by a numerous suite to the gates of the abbey. If, on the contrary, one of the members breaks down in his argument, or uses poor and inelegant phrases, or if he violates a rule in logic and adopts his words accordingly, they proceed to disfigure his face with red and white and cover his body with dust and dirt, and then carry him off to some deserted spot or dump him in a ditch.'

Clearly, this was nowhere near the Buddhism preached by the Founder in sixth-century B.C. Magadha. There still existed ascetic monks who travelled barefoot, slept in the open, begged their way on leavings of food, and preached to the villagers or forest savages in country idiom; but their status and numbers diminished steadily. The monk's prescribed garment of discarded rags pieced together had been replaced by elegant robes of fine cotton, excellent wool or imported silk, dyed in the costliest saffron. One feels that the great Teacher (who had passed through Nālandā village on his last journey on earth) would have been laughed out of the exquisite and magnificent establishments that ran in his name, unless perchance he could prove himself by some miracles. Such miracles had been derided by the Buddha, but were now the mainstay of the religion, so that reports of supernatural feats by many Buddhas proliferated. The most primitive fertility rites reappeared, sublimated in form, as Tantrism, which not only generated new sects but even penetrated Buddhist, Jain, and brahmin theology. The orthodox doctrine, too, had been covered by rank growths just as the pristine rules of monastic poverty and simplicity had been superseded. The Great Vehicle (*mahāyāna*) mentioned above openly took to this elegant life of body and mind during and after the second century A.D. The Hinayāna ('Lesser Vehicle', so called in contempt by the Mahāyānists after the bifurcation) preserved some outward forms of primitive austerity. They also retained a fixed number of Pāli scriptures where the 'Great Vehicle' wrote and rewrote whatever they liked in Sanskrit. The Mahāyāna canon as preserved in Tibetan and Chinese translation forms a whole library by itself, while countless books have been lost untranslated along with the original Sanskrit. The basic difference in monastic practice was trivial, for the Hinayāna monasteries also held ample grants, administered in the course of time (as we can see from their survivals in Ceylon and Burma) each by some fixed family whose younger males might be tonsured if necessary to hold the abbacy. Even before the schism, runaway slaves, savage tribesmen, escaped criminals, the chronically ill and the indebted as well as aboriginal Nāgas were denied admission into the order. The church and state had come to terms. The Buddha had correspondingly been turned into a regular counterpart in religion of the emperor (*cakravartin*) in civil life.

A prominent section of the original Buddhist discipline lays stress upon the disgusting and filthy constituents of the human body. The monk had regularly to meditate, detail by detail, upon the loathsome inner components of his own physical being. He was instructed to spend a good deal of time near corpse enclosures to observe human carrion being devoured by vultures, jackals, or worms. But no one would ever guess this from the finest specimens of Buddhist art. The multitude of diademed Bodhisattvas, magnificent women in opulent but highly revealing costumes, and their handsome male companions stretched unbroken from Gandhāra and Bhārhut to Ajantā and Amarāvati. No rotting half-eaten corpse, no leprous beggar with festering sores mars the smooth harmony of sumptuous frescoes and reliefs to remind the monk of the Founder's doctrine. Nor does the art portray the normal hardships of the poorest villager (*pāmara*), whose surplus the monk could eat, but whose misery was easily discounted on the callous theory that the suffering must have been deserved because of misdeeds in some previous birth.

Pāli records started by making Indra and Brahmā respectful hearers of the original Buddhist discourses. The Mahāyāna admitted a whole new pantheon of gods including Gaṇeśa, Śiva, and Vishnu, all subordinated to the Buddha. A few select goddesses found their way into this company, like the dazzlingly beautiful Tārā and the mother goddess Hāriti, who had originally been a child-eating demoness. Charms (*dhārani*) to be recited against snakes and demons entered the canon. At the same time, many an abbey had its respected patron *nāga* snake-demon. The Buddha, of course, remained above all the rest as a super-god in an inaccessible heaven of his own; but the number of past Buddhas was multiplied beyond limit, and a future messianic Buddha Maitreya added. Many popular folklore tales were adopted bodily as stories of the former births (*jātaka*) of the Buddha through which he had perfected himself for Buddhahood. Every branch of the doctrine, every new monastic rule was justified by writing in a new story about the Buddha, while relics of the Buddha's mortal body, worshipped everywhere, grew in size and quantity till they would have done credit to a whole troop of elephants. But the brahmins could and did play this game much better. The gods the brahmins wrote into their *Purānas* were in high worship, whether by the peasants or by the tribal chiefs who had risen to kingship. A classical case is that of the patron Nāga Nilamata of Kaśmir, whose cult had fallen into desuetude because of Buddhism, but was revived by the *Nilamata-purāna* specially written by the brahmins— who revived themselves therewith. Buddhism had never become a state religion in the sense of Islam or Christianity, nor did it use the state machinery for the suppression of any rival doctrine. From the very beginning the Order contained brahmins who might have renounced caste but retained their intellectual traditions. The current brahmin ideology (not ritual or cults) was often taken for granted, just as the brahmins had given up beef-eating and accepted non-killing (*ahimsā*) as their main ideal. The higher philosophies of both Buddhist and brahmin began to converge in essence. Neither admitted the material world as real. Certainly, neither

Śamkara nor the doctrines which he presents as his adversaries' main principles during the 'refutation' show the remotest knowledge of anything that could have been recognised as Buddhism by or before Asoka. It is difficult today to grasp just what the controversy was about, for the difference between the protagonists seems negligible in content, if not in form as well. As for the waning practical effect of Buddhism, we might note that Asoka had turned to the non-killing religion after a single gruesome campaign in Kalinga. In contrast, the devout Buddhist emperor, Harsha Śilāditya (A.D. 605–655) of Kanauj, fought incessantly for at least thirty years to bring most of India under his sway. For that matter, Jenghiz Khan (Temujin) and the Mongol princes who succeeded him conducted military operations over most of the Eurasian continent, notorious in history for their scale of carnage and destruction compared to which Alexander's campaign looks like a border raid; but these Mongol emperors, too, pass for good Buddhists. No Buddhist king, however, killed or crusaded for the glory or propagation of religion.

The state support that Asoka had given continued till the end of the twelfth century, when all monastic foundations in the north were finally looted and wiped out by Muslims. The Indo-Greek prince, Agathokles, showed Buddhist symbols on his coins as did the *dhammaka-dikaios* Menander. The Kushānas ushered in a new era of magnificent donations, which gave a secure base for the Mahāyāna; the dynasty lasted till the fourth century A.D. The gifts were never rescinded by pre-Muslim kings. The immediate successors of the Mauryans favoured brahmins. The first Śunga king celebrated a horse sacrifice in *yajña* style. This had no effect upon Buddhism, as is shown by the augmented Śunga structures at Sāñci. The *Mahābhārata* was prominently cited in Gupta land-grants to brahmins, from the fourth century; but at the same time Buddhist monasteries were renovated and their stipends increased. The first real persecution came early in the seventh century with King Narendragupta-Śaśānka of west Bengal, who raided deep into the Gangetic plain and destroyed many Buddha images besides cutting down the Bodhi tree at Gayā. All was quickly restored and made even more splendid in a few years by the munificence of Harsha. But the decline and precarious state of Buddhism was visible even as Hsiuan-tsang studied at opulent Nālandā. His nightmare of the bitter end was literally fulfilled about A.D. 655, when the great monastery was sacked and burnt down in the general disorder after the death of Harsha. However, the Pālas restored the financial position in the next century, and built several new *vihāra* foundations, including the huge abbey not far from Nālandā from which the name Bihār was later given to the whole province. The Senas, unquestionably Hindu kings in the modern sense of the word, continued the donations and had to fortify the Pāla monasteries in order to protect the treasures within from brigands. This only led to the buildings being stormed and sacked all the more thoroughly by a handful of Muslim raiders under Muhammad bin Bakhtyār Khalji, who swept through Magadha and west Bengal about A.D. 1200. The tremendous complex of *stūpas* and monasteries at Sārnāth which had grown up on the site of the first Buddhist sermon and about the locus of the Buddha's simple leaf hut was wrecked beyond recovery at the same time, thus ending a continuous tradition of refuge and meeting-place for ascetics which went back to the centuries before the Buddha. Sārnāth had survived Hun raids, violent Pāsupata intrusions and schism, and had just been restored as well as further enriched about A.D. 1150 by the 'Buddhist' queen of the 'Hindu' king, Govindacandra Gāhadavāla. The Koreans could still invite an Indian Buddhist monk during the fourteenth century, but not from any

FIG. 15. Signature of the Buddhist emperor Harsha, from a copper-plate land-grant to a brahmin (the Banskhera plate; Epigraphia Indica, vol. IV, opposite p. 210). The year was perhaps A.D. 628. Harsha wrote on the copper plate in ink, signing with the words 'by my own hand, of śrī-Harsha, king of kings'. The inked letters were then cut into the plate by the engraver.

of the classical foundations; it had to be from the south, where Buddhism was quietly fading away. For that matter, the minor non-Buddhist schools such as the materialist Lokāyatas and the near-Buddhist followers of the Sakyan Devadatta were known to survive in Magadha at least till the seventh century. They were not destroyed, but withered away in peaceful decay in a land that could tolerate many incompatible systems at the same time, but would not bother to make a permanent record of their traditions and doctrines. The question of the 'restoration of Hinduism' or of some king being Buddhist or Hindu is meaningless. Many people, kings or commoners, could support the later brahmin ritual, worship prehistoric gods barely made decent, and simultaneously give generous donations to Buddhists, Ājivikas, and Jains right through to the end. Harsha of Kanauj, whose support of Buddhism is not in doubt and who could forgive an assassin he had personally disarmed, styled himself 'High Follower of Śiva' (*parama-māheśvara*) in the land grants he made to brahmins like any other king of the medieval period. Moreover, his clan deity was the sun god, popular in the Panjāb since Persian influence entered again with the

Kushānas and created a new sect of 'Maga brahmins', presumably of Magian origin. Harsha correspondingly assumed the title *parama-bhattāraka* as well. Finally, one of his Sanskrit plays, the *Nāgānanda*, where he himself acted the part of the self-sacrificing Buddhist hero, is dedicated most devoutly to Gauri ('the White Goddess', i.e. Pārvati), consort of Śiva. Neither he nor any of the monks, whether Buddhist, Jain, Ājivikas or others, who gathered in their thousands along with the brahmins at the Ganges-Yamunā confluence every five years for a great distribution of gifts by the emperor, would have been conscious of any contradiction. The incongruities of modern Indian character noted in our first chapter had become current before Hsiuan-tsang visited India.

Still, this looks more like the corrupting influence of wealth than the victory of the village. As a matter of fact, the change had begun well before Asoka. About a hundred years after the death of the Buddha, in the reign of King Kālāsoka of Magadha, the monks of Vesāli had begun to accept and even to solicit cash gifts for the use of their small local chapter. This caused scandal among other Buddhist monks of the day. Ultimately, a council convened at Vesāli and attended by the most honoured members of the Order under the leadership of a monk Yasa condemned and suppressed the new usage as heresy. Monks were to accept nothing except food or small articles for immediate personal use. This was made part of the *Vinaya* canon thereafter. If we find the sumptuous monasteries of all schools so well endowed after this clear injunction, there must have been some powerful reason underlying the change. This basic reason is quite easy to trace.

The monasteries performed one of the tasks of the *cakravartin* universal monarch supposedly recommended by the Buddha, but nevertheless omitted by Asoka when he built roads, resting-places, water reservoirs, and public hospitals for man and beast. The accumulated monastic wealth often provided some of the capital so badly needed by early merchants and cara-vaneers in the Indian hinterland. The pioneer brahmins who, like Bāvari, penetrated the wilderness with at most a handful of cattle and a couple of disciples, could not do this. Nor could the brahmin *agrahāra* settlers with whom kings liked to seed the wilderness not yet brought under the plough, but ripe for opening up. This is one of the reasons why the two radically different systems could coexist side by side with no open conflict till the seventh century in the north and the ninth century in the south. It seems to me the main reason why Buddhism could grow for so many centuries after the ancient pastoral *yajña* against which it had protested so effectively had vanished under pressure of widely developed agrarian food production. This special economic function accounts in the main for the spread of Buddhism into the adjoining countries which never needed to invite the

182

brahmins to introduce the four-caste class system. Those lands had never known the vedic *yajña* and could hardly have loved for its own sake the intricate, rarified and virtually incomprehensible doctrine which a long line of distinguished Indian, Chinese, Tibetan and other monks translated so assiduously into several languages.

It is known that the first Buddhist missionaries who went to China were associated with overland merchants. What we know of the economic function of the Buddhist monasteries in general is in part from the Chinese records, too, confirmed by rather obvious but hitherto ignored archaeological features of the cave monasteries whose ruins dot the western Deccan. Both Chinese and Indian foundations belonged to the same Mahāsāmghika ('Great Order') school, a proto-Mahāyāna dispensation, or to other Buddhist sects that were very close in doctrine and practice. The Chinese documents prove that their Mahāsāmghika monasteries were instrumental in peaceful development of the Chinese hinterland; Buddhism in general brought a message of peace and non-killing. Monastic orchards, farms, cultivation by slave and hired labour, sales and loans to lay farmers and traders are all attested, along with generous charity in times of famine. Many of the contracts and some of the monastic accounts still survive. It is explicitly recorded that the routine followed in such matters was modelled upon Indian Mahāsāmghika practice. In fact, the pilgrims who came for a long course of study in India paid as much attention to monastery administration as to holy places of Buddhist pilgrimage and to the sacred texts. I-tsing, a hundred years after Hsiuan-tsang, notes even minor practices as to hygiene and daily life in the monasteries and cites with approval the specious arguments used by Indian monks to justify the use of silk robes. China, too, had the more austere primitive type of almsman-monk, who faded away just like his Indian counterpart.

The monastery at Kārle in western India was Mahāsāmghika though open to all Buddhist monks of any sect whatever. All the metal and the woodwork, except the once painted beams of the *caitya* vault, has vanished. The painting on pillars and walls is also gone. Presumably the Vesāli reform drove money-minded almsmen farther south, where they had not to trouble about state control or about the usage in Bihār. But the foundation is dated by radiocarbon to a pre-Asokan epoch. The sculpture is beautiful and even voluptuous, of handsome couples of opulent men and women dressed in the height of style, riding horses and elephants; hardly what one would expect in an assembly place for monks, but precisely what rich merchants would have liked. The artists must have been specially brought from some distance and employed at considerable expense. Moreover, the whole complex took a few centuries to complete, but the plan remains unitary. This means a continuity of design, finance, and administration. The connection with merchants and bankers (*śresthi*) from many distant places is obvious from the names of donors inscribed on various pillars, statues, and caves which they donated. Nevertheless, there were many other donors, apart from the many small anonymous cash gifts nowhere recorded, who helped maintain the abbey and finish the work. Some were high officials, others physicians and the like. The merchants' union (*vaniya-gāma*) of the locality appears on one pillar as donor; the institution became prominent through the Middle Ages, till Muslim conquest reduced its importance by introducing a new type of trader. The king and his governor confirmed gifts of whole villages after the Śaka dynasty of the original donations had been eliminated by Sātavāhanas in the second century A.D. But some of the donors are startling. Guilds of bamboo-workers, braziers, potters and the like appear in some monasteries not only as giving generous gifts but as paying interest to the monastery from moneys invested with them by a prince for a perpetual grant out of the interest of the trust fund. Finally, there are individuals: scribe, physician, blacksmith, carpenter, head fisherman, the wife of a ploughman and mother of a householder-farmer, and so on. No artisan or craftsman or worker of this sort could be expected to make enough money to donate anything important in normal Indian village life. The society then must have been of commodity producers, on a scale not familiar to later days in the Deccan, or indeed anywhere else in the country. The development of *sitā* lands and state enterprise on the *Arthaśāstra* model could obviously not have taken place in the locality of the cave monasteries, for most of them are even now in the undeveloped wilderness, whereas the very buildings of northern monasteries have often been ploughed under the soil. However, the Deccan cave monasteries all lie handy to the trade routes running from the western estuarial harbours (Kalyān, Thānā, Chaul, Kudā, Mahād) through the well-marked passes of the sheer Deccan scarp that lead up to the plateau. The new terminus Junnar, soon a second Satavāhana capital, is similarly ringed around with no less than 135 Buddhist caves.

There is no question of kings being converted here, for there were no kings at all in the Deccan at the time of the first cave monasteries. Official (not monastic) caves at the important Nānaghāt pass 30 kilometres west of Junnar record full details of the innumerable donations as *yajña* fees made over to brahmins by the Sātavāhana kings: cattle by the thousand, elephant, chariot, horses, coined money, and so on. Besides the *yajña*, however, special mention is made of the Sātavāhana worship of Krishna and his strong ploughman brother, Balarāma-Samkarshana. In other words, the Bāvari tradition persisted and the northern developments of brahmin religion came south ready-made. Yet the Sātavāhanas continued to support all the

184

cave monasteries. The cave at Bhājā with the famous *dvārapāla* guardians might even have been carved out primarily by royal support, to judge by its structure. But the *caitya* façade has collapsed, with loss of the major inscriptions that might have been expected.

Some of the recorded gifts to Buddhist monasteries are, remarkably enough, made by monks or nuns. The very fact that they had the money to pay shows that the decisions of the council of Vesāli had been openly flouted or quietly suspended. Formerly, the entrant into the Order had first distributed all his worldly possessions and then renounced the worldly life. Now he brought his money and experience of money-making into the monastery. At Kārle, the wealthy lay-follower Budharakhita donated a costly assembly hall in his own name. The same name is later inscribed above a cell at the end of the complex, which he apparently used as his chamber when he renounced the world. Some of the cells in the main body of the *vihāra*, whether at Kārle or in any of the other monasteries of the region, show inner compartments without light or ventilation which could only have been meant for the safe-keeping of precious goods. Most of the outer cells had strong wooden doors which could have been barred from within and carefully locked from without with a peculiar chain arrangement. This indicates the presence of substantial wealth. The monasteries were important customers for the caravans: cloth for the monks, incense and costly perfumes for the service, metal images, metal lamps in large numbers (the soot still blackens all the ceilings) were not locally available. It is also obvious that these abbeys were important stages on the journey, resting-places for the caravaneers, as well as supply houses and banking houses. At Junnar, for example, it would have been more convenient to group the caves closer together, but even when on the same hill, it is noticeable that they are in small groups spaced as widely apart as possible. Each group was patronised by a different set of merchants, which may account for the lack of cohesion, a financial counterpart of the diversity of sectarian doctrines.

This system and the monasteries that it supported passed away when Buddhism had become a drain upon the economy instead of a stimulus. The long-distance luxury trade, especially from the north of India and overseas from the Roman empire, was surpassed in volume by predominantly regional barter in essentials, under a totally different class of merchants. The interruption of the overland trade routes and the virtual collapse of the Roman empire in the third century A.D. might have been supplementary factors. Secondly, the growth of villages and towns found the monasteries inconveniently situated for trade and finance on a large scale. They could not be shifted inasmuch as religion required an isolated spot for the prime duties, which were, after all, monastic, not financial. The long caravans gradually dwindled to groups of Banjāras (*vānijyakāra* = merchant) and Lamāns (*Lambamāna*) that still exist. The powerful guilds were broken up, their members scattered through distant villages; or they shrank to miserable caste groups of producers who travelled for meagre gain from place to place, as bands of the Burūd bamboo-workers and basket-makers still do. Production increased, but commodity production per head and the incidence of exchange over long distances both declined. From about the sixth century the passes were guarded by forts, a new feature of the feudal landscape. Their ostensible duty was protection of kingdom and travellers, but all they really accomplished was collection of tolls from the caravans. Worst of all, the immense amount of precious metal, brass, and bronze locked up in the monasteries was badly needed for currency, utensils, and tools. Even the Chinese emperors had ultimately to issue decrees forbidding the use of metal for images in the Buddhist temples and monasteries. In India the necessary economic measures often appeared with theological trappings, as a change in religion. The monasteries had to go, but their mark was not erased. The ancient mother goddesses whose primordial cults had been situated near the monasteries and displaced by Buddhism sometimes returned to the identical spot. Occasionally, they occupied a deserted monastic cave; at Junnar the old name Mānamodi of the mother goddess can be traced through the ages to the same place. At Kārle the great stone *stūpa* is identified with the goddess Yamāi. But the blood sacrifices of these goddesses at Buddhist sites were either abandoned or moved to a long distance. The northern Kushāna plough still to be found in a few parts of Mahārāshtra is generally close to these Buddhist caves. The great sixteenth-century Marātha saint Tukārāma identified the Buddha (of whom he knew very little) with his god Vithobā. That he meditated in the same Buddhist caves and composed his simple religious verses there is surely not an accident.

The economic root cause of such changes is shown much more clearly in another context. King Harsha of Kaśmir (A.D. 1089–1101; not to be confused with the seventh-century emperor Harsha) systematically melted down all metal images throughout the length and breadth of his kingdom, with just four exceptions. The work was carried out under a special 'minister for uprooting gods' (*devotpātana-nāyaka*). Each image was publicly defiled by leprous beggars who voided urine and excrement upon it before dragging it through the streets to the foundry. Not the slightest theological excuse was offered. The king did have a Muslim bodyguard of mercenaries, but went out of his way to offend them by eating pork. This Harsha was nevertheless a man of culture, excellent littérateur, connoisseur of drama, music, and ballet. He supported brahmins within reason and honoured a Buddhist preceptor whose pleading, in fact, rescued the four images, two of the Buddha. The metal was needed to finance the king's desperate and expensive wars against rebellious Dāmara barons. Islam took over in Kaśmir in the fourteenth century without striking a blow and without subsequent looting or persecution.

7.3. Political and Economic Changes

Indian dynasties after the Mauryans are fairly well known, though the chronology is never precise, nor the extent of any territorial rule certain. The individual kings remain submerged in the pleasant obscurity of fable. Nothing like court annals exists except for an outline covering later Kaśmir and perhaps the genealogy of Cambā rulers. Still, one may pass the major names under review. The main divisions are the Kushāna, Sātavāhana, and Gupta periods, before Harsha and the decline. Many valiant kings raided back and forth across the sub-continent. At the village level, however, not much attention was paid to whatever happened at the top. This is perhaps the whole point of the story.

The half a dozen Mauryans who succeeded Asoka may have ruled more or less concurrently over the several parts of his empire, for each section had its own major problems. That the successors made no further change of basic policy is clear. Asoka's grandson Daśaratha presented the Barābar caves to the Ājivikas, while a successor Samprati is supposed to have died in the Jain faith. The Mauryan name retained its prestige long after royal power had vanished. The 'last descendant of Asoka', Pūrnavarman of Magadha, restored the Bodhi tree and the Buddhist foundation at Gayā after Śaśanka's destructive raid. Bāppā Rāval, the traditional founder of medieval Rajput clans, displaced a local Mauryan in Rājasthān to set up his own rule. Such petty 'Mauryans' were known as far south as Goa, down to the tenth century. Some of the enduring lustre of Candragupta Maurya may have caused the Marātha name Candrarāv More to become the title for which it passed in the seventeenth century.

The last Mauryan emperor Brihadratha was killed about 184 B.C. at an army review by his own commander-in-chief Pushyamitra of the Śunga clan. The Śungas revived the *yajña*, rather ineffectively to judge from their feeble military performance. A barbarian risen to power, Khāravela, raided deep into the heartland from Kalinga, reversing Asoka's victory. The Greeks had already 'conquered India' in their own parlance by taking the Kabul valley from Subhagasena, a provincial governor of the Mauryans. They advanced into the Panjāb under Eukratides. The famous Menander set up his capital at Sialkot, whence he raided into the Gangetic basin as far as Fyzābād and perhaps up to Patnā. The territory about Ujjain remained the unshaken mainstay of the Śunga rule, but even here the Sātavāhanas had made inroads from the south by the first century B.C. Apart from this tale, miserably gleaned from scattered, casual references, we have only discordant king lists. Yet the period was important for Indian culture. The matchless sculpture and architecture of Sāñci, where the Buddhist monuments are the oldest in India to survive almost intact, provide continuity down to the high Gupta period and are in a class apart. Patañjali's grammar and Sanskrit prose, mentioned earlier, also belong to the time of Pushyamitra Śunga. A Greek Heliodoros, ambassador of the Antialkidas who ruled at Taxila, dedicated a pillar with eagle capital near Bhilsā. There he proclaims himself a devotee of Vāsudeva; the language of the pillar inscription is Prakrit, with demonstrably Greek word order. This gives us priceless information about the spread of the Krishna cult. The dark hero of the Yadus was still not raised to the status of all-god or an incarnation of Vishnu-Nārāyana. Other statues and inscriptions of the time show that his ploughman brother Samkarshana and occasionally some other Yadu heroes enjoyed almost equal status. In other words, the cult had not shed its tribal features though the tribe had long vanished. The Śungas retained their hereditary title of *Senāni* (commander-in-chief) after mounting the throne, but in spite of this and the *yajñas* their success lay more on the parade ground and in fields of culture than in battle. Kālidāsa's play *Mālavikā and Agnimitra* deals centuries later with the love story of Pushyamitra's son, a viceroy at Ujjain. The Śunga claim on brahmin memory was of some use after all, though not strong enough to prevent the Kānvāyana brahmin minister of the tenth and last Śunga from assassinating his master to usurp the throne, which thus passed to a brief-lived brahmin dynasty.

The question of Greek influence upon Indian drama, epic poetry and culture is variously handled according to the particular critic's own prejudices. It will be avoided here for lack of evidence, which in any case shows that the influence was negligible. The Indians did borrow from Greek (or earlier) astronomy; Greek geometry, so brilliant an intellectual achievement, took no hold whatever. Algebra was the special Indian invention. The prime Greek contribution to mathematical thought, rigorous proof of theorems from clear-cut hypotheses, passed unnoticed in India. Indian influence upon immigrant Greeks has already been discussed. The diminishing Greek kingdoms of the Panjāb were finally mopped up by the Śakas who pushed in from the west about 50 B.C. These barbarous intruders soon became civilised in the brahmin sense of the word, as noted from the case of Rudradāman. They occupied several trade ports on the western coast as well, branching out into small kingdoms with shifting boundaries.

The real cause of development of the west coast was the coconut. This coconut tree, which forms the basis of the whole coastal economy today, seems to be an import from Malaysia. It was being propagated on the east coast about the middle of the first century B.C. and reached the west coast a century later. By A.D. 120 the Śaka Ushavādata, son of Dinika and son-in-law of the reigning king (title, *khakharāta*) Nahapāna, began to give away whole plantations to brahmins, each one containing several thousand coconut trees. Ushavādata was generous to the Buddhists as well, but there were no cave monasteries on the coast within his reach. The coconut, now to be found in every Hindu ceremony and ritual, was rather poorly known in many parts of India before the sixth century A.D. This provides a useful comment upon 'timeless and immutable' Indian customs. The wood, fibre, wine, and other products of this tree are also of the utmost value; the nut itself provides 'meat' for cooking and when dried an excellent food oil, used also for soap-making. The western coastal strip (where the coconut can grow well because of heavy rainfall and hot climate) could not have been profitably cleared of its dense forest, let alone settled with its present crowded population, without this tree and the heavy commodity production based upon its exploitation in full. The trade up the few passes of the sheer Deccan scarp gave a longer lease of life to caravans; they took salt and coconuts up to the plateau to exchange against cloth and metal vessels, as well as the grain of the uplands.

The Kushānas held the north as a great imperial dynasty from A.D. 78 to the third century, then gradually declining till their extinction in the fourth by attacks from east and west. Because they ruled their Central Asian homelands as well as the Panjāb and Uttar Pradesh, the old *uttarāpatha* trade with its extension into the Asian heartland was revived; therewith went Buddhist doctrine and Indian culture. The founder of the dynasty, Kanishka I, seems to have issued coins only under the magnificent style and title 'Great Saviour', *soter megas* or *mahā-trātā*, without a personal name. The Kanishka of the gold coins was probably a grandson of this first. The founder had been a tribal chief, deified in Vedic and Iranian style by the Surkh-Kotāl inscription. The successors patronised all religions in the grand Asokan manner, building the greatest known *stūpas*. Their coins are marked variously with the Buddha, with Śiva and his sacred bull, with the name of the mother goddess Nanaia (Chinese, Nai-Nai). Kushāna mints knew and used Alexandrian technique, familiar at that time to the Roman emperors, who seem to have employed designers from the same metropolis. The progressive disappearance of silver coins shows that northern trade was increasingly in the costliest luxuries such as silk, saffron, jewels, wines, and other articles for the great nobles. The peasants had to manage locally by barter. The *Arthaśāstra* mode of production and the state monopoly of metal had unquestionably been abandoned. For that matter, Śunga coinage was trifling and miserable in appearance as compared with the magnificent portrait coins of the Indo-Greeks. The period of punch-marked coins had passed in the north after the Mauryans, though the old coins circulated along with newer die-struck or cast currency. That Rudradāman, Nahapāna and their successors struck many silver coins shows the difference between a rich northern empire where the commodity exchange was mainly in luxuries and a newly emerging society in the south and west where trade and manufacture was also in more essential goods. It is not easy to imagine second-century blacksmiths and fishermen in the north rich enough to make important donations to monasteries, as so many of them did in the south.

The Sātavāhanas, of whom a good deal has already been said in passing, rose from chiefs of the obscure 'Horse People' of Bāvari's day to be kings over a four-caste society in brahmin style. Their origin was traced in later ages to a brahmin widow ravished by a 'Nāga' at a pool of the Godāvari river 'in days when Paithan was a hamlet'. It should be understood that though copper and iron were in great demand in the peninsula, the Sātavā-hanas also gained from long-distance luxury trade, here with the Roman Empire. Mediterranean coral was also prized by Indians, as Indian chalce-dony and agates were in the west. Lead, copper and silver, wines and slaves for household service, concubinage and entertainment, the art and crafts-manship of the Romano-Greek world had an Indian demand shown both by documents and archaeology. Indian cloth, spices, ivory, and leather goods were exported in exchange. Finance and working capital necessary for the rapid growth of guilds and of new settlements came from the (traders and) monasteries, as noted earlier. The Deccan had had large groups of neolithic pastoralists, mostly cattlemen, boolying up and down the river valleys. Their memory and prehistoric megaliths still persist, along with an occasional cult spot that can be traced back to their time. Agriculture needed only knowledge of the heavy plough and of iron-working, both originally supplied from the north. But the fertile black soil, so famous for the cotton grown on it, is gathered in relatively small pockets, not capable of bearing a continuous settlement as in the alluvial northern river basins. So we first hear of the *gulma* army company used as a police unit by itself in Sātavāhana inscriptions. It meant that the powerful stand-ing army, without which resistance to any well-organised invader was not possible, would decline in the absence of joint large-scale drill and combined manoeuvres. But it was cheaper to maintain the armed forces as small units scattered over the land, another stimulus to later feudalism. Prakrit literature developed its finest output under the Sātavāhanas, whose rule faded away in the third century. Most of the works are now lost; some, like 'The Ocean of Story' (*Kathā-sarit-sāgara*) remain only in Sanskrit metrical versions. The anthology *sattasai* of 700 verses ascribed to the Sātavāhana king, Hāla (but actually with many later additions), shows grace and charm, though of a genre character. This was the period when small towns manufactured the bulk of trade goods in the Deccan through craftsmen's guilds and built up some sort of a civic culture. The tradition is represented by the 'man about town' (*nāgaraka*) of the *Kāmasūtra* of Vātsyāyana. This book, written during or just after the Sātavāhana period as the last of a long tradition, is deliberately modelled upon the *Arthaśāstra*. The subject, however, is the science of sex, not that of the state. All aspects of sex life are treated frankly and scientifically: social, individual, physical, psychological, the family and modes of voluptuous enjoyment; yet the book is not pornography nor comparable to the salacious Alexandrian treatises on aberrant sexual practices which were then so fashionable in the Mediterranean region. The art of love in the *Kāmasutra* is by no means on the Chateaubriand plane of ideal pining; but for all its frank sensuality, there is a certain naïve simplicity about it characteristic of the time and country. The *nāgaraka* who visited the countryside for a while was advised to set up clubs among his country cousins for cultured conversation, refined story-telling, graceful actions, music and song, dance and drink along with the full range of love-making in a civilised manner. The love life of the Sātavāhana court is also referred to in some passing examples. Finally, the patron *yaksha* of Paithan, known well before the fourth century A.D. as Khandaka, became the local Śiva. His cult had spread all over Mahārāshtra under the original name Khandobā, with centre at Jejuri and a powerful following among all castes. The special ministrants, male and female, still manifest the frenzied primitive nature of the original worship. Of course, brahmin priests skim off the main profit, as would be expected of so paying a religious proposition.

The east coast and the extreme south also developed greatly during the Sātavāhana period, though the latter region was never under their rule. The great Buddhist centres at Nāgārjunakondā by the mouth of the Godāvari river, and at Kāñci, were founded before the second century; both show the same process at work as elsewhere in the period, namely inland and overseas trade with civic development under the stimulus of large monastic foundations that accumulated as well as supplied capital.

Happy hunting for professional historians is provided by the list of southern dynasties: Ikshvākus, Pallavas, Bānas, Kadambas, Cedis, Kalachuris, Cālukyas, Colas, Pāndyas, Ceras and many other kings make a nice but generally meaningless list. The details may be studied in books on medieval Indian history, which generally neglect to point out the mutual acculturation. The 'higher' brahmin culture was imposed upon or adopted by tribesmen while primitive elements were reciprocally absorbed by the brahmins.

Between the last Sātavāhanas and the first Guptas (fourth century A.D.) lies an interlude of small invasions and aboriginal chiefs trying their hand at kingship. Among these last were several Nāgas of the Gangetic plain and also of the wilderness that reached down the centre of India towards the Deccan. Some Bhils had made their try, to be slaughtered about 57 B.C. by the Śakas invited by the Jain *acārya* Kālaka, whose sister had been violated by a Gardabhila king. Numerous small kingdoms constantly at war had sprung up over the greater part of the country, though there was still plenty of forest and undeveloped land. Society remained predominantly agrarian in a generally disturbed land.

The first two Guptas, Śrigupta and Ghatotkaca, are mere names, known only through respectful mention by the real founder of the line, Candragupta I (A.D. 320–35), son of Ghatotkaca. The names of the rest of the dynasty end in *-gupta*, whence the names 'Gupta kings'; the dynasty could claim no respectable ancestry and apparently not even a high tribal origin. Each king assumed numerous other subsidiary titles at will, which complicates the historian's task. The marriage of Candragupta I to Kumāradevi of the Licchavis was a great step in securing recognition for a line that had no clan basis like the Mauryans and whose origins always remained obscure. Coins were struck in the joint names of this king and queen, while the son of the union does not fail to brag about his mother's lineage. Candragupta I consolidated, as far as can be conjectured, the new dynasty's hold over Kosala and part of Magadha. The final conquest came under his son Samudragupta (*c.* A.D. 335–75), who boasts of having subjugated the whole land. His (posthumous) panegyric carved on an Asokan pillar shifted from Kosambi to Allahabad fort makes a powerful contrast in language, style, and content with the adjacent simple words of the great Mauryan. The *prasasti* in high Sanskrit with ornate, long compounds is purely an announcement of triumphs. King after king is named as exterminated, vanquished in battle, or suing for friendship. There had been no other Indian kings in Asoka's day worth the title. The clearing out of these new and petty or old and decaying kingdoms by Samudragupta meant peace and prosperity for the country. The accumulated surplus looted from the numerous defeated princelings helped maintain a luxurious but cultured court and powerful army for a long time, yet with the quite low taxes commented upon by Chinese pilgrims and attested by the copper-plate charters of these Gupta kings. However, the significant military achievement has been lost to sight in the roll of victories. Samudragupta exterminated nine Nāga kings in Āryāvarta proper and 'reduced all kings of forest tribes to servitude'.

The jungle kings are not important enough to be named individually like the Nāga rulers, but obviously represent an earlier stage of the same phenomenon. The innumerable forest chiefs were strengthened by the intrusion of small-scale agriculture to become raiders upon older settle-ments on a scale which might be petty in each case, but was a major nuisance in the aggregate, seeing the extent of the mischief. Samudragupta cleared the Gangetic heartland of this last obstacle to peaceful food produc-tion. Forest tribes of various kinds, more or less advanced towards food production and kinship, remained in marginal regions: Nepal, Assam, and the central Indian jungle. The move begun in sixth-century Magadha, carried on as land-clearing by the *Arthaśāstra* state and left incomplete by Asoka's 'emissaries of the *dhamma*' to the *ātavika* chieftains, was thus completed by force at the end of the fourth century. The *ātavika* problem could be ignored after the Guptas. Candragupta II (A.D. 379–414; styled Vikramāditya and the subject of many legends), married a Nāga princess, Kuberanāgā, not to mention other queens including his brother's widow, Dhruvasvāmini, rather romantically rescued and won. This was the king in whose reign Fa Hian visited India to find a land completely at peace and prosperous beyond words. The daughter of Kuberanāgā and Candra-gupta II was given to the Vākātaka king of the Deccan and reigned as the regent during her son's minority. Thus most of India and freshly won territories extending into Assam, Afghanistān, and possibly towards central Asia were then part of the Gupta empire or within their sphere of influence, while Bengal was really opened up for the first time. Patnā was still a good-sized city, though the Asokan palace lay in ruins.

(The process of decay was so long and gradual that a book like the present could be terminated at any date after Harsha. Harsha's was the last great personally administered empire without a feudal basis reaching down to the villages. The first Islamic raid under Muhammad ibn al-Kāsim [A.D. 712] penetrated as far as Multān, and receded; but the Arabs soon made a permanent occupation of Sind, which joined their advance along the Makrān coast, thus restoring the ancient Indus trade route. As the best sailors and most enterprising traders of the day, many Muslims held the official position of port-master or the equivalent under Hindu kings, as happened at Goa, Sanjān, and other places on the west coast. Their small trade colonies stretched as far as Canton within a century of the Prophet's death and had their religious rights carefully protected by local rulers—a compliment that was decidedly not to be returned. Iconoclasm was the great excuse for the serious raids that began with Mahmūd Ghaznavi. In a series of incursions that lasted till A.D. 1025 he looted and destroyed the finest temples of the north, including those at Mathurā and Banāras, and the incredibly rich shrine of Somanāth in Kathiāwād. The spoils formed the great attraction for all invaders after him, while clear and accurate accounts of India written by many Arabic scholars—none greater than Al-Birūni [A.D. 1031]—were an excellent guidebook. The permanent occupation of the north came with the conquest of Muhammad Ghūri, whose armies overran both the great northern river basins by A.D. 1205. The agents he left behind to administer the land from the strategic headquarters of Delhi soon became independent and set up their own Muslim dynasties, beginning as the emperor's slaves but allowing the ablest slave generals to rise to the throne. The looting of the Deccan began with Alā'-ud-din Khalji nearly a hundred years later, to be completed by his general, Malik Kāfūr, by A.D. 1312. A viceregal agent, the Nizām-ul-Mulk, remained in the Deccan, but again the Muslim empires regularly fell apart into provincial kingdoms with their own feudal administrations.)

This was no longer the *Arthaśāstra* type of empire, nor was it necessary to take special aid from religion as Asoka did. The religions already existed in great force; the Guptas supported them all generously as a matter of course. The final adoption of the Sanskrit language for inscriptions marks a broad, well-developed upper class allied to the brahmin priesthood, but on the best of terms with the Buddhists as well. However, the most significant move which accounted at once for initial Gupta prosperity and later decline lay at the village level. In the first place, peace and the reduction of forest chiefs meant a sudden spurt in village settlement, this time by private enterprise. Traders profited from the increased production, as the crown did from augmented revenue; but the towns and cities could not meet the new demand for village essentials. Guilds still flourished, from silk-weavers to oilmen; but it was impossible for guilds to supply all village needs regularly with any profit for themselves. The transport problem would be insoluble for centralised production on any large scale. The progressive lack of silver coinage has already been pointed out. This mainstay of the market in utility goods was no longer necessary, while the gold coins show that trade in luxury articles still flourished. No hoards and few specimens of silver coins struck in the Gupta period have been found. Asoka had managed on an inflated silver currency; Śakas and Sātavāhanas on smaller bits of silver, and the latter at times on pewter or billon coins. But obviously the total amount of coin in circulation was not sufficient to support commodity production on a scale consonant with the increased population and growth of new village settlements, such as we should have expected with the *Arthaśāstra* economy, for example. It is known that officials were paid by income from fixed plots of land, though not in hereditary feudal grants as yet. Corvée labour was exacted for public works, but paid for and not taken in lieu of taxes from the poorest classes as it would be in feudalism proper. The system bore the seeds of feudalism, but was not feudal till the end of the sixth century. The main problem was of servicing the village to make it self-contained without commodity production and cash payments beyond the absolute minimum.

This problem was solved by the system of village artisans. Each village of any size now had its blacksmith, carpenter, potter, priest, skinner of dead cattle, tanner, barber and so on. Later, the number of these 'village artisans' (*nāru-kāru*) was fixed at twelve. Each of them was assigned a plot of land to till in his spare time, or by the labour of other members of his own family. In addition, each was to receive a small share (Marāthī, *balutem*) of the harvest from every *kutumbina* peasant cultivator family. The village of this period administered its own land and internal affairs by *sabhā* council. There was still plenty of wasteland, the permanent assignment of which needed royal or later feudal-baronial sanction. The village artisans were thus an integral part of the village system, not people who moved about freely to dispose of their services; at the same time, if their payment did not suffice, they could always set up on their own as cultivators, so that there was a fair balance between technical needs and payment fixed by tradition. Though members of several different castes, none of which could be the main local peasant sub-caste of cultivators and plot-holders, the artisans showed remarkable solidarity among themselves as a group. Their duties were fixed by custom: e.g. making and maintenance of the ploughs, axes, and digging tools, supply of a fixed number of pots per family per year, etc. Additional work was generally paid for either by extra grain or by special invitation to feasts at ceremonies like weddings, processions, funerals and the like with which the extra work was connected. The village community thereafter became a tight, viable, closed unit. Even during the worst days of Muslim feudal oppression the village would protect itself by the last desperate action, namely desertion *en masse*. This, of course, implied the availability of fresh land somewhere else for settlement, and hence is not possible today. In addition, there was the protection afforded by the caste system, whereby other members of the caste in other villages were obliged to help their fellows in distress. The worst features of caste were developed by village life, but that there was such a major

195

compensating factor which preserved the institution of caste must also be remembered.

It is obvious that the guilds would break up as soon as this type of village production became the norm. Plots for the village carpenter, etc., are first mentioned in Gupta charters. The contribution of the Gupta period was therefore double-edged: immediately, very profitable for all; eventually, fatal to the advance of a powerful and cultured society. The insularity of the village was to be unshakable hereafter. The peasant would witness the ruin of empires with equanimity while concentrating upon his increasingly miserable patch of land. Salt and metals, brought in by poor caravaneers on barter, never constituted enough exchange with the outside world to raise the level of village culture. Only the occasional fair or pilgrimage relieved isolation to a trifling extent. The cities declined rapidly, Patnā becoming a village by A.D. 600; the royal court and camp amounted to a moving capital.

These changes were reflected in medieval temple-building, in the emergence of a number of dynamic regional schools of sculptural architecture. These monuments were usually built at the focal centres of political power and reflect, on the one hand, courtly ambition, and on the other, the popular-cult basis of medieval Hinduism. The larger shrines profited by royal land grants, gifts from worshippers, sale of charms and indulgences, fees for the remission of sins, ceremonies for peace to ancestral souls. Worst of all were the substantial profits from temple dancing-girl prostitution. Most of the cash was locked up in precious images or jewels for the gods; or just pocketed by the priesthood and their parasites (some of whom were moneylenders and merchants not publicly accountable for the temple funds in their possession); the temple buildings would often be allowed to fall into decay. No Hindu temple approached the Buddhist monastery as centre of learning. The feudal court might attract scholars from all over the country during a particularly generous reign, but there was neither certainty nor continuity. The gathering of talent would vanish with the death of the patron, as, for instance, with King Bhoja of Dhāra, or Harsha of Kanauj. Sacred places like Banāras contained a few individuals unconnected with temple or court, each of whom took a handful of poor but intelligent disciples to keep alive some of India's intellectual heritage. The average village brahmin rarely went out to learn anything, though he continued to enjoy rights, privileges, and immunities granted to his pioneer ancestors. Some villages could dispense with the brahmin altogether, for the village cults could be served by non-brahmin *gūrav* priests under the same terms; ritual was sometimes performed by others than brahmins for most of the lower castes; but the calendar, forecasting lunar dates of observances and the like, implied a minimum literacy, not possessed except by the trained brahmin or the Kāyastha official.

The village originally held all food-producing land in common. Plots were assigned to settlers according to the need and manpower of each family, by decision of the village council. Land was of no value in itself as property of the individual at that stage; sale of land for cash is known to have been rare, and whenever it took place, as at Nasik, where Ushavadāta paid 4,000 pieces of silver to a brahmin to transfer a field to the use of the Buddhist monastery, it implies rich trade in the neighbourhood. Inasmuch as the main body of settlers was formed of one or two *sajāta* kinship groups as a rule, membership of the group and tenure of land went together. Expulsion from the community meant simultaneous loss of caste and of the right to till land in the village, hence exile, which was about the heaviest punishment the village could inflict upon refractory members. All armed force was wielded by royal officials or later by local barons; the village (though liable for compensation to any stranger who suffered loss because of robbery committed within the village boundaries) had little force at its disposal. Royal grants specifically mention 'Not even to be pointed at, let alone entered by any king's official' as a special privilege, a superlative boon to the village people and to the grantee of the village revenues. The officials themselves acquired new titles with the move to feudalism: *sāmanta* (which originally meant neighbour, neighbouring king, now also 'baron'), *thakkura*, *rānaka*, *rāüta*, and so on. The local variation was unlimited in form, but the substance was much the same. The main baronial task, camouflaged by the attempted preservation of older custom, was to collect the revenue in kind, and pass on a portion, converted into cash, to the state (king). In addition, the baron was supposed to serve in the regular army at need, with a statutory number of armed followers, including horsemen, equipped at his own expense. Inevitably, the assignment of wasteland on fee became a royal or feudal privilege and led at times to the creation of two classes of peasant-farmers in the village, the older 'permanent' settlers who paid a regular tax whether they cultivated the land or not, and the 'late comers' who might work on their assigned fields without right to vote in the village council, but paid only a share of the actual yield. The baron might add value to the land by undertaking works beyond the means of a single village, e.g. dams, canals, etc.; the villages concerned naturally had to pay him more taxes. Eventually, fields were assigned within the village to a special class of retainers on condition of personal military service by the holder or his heir: feudal tenure in its ultimate form. The merchants and manufactures under their investment were concentrated in a few special centres and port towns. The vanished guilds were replaced at need by much looser *goshthi* associations for restricted purposes; as for example the construction of a temple for which a single *goshthi* could include people such as the viscount, the merchant, the peasant, and the temple dancing-girl prostitute. Merchants' associations regulated competition and received special charters from the king guaranteeing them and their artisans immunities from interference by the feudal lords and minor officials.

7.4. Sanskrit Literature and Drama

Something remains to be said about culture in the formal sense. It would be difficult to treat of Indian music, which has an uninterrupted tradition from the oldest times but no reliable history. It has always been chamber music for the finest ear, with the octave divided into twenty-two notes. Indian music has well-defined modes with delicate melody and rhythm, but no accent, and neither harmony nor counterpoint as in Western compositions. While Samudragupta is portrayed on some of his coins with a lyre, nothing is known of the tunes of the fourth century. For that matter, playing upon the bamboo flute was a speciality of the Śabara jungle-dwellers, who presumably invented the flute itself. Dances performed by specialist professionals before the gods, or for major festivals, and sometimes at weddings or other family ceremonies, were adopted from tribesmen, as has been noted for the *gondhal*, of Gond origin. The visual arts, easier to appreciate, require a large number of illustrations. Sculpture and architecture have been badly served by the rather poor archaeological record now available. The destructive climate, vandalism and negligence have wiped out most of the painting. These arts were secondary to religion or to court ostentation. Craftsmanship was duly prized, without giving any Indian artist the prestige and social standing of a Pheidias or Michelangelo. The traditional Sanskrit books on architecture and iconography are contradicted by the specimens actually found. The writer of the book was generally a brahmin, the craftsman almost always came from a lower, unlettered caste, with the exception of a calligrapher or illuminator of manuscripts. Religious convention insisted upon primitive types of images, while patrons naturally wanted the gods, however ill proportioned, to be dressed and ornamented in their own human image, in the height of current fashion. Appreciation of Indian art for its own sake is a modern taste acquired by most Indians from foreigners—who had till recently despised that art as crude and uncivilised native workmanship.

There remains literature, preserved and still prized by Indians for its exquisite qualities. Nothing is known of Śiśunāga or Mauryan secular writing, if any then existed. Only Hāla's anthology survives of Sātavāhana production. Sanskrit literature has perforce to be discussed because writing in the various Indian languages really began after the period with which this book is concerned. Here we must always except whatever had been written in the Indus valley, which at present seems lost beyond recovery, except for the few, brief, undeciphered seal legends. I have also to leave old Tamil out of consideration. The drama, indeed, had primitive and cultic beginnings. Several Rigvedic hymns need a chorus or have to be acted out by two or more characters. The most famous example is the Urvaśi and Purūravas story. This appears as a staged dialogue in the oldest Veda, a dramatic substitute for what had originally been the sacrifice of the male in a fertility rite after a sacred ritual wedding (*hieros gamos*) with an *apsaras*. The Vedic Purūravas pleads in vain to be spared, while Urvaśi calmly rejects the plea. The theme gradually changed into a romance of separated lovers. Chants and dances are a regular feature of Sanskrit drama, as of primitive fertility rites. The obligatory *nāndi* prologue and benediction show that Indian stage performances originated in 'Mystery Plays'. There was always a musical accompaniment for verses set into prose dialogues to be sung in the manner of an operetta. The dance also remained, though not always included in the extant stage directions. In addition to group dances, individual characters had to mime various sentiments according to conventions which enabled them to tell the story almost without a word being spoken, as in the modern *Kathākali*. The very word *nātya* for 'drama' also signifies the miming dance. The normal play meant an all-night performance, though theatre caves for possible daylight use have been found.

Such auxiliary entertainment with themes often drawn from the great epics attracted audiences that need not have understood the Sanskrit of the upper classes for and by whom the plays were written. Leading male characters of the dramas speak polished Sanskrit, the women and servants only Prakrit. This was originally taken from life. Even now, in out-of-the-way places, the speech of cultured men differs materially from that of their generally uneducated womenfolk and of the men of the lower orders. However, the aristocrats at home would have to address the more ignorant members of the household in Prakrit, whereas they never condescend to the vulgar tongue in the plays. Later use of dialect on the stage became pure convention. Fewer people understood the dead Prakrit—dead because of rapidly changing spoken languages—than understood Sanskrit. Rājaśe-khara in the ninth century obviously wrote the lesser parts in Sanskrit and translated them into Prakrit according to set formulas; convention had become much stronger than invention.

Though this method of construction excludes the purely metrical drama, the obligatory songs meant that the playwright had also to be a poet. The 'cultivated' dramas never completely replaced primitive play-acting; which may be seen to this day at country fairs as song-and-dance or *tamāsā* performances presented by wandering low-caste minstrels of the sort once excluded by the *Arthaśāstra* from crown villages. The first known refined plays were presented by the Buddhist monasteries on specific anniversaries. They are attested by central Asian manuscript fragments and by Chinese pilgrims' reports. The secular life and conversion to the faith of a hero such as Sāriputta, Moggallāna, Kassapa, or the great renunciation by the Buddha himself were presented on the stage to large audiences. The first eminent Sanskrit playwright and poet known is, accordingly, the Buddhist Aśvaghosa who set the norm for later dramatists and versifiers. His poem *Saundara-nanda* on the ordination of the Buddha's half-brother and death by heartbreak of his beautiful wife gives full treatment of the princely splendours and frank love-making that all monks had to renounce. Indeed, the theme must have supplied motives for other forms of Buddhist art, as it survives in a magnificent fresco at Ajantā. Another such poem, 'The Life of the Buddha', has been added to by various hands, so that the Chinese translation does not entirely tally with the Sanskrit text; but the core is of Aśvaghosha's composition. His plays are lost (except the fragments of a *śāriputra-prakarana*), but stanzas given in his name by anthologies may have been declaimed on the stage as part of some play by him. In fact, with many later poet-dramatists like Vallana of the Pāla period, nothing survives except such vestigial stanzas culled from their lost dramas. Buddhist or not, the plays took on the colour and tone of the class for which they were composed. Erotic themes (*śringāra*) remained a main feature. Indian literary conventions about love were quite uninhibited. The Buddhist Sanskrit plays are as incongruous in their own way as the sumptuous paintings and voluptuous decorative sculpture of the celibate Buddhists' abbeys. The life of a court verging towards feudalism was reflected as far as tradition and stage conventions would allow.

Bhāsa, remembered only as an honoured name, was resurrected early in this century with some plays discovered in Kerala. The later stylised forms and conventions are not followed, so that controversy still rages about their authenticity; but the genius of the playwright is not in doubt. The finest is undoubtedly the 'Dream of Vāsavadattā' (*svapna-vāsavadattam*), drawn from the ancient Udayana cycle of romance. Queen Vāsavadattā is persuaded by the high minister to have it announced that she has perished in a conflagration, so that the devoted king could be led to make another politically advantageous marriage which he would otherwise have refused. The king continues to dream of his lost love, who is actually serving disguised as a maid in the inner apartments. In some poignant, unforgettable passages, she mingles in the king's half-waking dreams without daring to wake him fully. Polygamous society made the ultimate happy ending possible.

The greatest name in all Sanskrit and perhaps all Indian literature is of Kālidāsa. Nothing whatever is known of his biography, but he came after Bhāsa and could only have written for the Gupta court, probably of Candragupta II (Vikramāditya) of Ujjain. Of his poems, the graceful 'Cloud Messenger' carried an exiled Yaksha's love-message to his distant pining lady. The whole Indian landscape that the cloud must traverse is beautifully delineated. 'The Lineage of Raghu' gives Rāma's ancestry and may refer indirectly to some Gupta conquests. The incomplete *Kumāra-sambhava* tells of the birth of Skanda as a child to Śiva and Pārvatī, born to destroy a demon who troubled gods and men. These three poems rank at the summit of Sanskrit poetry by their metrical and verbal perfection. The themes are brahminical, drawn from epic and *Purāna*. So also are the plots of Kālidāsa's dramas, except the 'Mālavikā and Agnimitra' based on Śunga history, and connected with the Gupta court through Ujjain. The Urvaśi-Purūravas story is transformed into the ultimate romance between mortal king and immortal nymph, as 'Vikrama and Urvaśi'. The title may allude to the reigning Gupta king; the Purūravas of the play deals upon equal terms with Indra, ruler of the heavens. The supreme achievement, both in literature and stagecraft, is acknowledged to be the 'Recognition of Śakuntalā', where the theme is the union of King Duhshyanta with a half-apsaras Śakuntalā. The story is taken from the *Mahābhārata* epic, but the handling of the love scenes is strikingly original. The hero (distracted by a curse) is unable to remember the heroine who suddenly appears at court with a son she claims to have borne him. Kālidāsa plays upon human senti-ment and emotion with unequalled power. Second only to Kālidāsa was Bhavabhūti, whose 'Later Life of Rāma' is again a drama drawn from the epic. His 'Mālati and Mādhava' deals with lovers who have to undergo the deadliest of trials, including the possibility of being offered up as human sacrifice; the staging must have shaken the audience beyond measure. Bhavabhūti was a brahmin and a poet of rank, belonging presumably to the first half of the eighth century. As usual, little is known of his actual life and career. Many other poets and dramatists are known by even less, just the name or an occasional stanza that remains in an anthology, or some casual fragment culled from a worm-eaten manuscript. Māgha, Bhāravi, and other poets are more fortunate in being represented by some complete works, still read with pleasure. The *Jānakiharana* ('Abduction of Sita') by Kumāradāsa had to be restored from a literal Ceylonese translation, later confirmed by south Indian manuscripts. The few names mentioned here in passing were by no means the only authors of note. The Emperor Harsha, whose writing of and acting in the play *Nāgānanda* has been mentioned earlier, composed other dramas of which two still exist. The tradition worked vigorously even in the late ninth and early tenth century with Rājaśekhara, himself a wealthy feudal landholder and patron of many poets; he wrote rather artificial dramas, polished verses, and considerable works on poetics. The grand manner declined after him, but did not by any means vanish; kings and princes not only patronised poets but tried their own hand at versification for some centuries to come. Many poets of the Pāla court are known by name, some of them Pāla princes. King Bhoja of Dhāra was both patron and writer of merit. The Gāhadavālas in the twelfth century supported a good poet Śri-Harsha, not to be confused with the emperor; his poem on the Nala-Damayanti romance is as fine a work of its sort as any. The last considerable northern centre of Sanskrit literature and drama was at the court of King Lakshmanasena of Bengal, whose kingdom was mostly overrun by the Muslims by A.D. 1200. The decay is clear and palpable even before the Islamic conquest.

One play remains in a class by itself, 'The Little Clay Cart' (*Mricchakatika*) of Śūdraka. The author is supposed to have been of royal lineage, connected in some way with the Sātavāhanas; but as usual nothing is actually known of him. The play closely follows and extends a fragment ascribed to Bhāsa, but flouts convention by ignoring court life and epic incidents in its choice of theme. The hero Cārudatta is a brahmin caravan merchant fallen upon hard times. The heroine is a wealthy, beautiful, accomplished and cultured courtesan Vasantsenā, pursued unsuccessfully by the king's ill-bred brother-in-law Śakāra, who is also the local governor. This boorish villain, foiled several times, finally strangles the heroine and leaves her for dead, but accuses the hero of her murder. There is a secondary love story and a revolution led by a popular rebel who succeeds just in time. The heroine is revived and the hero rescued from the execution block. The Prakrit spoken by various characters has provincial variations that seem to be modelled upon life. Except for a needlessly prolonged descriptive passage about the magnificence of Vasantasenā's establishment, the play preserves all the unities, balances emotion with action, relieves pathos with humour, gives scope for good acting and presentation, yet reads very well. It is one of the two works that anyone wanting to enjoy the characteristic flavour of ancient Indian literature (without too many long explanatory footnotes) should read in any available translation.

The other book recommended is in prose: 'The Ten Princes', left incomplete by the author Dandin and supplemented by at least two other pens. For verve, gusto, knowledge of all strata of society, full range of picaresque and romantic adventure, controlled exuberance and delicate irony, there is no other Sanskrit work that will stand comparison. Dandin was a southerner, best placed in the early seventh century A.D.; a poet and literary critic of ability, as well as master of prose and one of the really well-read men of his day. The one trouble with his prose is due precisely to his absolute command of Sanskrit, which led him into untranslatable play upon words. This immediately became a disease with lesser writers, the parallel of Indian painting and sculpture where technique and craftsmanship destroyed art. The weakness was inherent in the very structure and development of the language. As Patañjali said, 'Words are eternal. One may go to a potter and order a particular type of vessel; no one goes to a grammarian to say, "Make me such and such a word".' The term *padārtha* for a 'material object' signifies 'word-meaning'. Idealism is built into the language, and if new words could not be made, the writers never denied themselves the exhilaration of putting old ones together in endless combinations with new meanings. The *Brāhmanas* and *Upanishads* use many childish etymologies to extract some convenient new meaning out of old ritual terms. The theologians took the next step of making the whole external world unreal, to entangle themselves in abstruse theories of word-meaning. With the writers, the trick was to get several different meanings out of the same long compound, which could be factored in more than one way, Sanskrit being what it is. It needed infinite leisure to indite or to read such compositions; but by the end of the twelfth century this fashion had reduced a good deal of Sanskrit writing to the intellectual level of a crossword puzzle. The style was set by another great writer, Bāna, whose *Kādambari* has compound words that go at times to several lines each in printed editions. But his skill was such that the very name of the book, actually the name of its heroine, has now come to mean a 'novel' or 'romance' in Indian languages. Bāna was one of the Emperor Harsha's court poets. His 'Life of Harsha' is a masterpiece of Sanskrit prose. A romantic biography of little use for accurate historical or physical detail, it contains priceless descriptions, as of the misery, panic, and havoc caused by the devastating march of a friendly army through its own territory. The earlier *Vāsavadattā* of Subandhu might have led to something like the *Arabian Nights* story-teller's tradition, but the *Kādambari* killed Sanskrit prose effectively as a literary medium.

The 'Ocean of Story' (*Kathā-sarit-sāgara*) has its roots in the pre-Mauryan stories formed around the dashing and gallant King Udayana of Kauśāmbi. A massive collection of stories from this cycle made in the Paiśāchi ('of the goblins') language by one Gunādhya was acknowledged by later writers as their inspiration; being now completely lost, the existence of the author and the collection is sometimes contested. The versions

203

of Budhasvāmin and Kshemendra are the veriest doggerel; that of the Jain Somadeva (c. A.D. 1075) of a somewhat higher literary quality, though by no means great poetry. The content shows that the stories were written to please merchants and artisans as well as men of the higher castes. The mark of the Prakrit and of Sātavāhana's *nāgaraka*-burgher taste is unmistakable as contrasted with the courtly Gupta style. Dandin and Bana drew inspiration from this story collection, which combines natural and supernatural in typical Indian style. The stories which form the best-known Indian contribution to world literature, however, are in the collection *Pañcatantra*, a set of fables in the style of Aesop compiled for the edification of princes who could not be troubled to go through a course of literacy. The influence of the *Arthaśāstra* is clear; the supposed narrator Vishnuśarman must be modelled after Cānakya, who bore the same personal name. This collection reached the west through Syriac and Arabic translations (*Kalīla o Dimna*) as the fables of Pilpai.

The literary lamp flared up magnificently just before going out. The last supreme effort is Jayadeva's *Gita-Govinda*, a musical poem in dramatic form about the mystical union of Krishna with his inner love Rādhā. The original lascivious myth and legend is sublimated, though the reader may find the text erotic enough. The music that pervades the poetry raises Jayadeva's great work above all others on similar themes. But then Jayadeva had had an entirely different career from the other Sena court poets whom he joined in later life, about A.D. 1200. As a brilliant but poor brahmin youth, he romantically wooed and won a beautiful girl of his own caste. Together they wandered through the countryside as minstrels. She danced to the accompaniment of his songs, composed in country language and set to his own tunes. Some of his vernacular poems and musical modes have survived. The *Gita-Govinda* might even have been drafted in the common idiom before being transferred to Sanskrit for the court. In addition, Jayadeva presaged the dawn of Vaishnava reform. This reformation appears in the guise of a bitter theological controversy between the *smārta* followers of Śiva and Pārvati as against the Vaishnavas, who worshipped Vishnu-Nārāyana in some form. In Bengal the great Vaishnava name is that of Caitanya (1486-1527). The movement came to a head much earlier in the south, with Rāmānuja (twelfth century) as against the Śaiva followers of Śamkara. The quarrel led to the breaking of heads and lasted till late into the nineteenth century. How little religion really had to do with the heart of the matter is obvious from one simple fact. Both sides ignored and even served faithfully the Muslims who had conquered Bengal, the very invaders who smashed up the images of all sects and slaughtered sacred cattle, whether two-legged or four-legged, to trample rough-shod over all brahmin

FIG. 16. Hari-Hara, combined deity with the attributes of Śiva for the right half-body, and Vishnu for the left. From a modern bazaar chromo lithograph, used by devotees in place of the costlier images of metal or stone. The cult was prominent from the ninth century onwards, but failed to reconcile the growing antagonism between two different classes of larger and smaller landholders, which appeared as the theological quarrel between the worshippers of Śiva and Vishnu.

convention. The real underlying struggle is known to have been between the great feudal landlords who worshipped Śiva and his consort goddess, as against the smaller but more enterprising entrepreneurs who opted for Krishna or Vishnu-Nārāyana. A brief move to combine the two deities into one as Hari-Hara failed, though the much earlier hermaphroditic combination of Śiva with Pārvati and the marriages of the gods to mother goddesses had succeeded, as did the incarnation method of gathering many cults into one. The reason was that the earlier religious fusion meant a more productive society, as for example of pastoral and food-gathering elements that went on together to food production. Now there was not enough to go around; combined cults led to no ultimate, substantial increase in production. Hence the acrid controversy. But when the new form of Vaishnava life was first made known the simple people of entire villages would dance in joy, often going to the next village to communicate their exhilaration—a miraculous ferment in the otherwise deaf and passive units of Indian rustic life. That the villagers at Jayadeva's birthplace Kenduli still celebrate his anniversary with song, music, and dance is due to other causes than the exquisite poem which only the learned can understand. His appreciation of pure beauty was derived from first-hand knowledge of how sadly such beauty was needed in ordinary life.

Numerous anthologies mark the progressive drying up of the springs of originality in the century just before Jayadeva. The oldest known anthology of classical Sanskrit verse was compiled about A.D. 1100 by the titular *pandita* of some Buddhist monastery (probably Jagaddala) in or near the Rajšāhi district of east Pakistan; it had to be edited from manuscripts preserved only in Nepal and Tibet. The most characteristic of such collections passes under the name of Bhartrihari, who may have existed as a real person, an indigent poet of considerable ability. The new type of verse speaks of poverty and helplessness—of the brahmins, of course—in the face of caste and social convention which allowed no escape except through the parochial and overcrowded priesthood or the arbitrary and galling patronage of petty feudal princelings. The consciousness of talent withering away unused led to a new poetry of frustration, usually in terse epigrams. Thereto were added stanzas on lower-middle-class morality (*niti*) and some erotic verse which shows literary wallowing in luxuries well beyond the poet's reach. Lastly came the inevitable concomitant, a quite imaginary 'renunciation' in the distant future of the so-so life that the poet actually lived. Verses of Bhartrihari type are now used as handy platitudes by Indians with some classical education and unwillingness to work at the manual and mechanical trades.

The question naturally arises: Was there no Sanskrit literary work that gave form to the Indian character in the same way that Cervantes's *Don Quixote* set its stamp upon the Spanish literati? The one book that comes nearest to such a position is the *Bhagavad-Gitā*, 'Song of the Blessed Lord', called the *Gitā* for short. Though its composition can hardly have been possible before the end of the third century, the work is put into the mouth of Krishna and inserted into the greatly expanded *Mahābhārata* epic. Here Krishna appears as the divine exponent of a complete and rather intricate philosophico-religious doctrine; this was a new position for the god, the nearest to it being a solitary reference in the *Chāndogya Upanishad*, where a

Krishna 'son of Devaki' appears in passing as a human pupil of the seer Ghora Āngirasa, but nowhere as a teacher or all-god.

The basis of the *Gītā* develops as follows. The Pandu hero Arjuna felt revulsion at the impending slaughter of kinsmen and lay down his bow just as the two armies had begun their movement to join battle. His charioteer, none less than the dark hero of the Yadus (the Yadu tribe fought on the other side, curiously enough) successfully exhorts him to do his duty. The fratricidal advice is given in over 700 tightly woven stanzas whose quickest recitation would have taken, say, three hours, by which time the whole battle might easily have been lost. Krishna, now proclaiming himself the all-god, expounds every contemporary system of philosophy in turn as his own, without naming any of the numerous doctrines outlined in crystal-clear verse. Since all views come from the one god, there is no polemic, though Vedic *yajña* and ritual in general are slighted with a passing sneer. The pure life, non-violence, absence of greed and of self-seeking are extolled. When puzzled Arjuna naturally asks 'Why then do you ask me to kill?' the god neatly glides away to the next point of his exposition, leaving the direct question unanswered. At a critical moment the divine character reveals his true self, shows that he is the creator of all beings and their destroyer as well. He fills the whole universe, heaven, earth, and several underworlds; as all-destroyer, he has already devoured all members of both the mighty hosts about to fight. Arjuna would commit no sin in killing a kinsman dispassionately. So long as one has absolute faith in the absolute god, the ultimate gain of union with that god in life not of this world is assured to him. If Arjuna won the purely formal and symbolic battle, he would have the further joys of universal sovereignty in this world as a bonus.

This divine but rather scrambled message with its command of expository Sanskrit is characteristically Indian in attempting to reconcile the irreconcilable, in its power of gulping down sharp contradictions painlessly. The choice of all-god, dictated by his spreading personal cult, is as incongruous as if Herakles were to spout an abstract of the New Testament synthesised with all major Greek philosophical works as his own unitary doctrine. Krishna's philandering with the milkmaids, dalliance with mother goddesses, killing of his own uncle and invariably crooked advice in the *Mahābhārata* epic hardly inspire confidence in any morality he might preach. In fact, it took some time for the great work to catch on. Even in its own day it did not serve the main purpose of the brahmin redactors of the great epic. An insipid sequel called the *Anu-Gītā* was therefore read out in the same epic by the same god to Arjuna after the total victory. This merely praises brahmins and brahminism. No one bothers to read it now, whereas the first *Gita* eventually went on from strength to strength. The rather simple reason lies in the transformation of medieval society.

Hsiuan-tsang mentions a brahmin's forgery, written to incite a king to war against his own cousins. The context shows that this must have been the *Gita*, and that it was by no means considered the quintessence of brahminism that it became later. The first outstanding brahmin to use it was Śamkara (*c.* A.D. 800), whose comment is standard even now, though he was supposedly a follower of Śiva and though the *Gita* summarises a good deal of Buddhism quite efficiently in the mouth of Vishnu incarnate. The rival leader Rāmānuja later drew quite different inspiration from the same *Gita*. The book was brought down to the common people in a splendid Marāthi verse exposition by Jñāneśvara. Composed at the end of the thirteenth century, it occupies a position in Marāthi analogous to the contemporary but highly contrasted *Divina Commedia* in Italian. Even in modern times, Tilak and Gāndhi drew their own conclusions from the *Gita* about the spiritual foundations which they believed necessary for the Indian national liberation struggle. That so many different people could draw such varied guidance from the same document is due obviously to its containing so unbelievable a variety of divergent ideas. Its divine sanction made it the one orthodox book which could be used to reach conclusions disagreeable to orthodoxy. It kept alive some vestiges of the spirit of dissent in the age of superstition which it did so much to promote. But why should it gain authority at all when its beginnings remain so obscure? All puranic works are spoken by some god or other, some even by Krishna himself, but none other had the same force. Why?

The extraordinary success of the *Gita* was due to its new doctrine of *bhakti*, unflinching loyalty to a god whose rather questionable personal record was not allowed to stand in the way. This suited the feudal ideology perfectly. Loyalty links together in a powerful chain the serf and retainer to feudal lord, baron to duke to king. It is the ideological basis of feudal society, however uninspiring and deficient in character the actual human objects of their vassals' loyalty may have been. It was just this loyalty that lay at the base of feudalism which led to the strengthening of many primitive practices in a context that could no longer be called barbarous. Court nobles cut off their own flesh publicly to appease the evil spirits that were killing Harsha's father through some incurable disease. Gānga and Pallava nobles of the south would offer their own heads, cut off before some god or goddess, for their royal master's welfare; this is attested by numerous inscriptions and sculptures from the eighth century onwards. Many vassals proclaim their determination not to survive the overlord for a single moment. That they would actually leap into the flames which consumed their royal master's corpse is reported even by Marco Polo; the desperate act cannot be taken as an extension of the custom of *sati* which is recorded with increasing frequency among the ruling classes from the sixth century, and which can be traced back through Greek accounts to prehistory as the feudal nobles' actions cannot. Precisely with the dawn of the final stage of Indian feudalism do we get Śaṃkara and the promotion of the *Gītā* to the summit. The incongruities of the *Gītā* are entirely 'in the Indian character'; but the Indian character was not fully set in its familiar mould till the feudal period. When gunpowder had blown Arjuna's bow and later feudalism off the map, the Indian intellectual still turned instinctively to the *Gītā* to find some way of coping with patriotic needs in the new world of banks and shares, railroads, steamships, electricity, factories, and mills. The prestige of the book has waned as India comes to grips with her modern problems. The *Gītā* is honoured oftener than read, and understood far less than it is recited. After such mixed ideas are displaced by clear-cut thinking based on a firm grasp of material reality, the work may still furnish some aesthetic pleasure for its power of expression and peculiar beauty.

This final remark might even serve as epitaph to the whole of ancient Indian culture.

ADDITIONAL NOTE

Recent but still unpublished work by the department of history of the Aligarh Muslim University throws considerable light upon two most important points; the beginning of the iron age in India and Aryan expansion into the Gangetic basin. The excavations at Atranjikherā (in UP) under the direction of Prof. Nurul Hasan and R. C. Gaur yield a clear pottery sequence which fits in with B. B. Lal's work at Hastināpura. Iron first appears, if I have not misunderstood the explanations given me at Aligarh, with the painted grey ware in strata dated at 1000 B.C. or earlier by radio-carbon. Below lies black and red pottery, associated with a little copper, and preceded by a pre-metal layer of ochre-washed pottery. Underneath this lies the natural, undisturbed soil. One possible interpretation is that the ochre-washed ware, rather badly fired and deposited in a thick widespread layer which shows neither hearths nor floors, came from seasonal camps of pastoral boolies. The black-and-red ware lies over a more compact area, and indicates a more permanent type of settlement of people whose presence inhibited the earlier ware, which ceases abruptly without any large sterile intermediate deposit. The people of the second deposit may have affinities with similar types in northern Rājasthān; but the Aryans picked up their pottery technique wherever they went. The painted grey pottery should be called Pūru ware; its association with iron is remarkable. The new metal is found in substantial quantities, which indicates permanent land clearing and real agriculture. Moreover, the increase of the metal rapidly drove out the painted ware in favour of plain, utilitarian grey pottery. From this point, the progress into history is rapid, but extensive archaeology and publication of detailed reports must necessarily precede more definite conclusions. It may be mentioned that field surveys by the Aligarh team shows many other deposits in western UP (Etah district) with a similar structure so that the results presented here are not confined to one spot.

Index

This is not comprehensive, but added explanations may facilitate use as a glossary and simplify reference to other works. The letter *c* is pronounced as palatal *ch* in Romanised names and words: Candragupta for Chandragupta.

Bhāravi, Sanskrit poet, author of *Kirātārjunīya*, 201

Bhārhut, Buddhist monumental site, 16, 110, 179. *Illus.: sculpture, Plates 80, 81, 82*

Bhartrihari, Sanskrit poet and/or anthologist, 206

Bhāsa, early Sanskrit dramatist, 200–1

Bhavabhūti, Sanskrit dramatist and poet, after Kālidāsa, 201

bhikshu, 'almsman' (*see* monk); no longer had to beg for alms, 178

Bhīl, tribe, 14, 43; petty first century kings, 192. *Illus.: sisters married and unmarried, Plate 28; winnowing wheat, Plate 34; drawings on wall, Plate 35*

Bhilsā, (Vidiśā) trade centre, 112, 139; Heliodoros pillar at, 188

Bhīmā, Deccan river, 36, 39

Bhoganagar, station on *uttarāpatha* trade-route, 112

Bhoja, tribe, 116; king of Dhārā, prolific Sanskrit writer on many subjects, 167, 202, son or step-son of Nāga princess, 168; patron of learning, 196

Bhrigu, brahmin exogamous clan; etymologically, 'Phrygian' and on the wrong side in the Ten-Kings battle, 82; prominent in Mahābhārata redaction, 95

Bible, 60, 71; relatively greater historical value, 78

Bihār, (*see also* Magadha), 14, 15, 21, 50, 150, 168, 183; mineral wealth, 89, 90, 125, 140, 163; name derived from *vihāra* = Buddhist abbey, 180

Bimbisāra, sixth century B.C. Magadhan king, 102, 110, 120, 124, 127–9; low or obscure origin, 128

Bindusāra, second Mauryan emperor, son of Candragupta, father of Asoka, 139, 140, 148, 157, 158, 161. *Illus.: coinage, Fig. 14, p. 158*

bird-mask, terra-cotta figurines, 68

Bodhi, (Mahā-bodhi) Pipal tree under which the Buddha attained enlightenment, 110; cut down by Śaśānka, 180; restoration by Pūrnavarman, 187

Bolhāi, mother-goddess on prehistoric megalithic shrine, 48. *Illus.: Plate 42*

Bombay, (city), 7

booly ,(transhumance, seasonal movement of cattle and owners), 39, 42; of late vedic *grāma*, 88; in Deccan river-valleys, 190; in Krishna legend, 116; pottery deposits, 209

Borgia, Cesare, 126–7

bourgeoisie, modern Indian ruling class, 2, 3, 6–8; foreign, 2, 6, 7; effect upon tribal life, 44; 52, 127

bow, 43, 64; supremely powerful Indian weapon, 135, 171. *Illus.: Plates 31, 93*

Brahmā, (eventually creator and senior god in brahmin pantheon) as divine essence, 102; reduced by Buddhists to respectful hearer of the Buddha, 179

Brahmadatta, legendary king of Banāras, 123

Brahmagiri, megalithic site in Mysore state, 91, 139

Brāhmana, post-vedic liturgical works; 87, 101, 102, 203; *Śatapatha Brāhmana*, 90, 102, 103

Brāhmī, alphabet, 88

brahmin, (priestly class-caste), 15, 26, 46–52 *pass.*; 82, 83, 86, 87, 88, 102, 103, 112, 113, 118, 150, 159, 191, 198; new in Rigveda but monopolised higher priest-craft, 83; peaceful penetration of wilderness, 86, 94, 111–12; control of tradition, 92, 95 and re-editing to order, 170, 179; could intermarry with Nāga aborigines, 93–94, 119; *b* breaks tabu on food cooked and soiled by low caste, 104; supposed heavy gifts to, 102; later *b* served all caste-groups as priest, 104, 168–9, 173; no brahmin in Sakyan and similar undifferentiated tribes, 108; *b* girl offered in marriage to the Buddha, 110; mixed racial character of, 119; *b* theorists of state-craft, 121; as agents provocateurs, 130; as ministers of state, *see* Kautalya, Vassakāra, Kanvāyana, Hemadri, Lakshmidhara; *b* priest bound by contract to perform sacrifice, 156; transformation after Asoka, 166–76; long and rigorous course of education, 166, but later many *b* hardly literate, 175; change to non-vedic rituals, 168; role in changing

Catur-varga-cintāmani, of Hemādri late thirteenth century work on ritual and state administration, 173

caves, 48, 115; European ice-age, 61; Buddhist monastic, 48, 107, 140, 160, 184; official (customs) caves by Nānāghāt pass, 184. *Illus.: map of Buddhist c. in Deccan, p. 169; c. drawings at Mīrzāpūr, Fig. 8, p. 115*

Cedi, medieval southern dynasty, 192

celibacy, 104, 106, 111

celts (tools), Indus, 64; first millennium Gangetic, 89

census, 52

Central Asia, 10, 11, 41, 96, 160, 163, 193; epicentre of Aryan waves, 77; joined to India under Kushānas, 189

Cera, (autochthonous tribe and) medieval dynasty in south-west, 192

cereals, grain, 34, 42, 71, 108, 126, 152; cultivated and milled by state, 150; low-grade derived from food-gathering days, 45; Indus urban granaries, 54, 70; Yajurvedic list of cereals, 85

Ceylon, 9, 96, 110, 160, 178, 201

chalcedony, (stone), 35–37, 42; old European demand for, 190

chalcolithic, (archaeological misnomer for early copper age), 91

chariot, (horse-drawn), 80, 82, 84, 104, 107, 115; obsolete in warfare after Alexander, 135; among Sātavāhana gifts to brahmin sacrificers, 184. *Illus.: cave drawing, Fig. 8, p. 115*

Chaul, (Greek Semylla) west-coast creek port, south of Bombay, 184

Chenchu, aboriginal Āndhra tribe, 43

Chin Hsi Hwang-ti, first Chinese emperor, 144

China, 6, 7, 9, 10, 11, 29, 58, 60, 73, 75, 96, 97, 103, 109, 110, 127, 140, 157, 176, 178, 186, 193, 200; relatively ample historical sources, 9, 183; higher position of merchant class in first empire, 144; role of Buddhism in economic development, 183

Christianity, 9, 10, 11, 96, 97, 115, 179

citadel, Indus mounds, 66, 70, corresponding to Mesopotamian *ziggurat*, 68, 69; tribal citadels in fourth century B.C., 138

city, modern, 6 *seq.*, influence on rural economy, 17, 125; destructive effect upon senseless tabus, 49 and caste, 52; first Indian cities, 53–71 *pass.*, with remarkable organization, 54 *seq.*; ruin of Indus *c*, 71, 78; no Aryan Rigvedic *c*, 80, and few small late-vedic, 87; urban revival, 88–91, structure of new *c*, 100; residence in *c* interdicted for Buddhist monk, 107; difference between urban and rural life in Arthaśāstra, 157; civic records lost through indifference, 173; town culture in Sātavāhana period, 191; *c* production unable to meet village demand 194

clan, (exogamous human group), 33, 48, 49, 101, 116; clan cults, 82; totem and tabu in 50; clan law, 172

class, (social division), 88; caste as, 86, 87; *c* division implied in Indus cities, 54; new *c*'s with urban revival, 100–1; *c*-structure not necessarily changed with dictatorship, 127; *c*-basis of state, 143; new master-*c* grows within *Arthaśāstra* state, 143–4, 165; seven *c*'s (= castes + ascetics + artisans + bureaucrats + pastoralists) observed by Megasthenes in fourth century B.C., 146; state as mechanism for *c*-reconciliation, 165; brahmin help in maintaining *c*-structure, 167

climate, variation of, 1; seasons, 26; effect upon preservation of art, 198

cobra, (*see* nāga), complex position in cult and iconography, 94, 118; primeval, earth-supporting, 118, 170

coconut, 2, 46, 48; basic role in western coastal strip economy, 189

coinage, 127, 153–4, *pana* in Sanskrit, 80; first appearance seventh century B.C., 124; periodically checked by pre-Mauryan guilds, 124; Kushāna with Alexandrian mint technique, 189; decay with luxury trade, 190 194; in joint names of Candragupta I and queen Kumāradevī, 192. *Illus.: Fig. 9, p. 127; Fig. 10, p. 129; Fig. 11, p. 146; Fig. 12, p. 148; Figs. 13 and 14, p. 158; Plates 55 to 78 inclusive*

Cola, medieval dynasty in extreme south, 192

Sanskrit drama, 199. *Illus.: Plates from crown villages with other entertainers*, 150, 200; in Sanskrit drama, 199. *Illus.: Plates 23, 25*

danda-nīti, 'law of the Big Stick' = use of force by ruler to protect weaker elements of the population, 171

Dandin, seventh century A.D. Sanskrit writer, 202–3

Danube, (river) in prehistory, 58

Darius, (Dārayavahuś) name of several Achaemenid emperors; *D-I*, 73, 75, 108, 130, 134; Daric coinage in Taxila, 124

dāsa, slave or servant, originally ethnic non-Aryan, 81; Rigvedic *dāsa* kings, 83; as tribal slave, 83; as slave or unfree, 119

Dasyu, interchangeable with *dāsa*, but later brigand, 81

Daulatābad, (Devagiri) fort, seat of medieval Deccan administrations, 173

Dead Sea scrolls, 96–97

Deccan, (and Indian peninsula), 14, 35, 38, 40, 42, 43, 45, 46, 124, 126, 192, 193, 194; beginning of iron age in, 39; new sources of iron, 162, 163, 173, *see dakshināpatha*, 111, 122; baser coinage current in, 164; different terrain and transport, 125–6; trade caravans, 189; passes in Deccan scarp, 39, 184, 189; not to be settled by *Arthaśāstra* methods, 164, 184; special 'black-cotton' soil, 14, 190; cave monasteries, 183, 184, 185. *Illus.: map of passes in D. scarp, with Buddhist caves, p. 169*

Delhi, (Indraprastha), 90, 91, 92, 95, 162, 194; early emperors of *D*, 24

Demetrios, coin of, *Illus.: Plate 60*

democracy, tribal, 129; internal decay, 130, 173–4

demons, pre-Aryan killed by Indra, 79; *yaksha*, 110; Krishna a demon in the Rigveda, 115

deportation, for re-settlement, by force, of dangerous tribal groups, 145; of surplus population, to form new villages, 149; of Kalinga war prisoners, 149, 158–9

desert, 1, 14, 96; alluvial *d* essential for first urban cultures, 58–59, 71

despotism, different function in changing and stable society, 127

determinism, economic, 12

Deulgão microlithic site, 36. *Illus. (microliths from) Fig. 4, p. 36*

deva, ('god', later 'king' also) demon in Iranian, 77, 80

Devadatta, Buddha's dissident cousin, 111, 181

Devakī, Krishna's mother, 115

devotpātana-nāyaka, 'high minister for uprooting images', 186

dhamma, (*dharma*), religion, originally justice, innate law (of nature), ethics, 141; as equity, 161; changed meaning after Asoka, 165, 172; tool for reconciliation of king to subjects, 165, 193

Dhammarakhita, Greek Buddhist monk, Asoka's missionary, 140

Dhangar, nomadic sheepherder caste, 42; roots in prehistory, 43

Dhārā, (Dhār) capital of Bhoja Paramāra, 167, 202

dharma-mahāmātra, 'commissioner of equity', new Asokan ministerial office, 161

Dhārwār outcrop, handy source of iron in small quantities, 123

Dhenukākata, Greek trade settlement near Kārle, 140–1

Dhruvasvāminī, queen to two successive Guptas, 193

dictatorship, and change of class-structure, 126–7

diet, religious restrictions on, 1; cause of genetic change in physique, 21, 40–41; totemic specialization, 31; balanced *d* possible without taking life, 34; and need led to crop rotation, 44; effect of changed *d* on sexual function in pre-history, 47; Yarjurvedic range, 85

differentiation, within Aryan tribes, by caste, 86, 120; for absence of *d see* Malla, Licchavi, Sakyan

digging-stick, (*thombā*), 39, 44–45

dikaios, Greek equivalent of *dhammaka* on Indo-Greek coins, 141, 161, 180

Diodorus Siculus, Greek historian, geographer, philosopher, 134

Dionysos, (Bacchus), Greek god, equated to Indra, 117

INDEX

Dīrgha-Kārāyana, ('long' K; also Dīgha Kārāyana, Cārāyana), Kshatriya theorist of statecraft, 121 and Mallian high minister of Kosala, 128, 129, 130

Dīrghatamas, ('log darkness'), Rigvedic seer and river pilot (?), 90

disputations, public (originally discouraged by the Buddha) Mahāyāna style, 177

Divodāsa, Rigvedic Aryan chieftain, 81

doctors and veterinarians in Magadhan state service, 149; on Asokan trade routes, 161, 182

drama, 6, 198 seq.; origin in primitive ritual, 31, 199

Dravidian, linguistic, perhaps racial, group, 41, 73

Druids in Caesar's Gaul, similar to ancient brahmins, 160

Durgā, consort to Śiva, in her terrible aspect (see Pārvatī), 170. Illus. Plate 96

East, changeless or timeless, 16, 150, 189

East India Company, 7; pay-scale for drudge labour, 153

edicts, Asokan, 157 seq.

Egypt, 9, 10, 11, 27, 29, 54, 55, 58, 61, 62, 65, 68, 71, 76, 175

Eightfold Path, central Buddhist doctrine, 106, 108

ekapātram, tribal commensality, fourth century, 145, 174

elements, primary (in philosophy), 104

elephant, 60, 104, 107, 126, 133; proper military tactical use, 135; subsidiary use in army, 149; specially protected, 149; assigned to honoured Buddhist Mahāyāna monks, 176; among Sātavāhana gifts to brahmin sacrificial priests, 184

Ellora, site of Buddhist, Jain and Hindu caves. Illus.: Kailasa rock-cut temple, Plate 97

Enkidu, Sumerian Bull-Man; Indus counterpart on seals, 60, 65

epic period, 91–95, 117

equity (see dhamma)

Erāpatra, Nāga Rāja, pays devotion to Buddha. Illus.: Plate 82

erosion, with modern deforestation, 14, 35, 39

espionage, massive and universal in Arthaśāstra, 143; on caravans, 147. 155; to ascertain public opinion, 147; upon officials, 147; pay-scales for different grades of spies, 153; with assassination, 165

Essenes, 97

ethics, state above all e but citizen bound by, 132, 142, till Asoka, 163, 165

Eukratides, Greek invader of the Panjāb, 187. Illus.: (coin of), Plate 61

Eurasia, 29, 34, 35, 75, 180

Europe, food-gathering more difficult in, 34

evolution, 27; social, 28

Fa Hian, Chinese Buddhist pilgrim, 193

famine, modern, 6, 22; created slave castes, 101; Arthaśāstra precautions against, 155; Buddhist monasteries could alleviate, 183. Illus.: Plate 22

Fara, Mesopotamian archaeological site, 60

Fertility rites, 47, 61, 87, 105, 199; origin of Tantric philosophy and practices, 178

feudalism, 22, 24–25, 35, 60, 97, 101, 119, 127, 144; feudal accumulation turned into modern capital, 7, 11; formal survivals in other lands, 12; decay under British rule, 17; effect on Gond tribal chiefs, 43, on gods, 49, on caste 51; class basis of 143; held together by chain of personal loyalty, 143, 208; continuation of pre-feudal 'gift' taxes, 148, and of half-share cropping, 150; prelude to f, 166–209; feudal payment to officials by hereditary assignment of land, 154; without village basis in Harsha's empire, 193; uncertain patronage of learning, 196; developed at end of sixth century A.D., 195; main tasks of f officials and barons, 197. Illus.: Feudal labour, c. 1600 A.D., Plate 21

figurines, Indus terracotta, 68

fire, (see holi) religious, 47; control of, as tool, 39; Mohenjo-dāro destroyed by f 55, 79; land-clearing by f 58, 85, 90 and as sacrifice to god Agni; f as god, 77, 91, 117; land-clearing by fire forbidden by Asoka as by Mahābhārata, 162

INDEX

Pharaoh, 11, 29, 62, 71; special functions, 68–69
philosophy, (see Buddhism), new Gangetic in sixth century B.C., 102–5, 109; patronized by kings, 128, but not practised, 141, yet eventually reaches into state mechanism, 159; dissemination along main trade-routes, 120; fantastic medieval p's and village isolation, 175–6
Phrygian, etymology of Bhrigu, ?, 82
pigeons, carriers, 60; for Magadhan official messages, 148
pilgrims, 173, 175; Chinese, 85, 96, 175, 176, 183, 193; pilgrimages as making a dent in village isolation, 196
pipal (Ficus religiosa), sacred fig-tree, 50; totemic, 50; Buddha enlightened under, 110
Pippala House, ancient cairn at Rājgīr. Illus.: Plate 43
Piśuna, theorist of statecraft, 121
Piyadasi (Priyadarśin), 'of pleasing mien' Asoka's personal name, 157
Plato, 133, 141
plough, 16, 18, 19, 29, 44, 45, 85, 108, 112, 118, 119, 123, 182, 184, 195; lacking in Indus culture, replaced by harrow, 62, 69; ploughs with twelve-ox teams, 89; heavy northern plough in south, 186, 190. Illus.: Fig. 1, p. 18; Fig. 2, p. 19; Plates 14, 15, 32
Plutarch, on effects of fight against Poros, 138, 139
political economy, see Arthaśāstra; Buddhist ideal of, 113
Poona, 36, 37, 49
porterage, caravans, 126; in army service, 153
pottery, 27, 79, 155; in village life, 21; potter as bone-setter and priest, 21; in prehistory, 27, 29, 31, 65, 66; potter's disc and wheel, 45; Indus p, 54, 63; womb-jar, 83; NPG (northern painted grey) ware, 84, 91; p-kilns sufficient to reduce copper ore, 29, 89; Nāga p, ?, 94; NBP ware, 133; early villages of potters, 125; rich guilds of potters, 184; recent discoveries, 209, 210. Illus.: disc, Plates, 5, 9; wheel, Plates 6, 8; paddle, Plate 7; potsherds of second millennium, Plates 39, 40

Pradyota, dynasty of Avanti, 131
Prakrit, simpler language, in same relation to Sanskrit as Italian to Latin, 73, 167, 188; high secular literary development under Sātavāhanas (lost), 191; spoken by women and menials in Sanskrit dramas, 199; 'Ocean Of Story' Sanskritised from P, 204
Praśasti (panegyric), of Samudragupta (posthumous) at Allahabad, 192
Pravahana Jaivali, kshatriya Upanishadic philosopher, 102
Pravarā, river, tributary of Godāvari, 112
pre-history, chap. 2 pass.; general, 28–33, Indian, 33–40; survivals from, 40–52; 64, 78, 81
priesthood, (see brahmin), not always brahmin, 15–16, 21; lost contact with homeland of vedic religion, 78; only developing in Rigveda, 82
prince, training and precautions against (heir-apparent), 144–5
prisoners, rigorous Magadhan treatment of convicts, 157; Asokan palliatives, 162
production, means and relations of p, 11, 32; relation to historical process, 12, 41–42; village as early advance in p, 16; primitive survivals, 23, 40–45, 51 (see tribe); modes and stages of, 23; essential role in formation of society, 34, 86, 101, 120; as basis of caste, 50; in Indus culture, 58–62; in Arthaśāstra state, 152–7; p and formation of language, 167; shows different social structure in Deccan in second century B.C., 184
property (private), 26; in land and beasts, 44; influence of, 52, 86; temple property, 69–70; effect on tribes, 121, 126, 145; non-tribal possession of land needed for monarchies, 122
prostitution (see courtezan), hierodule, 68; as Magadhan state monopoly enterprise, 156–7; as source of temple revenue, 196
public works, 113
Pukkusa, Taxilan kshatriya (perhaps tribal name), 120

Date Due
